'She's the apple of my eye and smart as a whip, but females don't run companies!' Adam Scofield, the dynamic founder of a newspaper empire, was proved wrong by his granddaughter, Mary, the golden girl who did just that and became a public celebrity.

But behind the wealthy Scofield façade lay tragedy. Adam's ill-fated marriage to a wife who cared more for her religion than for him – till Venus, the fresh, young film-star gave him back his manhood. Harmon, Adam's adopted son, and Mary's father, the profligate wastrel with psychopathic tendencies. And Mary . . . three marriages and some hopeless affairs. Power is not an asset in bed. And money and influence can't bring back the daughter who's disappeared . . .

PUBLISHED July 78

EDITION 1st

PRINT No. 27,500

COVER PTR Acorn

Also by Morton Cooper

Morton Cooper

Rich People

CORGI BOOKS
A DIVISION OF TRANSWORLD PUBLISHERS LTD

To Innes Rose
With Lasting Affection

RICH PEOPLE
A CORGI BOOK 0 552 10771 9

Originally published in Great Britain by
W. H. Allen

PRINTING HISTORY
W. H. Allen Edition published 1977
Corgi edition published 1978

Corgi Books are published by Transworld Publishers Ltd.
Century House, 61–63 Uxbridge Road,
Ealing, London, W.5.
Made and printed in Great Britain by
William Collins Sons & Co. Ltd., Glasgow

ON A STARLIT August evening in 1934, Harmon Scofield celebrated his eighteenth birthday with his new girl friend, Eunice Hoffer, seventeen, in a dark, smoky cabaret off Wilshire Boulevard. They were served without questions because he dressed well, looked and acted older than his age, flashed a lot of money around, and spent it freely.

Eunice kept up with Harmon, drink for drink, and agreed at well before midnight that a drive to the beach in his brand-new Reo—his father's birthday present to him—was a fine idea. He bought a bottle of Old Crow to take along. He left nearly a hundred dollars in tips at the cabaret, gave the parking lot attendant a ten-dollar bill to fetch the shiny Reo, and grabbed Eunice as soon as they were inside the car. She giggled, and slapped his hands away, and announced that she was going to stay a decent girl all the way to the beach. They had known each other for more than a month. They had made love often, but not yet on a beach.

Harmon chose back roads to prove that the twelve-cylinder Reo could do a hundred miles an hour, could in fact do everything but tap dance. Eunice squealed as it tore through the lovely night, and they took turns at drinking from the bottle, and she urged Harmon to go faster, faster.

A Ford, moving at normal speed, suddenly materialized ahead of Harmon. He stomped hard on his brake, skidded, and slammed into the rear of the Ford so hard that its driver lost control of the wheel and careened headlong into the trunk of a tree.

When Harmon came awake in a Santa Monica hospital bed, he recognized Caleb Buckminster, his father's West Coast chief executive. Fearfully, urgently, he asked if Eunice was all right.

With luck she would be, Buckminster answered. The impact had hurt her badly: her cheekbones were pulverized,

5

her jaw was broken, her front teeth were broken off and pushed into her throat. With luck, he repeated; doctors were doing an emergency tracheotomy.

The passengers in the Ford, a family of four, had been killed outright.

Except for bruises and a deep gash in his knee that would make him limp for a month, Harmon Scofield was unhurt.

Unhurt and in the clear, for his father was Adam Scofield.

Adam Scofield, in the Depression year of 1934, owned fifty-one newspapers, coast to coast. He owned eleven national magazines and a Sunday newspaper supplement. He owned Scofield Feature Service, Scofield News Service, and Scofield News Photos. He owned oil, and timber, and coal, and cotton, and real estate, and a motion picture company and newsreels and a radio network, and a half-dozen other flourishing enterprises that included some governors and United States senators. He was huge and handsome and sixty-three years old, at the zenith of his power and influence, which were substantial enough to have arranged, without his knowledge of the accident, for the Ford and its passengers to have never existed.

Harmon insisted on being taken to Eunice, to be with her as soon as the doctors were done, even if she was still unconscious. "You've caused enough commotion for one night," said Buckminster, who revered Adam and despised young Harmon. "The best thing that ever happened to you is that I personally was contacted. As it is, there's no guarantee your little prank's going to be kept quiet."

"Look—"

"No, lad, you look. You lie there and don't take a step until I get the word you can be moved out. I have some questions to ask you, and I want straight answers. Does that girl have any family hereabouts, anybody who'll be especially put out if she doesn't show up for a while?"

"She lives alone in a furnished room in Hollywood. Why?"

"Don't ask me questions. Just answer them—it's the

6

middle of the night. I want her name, and where she lives, and where she goes to school or works. You had her bloomers in your pocket, you ought to know something about her."

"What're you planning, to make trouble?"

"Goddammit, shut up, you young pup," Buckminster said softly. "Would you rather answer my questions, or the police's? Four people wouldn't've died tonight if you hadn't been in an automobile. I'm trying to save your *skin*! Not for your sake—if you were my boy, God forbid, I'd've handed you a pick and shovel and thrown you out of the house when you were ten, right out on your tail, and you might've, you just might've, amounted to something. I care about your father and I care about avoiding this kind of publicity for him and for the Company. Is *any* of this penetrating your little skull?"

Harmon nodded and told what he knew about Eunice.

"Very good," Buckminster said, and rose heavily from the wicker chair. "Now, you're not to speak to anybody. If someone somehow gets past the guard outside this door, your name is Foster. That's it; no more. I'll let you know when there's something to know. If you want to pass the time, you might pray for the souls of the couple and their two children you and your bimbo lady friend killed."

Caleb Buckminster, an almost studiedly shaggy man of fifty-eight, padded to the empty conference room across the hospital corridor. He phoned Art Lowery, his own favourite private detective, whom the Company retained around the year and around the clock, told him what he knew of the Hoffer girl, and ordered Lowery to learn everything there was to learn about her, as soon as possible.

Then he opened his alpaca jacket, chewed the stub of a cigar, longed to resume the sleep he had been pulled from, and gazed through the window and waited. Caleb Buckminster's rimless, oddly prissy spectacles at once made one think of a thoughtful scholar, which he was and which he was not; he was an educated and frequently sensitive man, but he was also a man who would instantly bypass what

7

others perceived to be basic moralities if the Scofield Company could be benefited. He was aware of the hard-dying rumours, here in California at least, that he *was* the Scofield Company, that every startling innovation that had made the Scofield communications empire the most successful in the world had been his, that Adam relied on him at every major turn.

It was still appealing to hear, and, of course, pure rubbish.

There was only one man who ran the Scofield show, and that man was Adam, who was now, fortunately, in New York, three thousand miles away.

Presently Dr Morrow came into the conference room and closed the door. "She can breathe. She's not in danger," he said. "Her front teeth were on the verge of going into the esophagus. We removed them, and we reconstructed fragments of the cheekbone as best as possible. She won't be a pretty sight for a while, but plastic surgeons are doing wonders these days in—"

"We won't worry now about her looks, Doctor," Buckminster interrupted and gave him three thousand dollars in cash, inside a handshake. "I want to know how soon I can talk with her."

"Thank you," Morrow said, quickly pocketing the money without counting it. "Tomorrow we'll wire the jaw and reconstruct the mandible. Barring anything unforeseen, you can probably see her the day after tomorrow. I can't guarantee how much talking you'll get out of her. She won't be able to open her jaw more than a half inch."

"I expect to do most of the talking. One more question, and then I'll leave: How soon can you dismiss her? A few more days?"

"Oh, not under a week. She's young and she seems fit, but I'd want her here for a week at least."

Buckminster nodded. "Very well. The boy's to be told she can't be seen for several days. You know where to reach me." He decided against checking in on Harmon for the time being. The matter would correct itself. The kid this moment surely wasn't feeling any guilt or responsibility for

8

the family in the Ford, though he very likely felt something for the girl. If he hears now that she got her face broken, thought Buckminster, he'll need to be protective and heroic. The matter will correct itself when he sees her wired and toothless and not worth jumping into the hay with again.

He went home and back to sleep.

Art Lowery, the private detective, came through. Eunice Hoffer had run away from her religious Wisconsin farm folks a year before. She'd gone from one waitressing job to another in the Hollywood area, without making any lasting friends. There was no evidence of prostitution or even that she bummed around with lowlifes. A quiet girl, a shy girl, and none too bright. She met Harmon when he drove into the La Cienega diner where she worked, and ordered a hamburger and invited her out. She went, apparently not knowing he was Adam Scofield's son, presumably not knowing who Adam was, but just warming to a clean-cut kid who was attractive and who offered her company.

The day after her jaw was wired, Harmon was released from the hospital, having been told that she was still on the critical list and couldn't be seen, more likely finally believing Caleb Buckminster's warning that he couldn't expect to stay scot-free unless he kept away from the girl, now and forever. Buckminster went to the girl.

She looked mauled and badly frightened. "I'll be clear as glass, young lady," he said, close to her. "You're in a peck of trouble, but I can help you."

Distantly, through the wiring, she asked, "Who are you?"

"Your best friend. Four people died as a result of that joy-ride you and your friend took the other night. You weren't driving the car, but the law here claims that anyone in a vehicle that causes the death of innocent people shares the blame. Once the police know as much about you and what happened as I know, you can be arrested and go on trial and get into the newspapers that go everywhere, all the way to Wisconsin. Or you can take this thousand dollars I have here for you and disappear, the minute you're discharged from here. When's the last time you had a thousand dollars, all your own, at one time?"

"Harmon," she said weakly. "Where's Harmon?"

"Harmon? There is no Harmon, young lady, unless you want to get him mixed up in this extremely serious mess, too."

"No . . ."

"That's wise. He can't help you, anyway. I can. I can see that the police won't take you to jail, but only if you co-operate with me one hundred percent."

She agreed. His chauffeur drove him back to the Scofield Building. The girl was sedated, and it was vaguely conceivable that when her head was clearer she would realize that the thousand dollars she'd accepted was nearly no money at all. Buckminster chose not to be concerned. *If* it turned out that there would be ripples from her, Art Lowery had some contact who could have her . . . removed, neatly, without a trace. Buckminster, sitting back and lighting his first cigar of the day, hoped, fully expected, it wouldn't have to come to that. As for Harmon, the kid was dense but not entirely stupid. He knew what he risked losing—a horse choker of a family inheritance—if he decided to be a hero.

So that was that.
But it wasn't.
Harmon soberly promised Buckminster to forget Eunice, who was being generously taken care of; promised to go back to New York and say nothing to anyone, to say he'd injured his leg by falling off a horse.

He stayed away from the hospital for as long as he could, four days. The wires wouldn't let her open her mouth very wide, but he was able to hear and understand most of the words. "They're kicking me out of here tomorrow," she moaned as Harmon held her. "Where can I go, looking like this? I'm so scared, Harmon, and I feel awful! And I'm pregnant. . . Harmon, did they tell you I'm pregnant?"

He sat up, and blinked. "That Dr Morrow," she said,

"he examined me all over this morning, and I'm six weeks gone, Harmon. It must've happened that first time we did it, and you told me we didn't need a rubber because I was just over my period. It's your baby, Harmon, I swear to Jesus it is! You can't leave me in the lurch like this. Where'm I gonna go, what'm I gonna do? That man, he gave me a thousand dollars and told me to go disappear, just like nothing happened or there'd be trouble. Well, *this* is trouble, Harmon, and you just better know it, somebody better know it. Everything hurts. I can't even look at myself in the mirror. I'm an old lady without teeth and my jaw's gonna stay crooked, and my face, my pretty face, who's gonna want to look at me if it don't get all healed up?"

"Eunice . . ."

"Where'm I gonna go, back to Appleton? My folks hate me worse than poison. They always said I wasn't a nice girl, they hate me. I go back there with a baby in me, they'll—I don't even want to think about that. Harmon, honey, marry me! You have to take care of me. You won't regret it. I'll get pretty again and it'll be wonderful, we'll screw all day and all night and I'll be good to you, honey, we'll have this wonderful baby, he'll be a boy and we'll name him after you, and we'll always be in love, don't leave me, Harmon, oh, God, I got nobody. . . ."

Alone, Harmon Scofield walked a stretch of Santa Monica beach. His knee was killing him, but he was determined to walk without the cane someone—he forgot who—had given him. The beach up ahead was crowded with gulls, hopping awkwardly into graceful flight, beautiful creatures with a great sense of humour.

He thought of Stan Laurel and Oliver Hardy: "*Another fine mess you've gotten us into, Stanley.*"

"Another fine mess you've gotten us into," he said aloud, in Hardy's voice, and appreciated the joke and his talent for perfect impersonations, and grinned.

He had come to California for part of the summer, to stay with friends and to find himself, on Father's gentle, supportive proddings, after having been booted out of Harkins—the third school in four years—for rock-bottom grades and what they'd called "frivolous and immature behaviour harmful to the rest of the student body." Sure, he'd taken a few little things from other guys, more in fun than anything else. But he'd explained, hadn't he? and, besides, the whole thing was silly, trivial. He'd tried his best, he'd assured Father; some people just seemed to be jealous of him, to have it in for him, resented him because he had good looks and a darned good personality and liked to live life to the fullest. He was going to be number one in everything he tackled, the minute he was ready, what was everybody's big problem?

Mother had urged a stricter rein. Father had agreed, and then disagreed: "The boy's sowing his wild oats, Eugenia, that's all. When's he to enjoy himself if not now? Grades? Is that what these schools are so upset about? I couldn't have passed a school examination if my soul depended on it, and I'd say I'm an educated man. I'd be ashamed of Harmon if he got straight A's by rote and didn't have the gumption to go out and lick the world on his own. But he will. He'll be fine, Eugenia, you wait and see. All I did was flounder around when I was his age, too. He just needs a little time, that's all. He'll find himself, and when he does we'll have to stand aside so we won't get run over. Don't you go clucking on like that."

Only a few of the gulls flapped away as Harmon approached them. The wide, cloudless sky was bright and clear. The *Criterion*, Father's L.A. paper, had predicted heavy rain today. That amused Harmon as well.

I don't want to get married, he thought, stepping on shells, listening to them crack. I suppose I love her. She loves me; she never once asked me for money or about money; I gave her some last week and she asked me if I'd robbed a bank. Maybe I do love her. When we're screwing, it isn't only dirty, it's . . . well, it's different from the others, it's dirty and it's . . . *holy*. She looks like hell right now. She looks like the cat wouldn't even bother to drag her in.

12

I love her.

Yes.

I'm getting a hard on, just thinking about her, even looking like hell and all.

What's wrong with getting married if you love someone? I'll get specialists and she'll look like herself again. I don't think I want a kid yet. Maybe she'll have one of those— what do you call them?—miscarryings, where in a while she just stops having it. Or an abortion. She told me once she's a lapsed Catholic but she still believes in it. The Catholics are nutty on that abortion business.

Time, a little time. I'll get her face and her mouth all fixed, and around about the time she's going to have the baby, if she hasn't had the miscarrying by then, I'll get some-one, Chub Arthington or Herb Graham or one of the bunch who's really experienced, to dig us up a good old abortion doctor.

Yes.

I love her.

It can all work out just great.

I'll take Eunice home with me. No, I'll take her to New York, but I'll stow her away somewhere till she starts to look better; introducing her, the way she looks now, would take too much explaining. Mother will have a rupture for sure, anyway. She has me pegged to marry the Queen of England at least.

Father? That will be a problem, but not for long. He stomps and storms a lot about knowing what's best for everybody, but he wouldn't raise any hard hell with me. He wouldn't know how.

I'll put the proposition squarely to him: *I'm marrying a girl I met and deeply love, Father. I've decided I don't want to go to college, anyway. I go along with what you've said:* "*You have to go to school to be a doctor or a chiropodist. But why go to learn how to make money when the professor who's teaching you is lucky if he's pulling down a salary of two thousand dollars a year?*" *I'll go right into the Company, Father. We'll see that Eunice has good medical care, and she and I will scout around Europe till your grandson is born, and I'll go right into the Company. The business end of it doesn't interest me as much as the creative end. I'll start off as a reporter—maybe a column with a byline in* The Outlook. *There's a lot going on right now in Germany. I could get us important exclusive interviews, maybe even with Hitler. We wouldn't even need interpreters. I know German pretty well, and Eunice and I can brush up with books and lessons on the ship across.*

What's wrong with that? When he sees I mean business, that I'm going to get married no matter what, what's he going to do? Show me the door? Disown me?

It'll work. The right timing, the right soft soap, and it'll all work out right.

The sky stayed its glossy blue, and he cracked sea shells with his heel and thought, I'm not sure I want a child yet, I'm not sure I want to be saddled down.

I'm not sure I really love Eunice.

I love Eunice.

It'll work. Father scares Franklin D. Roosevelt. I wrap Father around my finger.

It'll work, he thought, and the following day he took Eunice from the hospital to his friends' house in Beverly Hill. Several days later, when she felt well enough to travel, he booked a bedroom on the train to New York, in spite of Buckminster's savage cries that he was insane, that now Adam would obviously have to be told everything. "Go ahead," said Harmon. "Keeping him in the dark was your idea, anyhow. The cops and the hospital were paid off, weren't they? What's your problem, Bucky?"

The train's bedroom was large and Eunice stayed in it throughout the journey, not in pain, because of the sedatives and the liquor, but embarrassed to be seen by anyone other than Harmon. Meals and whiskey were brought in. Eunice wore a veil, sometimes even during sex, and he teased her that he wasn't used to doing it to women he couldn't see. She giggled—God, how he loved that giggle! The trip was long and erotic and happy. He checked her into a quiet

14

hotel, under a fake name, in Times Square, and promised he would be back soon, and they made love, quickly, before he left. He remained happy and confident until he reached lower Broadway, where the Scofield Building was and where his father was waiting. His steps began to flag. Then he raised his chin and marched into the lobby, ready to wrap Adam Scofield around his finger.

Father barely mentioned the accident, for what was done was done and had been disposed of. He listened attentively and, for the most part, without expression. Harmon finished. And then his father spoke as he had never spoken before, in cold fury.

"Marriage? At your age? To a waitress? Have you gone insane?"

"No, just in love."

"Good Christ. 'Just in love.' Well, this foolishness stops here and now. If that whore comes anywhere near you again, or near any of us, she'll be missing more than just her teeth. It stops. You've had your fun and now it stops. If you're convinced college isn't for you, all right, it'll break your mother's heart but all right, you pick what part of the Company you think might appeal to you and we'll get cracking with it."

"No."

"What's that?"

"No. My mind is made up."

"You don't have a mind. I'm not even sure I could give you credit for a few brain cells. Well, let's see. You're my only child. When I die, you stand to take over the whole shebang."

Speaking calmly, feeling not at all calm, Harmon said, "Maybe I'm ahead of you, Father. Are you honestly threatening me? Are you saying that if I go through with this, you'll cut me off?"

"Without a plug penny. That's precisely what I'm saying."

"Come on, Father. You're all wound up, but you know yourself it's not the end of the world. I'm your son. I'm

15

Mother's son."

"That's true, and you have no right to spit in our faces like this, after all you've been given, after all the love we've showered on you. Without a plug penny is pre*cise*ly what I'm saying."

Suavely now though the voice was not quite so steady: "Okay. I have something over eight thousand dollars in my account which I closed out on my way here. Maybe you'd forgotten that account. A man and his wife can travel pretty nicely on eight thousand dollars."

"A man? I'm the only man I see in this room you impudent horse's ass! Harmon I *love* you! I'm not about to let you pitch your whole life away for some little slut that got you hot under the covers! If it's whores you're looking for, we can find you plenty to play with till you find a decent young woman for marriage."

"Just watch it, Father. You're not to talk that way about Eunice. I don't just love her, I respect her." He watched his father redden more and tremble, Father whose editorials praised the sanctity of marriage and home, Father who had turned his own whore into a movie star, a movie star who was still a whore. "You're the expert on whores, Father," he began. "When's the last time Venus Montgomery and you—"

Adam Scofield's huge hand raised and cracked hard against Harmon's head. "Get out of our sight and our life, you foundling-home garbage collector, and take your scabby whore with you! This is the day you'll regret till the minute you die, and I hope that's soon! You've just shut every door that was open to you. Congratulations! All I hoped for you and built for you, you're dropping in the gutter. Congrat—" He broke down and wept, and rushed to embrace his son.

Harmon moved away swiftly, fearful that he could be talked out of what he needed to do. Moving away yet standing his ground, he said, "That's plain melodramatic shit, Father, right out of the noble Scofield press. You don't understand real love, after all. You don't understand me, because you never tried to. So now you want me to be

16

your jumping jack or otherwise you want to be rid of me? Swell, you're rid of me. Live with that. Good-bye."

By May of the following year, most of the eight thousand and forty dollars had been spent. It had been spent on Eunice's dental work and plastic surgery, making her prettier than ever, it had been spent on long vacations in Europe and South America. As the time for the baby's birth came nearer, Eunice began to have prolonged fits of petulance and inexplicable depression, times when she wouldn't let Harmon touch her, much less make love to her. They were in Ocean City, New Jersey, when her labour pains started. At the hospital, Harmon demanded a private room. The cost of private care was quoted to him, a substantial down payment expected in advance. As his wife lay in the charity section, in labour, he stood at a hall telephone and desperately tried to reach, not his mother, who would sermonize and then probably refuse to help, but his father. Mr Scofield was out of town and unavailable, he was told. He was finally connected with Vivien Madden, Father's personal secretary, who knew Harmon. Sorry, she said, but she and everyone at Scofield around the country had their orders: no one was to help him, in any way.

"But my wife's going to have our baby in a charity ward, with all the bums!" he screamed.

"Sorry," he heard repeated, and heard a click.

Eunice had a baby girl. They named her Mary Elizabeth, after Sister Mary Elizabeth, the one person who had been kind to Eunice Hoffer when she was a gawky, painfully shy student at parochial school in Appleton, Wisconsin.

17

ONE

ON THE RAINY May morning of her fortieth birthday, Mary Scofield's private plane flew her from New York towards London, where the International Society of Newspaper Publishers and Journalists would, the following evening, confer on her its highest honour.

She expected to stay in London several days, for reasons besides her acceptance of the award. She would meet with Britain's new prime minister and members of the new cabinet, would look in on the Scofield Company's London bureau, would sound out reliable old friends on current political and social moods, and would go to bed with a motion picture actor named Rick Tovar.

Mary Scofield, slender and tall and uncommonly attractive, with luminous white skin and a fine-boned figure that surely was not forty years old, was often called the most powerful woman in America. It was said that the designation both embarrassed and secretly pleased her.

Her fortieth birthday also celebrated her seventh year as president, chairwoman of the board, and controlling stockholder of the Scofield Company, whose primary properties were a chain of six newspapers and three magazines, co-ownership of *The International Outlook*, a daily newspaper for Americans abroad; the leasing of four television stations and eight radio stations throughout the United States; and hotels in Manhattan and Washington, as well as corporate control of several dozen other subsidiary businesses acquired or founded by her grandfather, the late Adam Hurd Scofield. She retained final decisions on all major corporate and policy questions, and she maintained a working knowledge of the continual shifts and changes in the Company's many enterprises, but she preferred to limit her personal, day-to-day attentions to those Company interests that attracted her most—its flagship newspaper, *The New York*

18

Outlook, and its weekly news magazine, *Scofield's*—frequently switching hats from publisher to editor.

Heads of state and industry, and leaders in the arts and sciences, were acutely aware of what and who she was.

Those who knew Mary Scofield and liked her personally called her the Velvet Claw, a tough commander with warmth, wit, direction, and a genuine sense of fair play.

Those who believed they had cause to fear or hate her insisted she prowled about in a lifelong search for a mislaid penis, that her seeming equanimity hid vast storehouses of vindictiveness and insecurity; they granted that she was indeed feminine and tough and beautiful, but swore that her vaunted social consciousness was restricted to those who rushed to fawn over her.

No one denied that, by inheritance and by her own hard work, she had turned a foundering publishing empire into a solid financial success. Undeniably Mary Scofield, thrice divorced, was a very wealthy woman and a woman of incalculable influence.

As she rested this day in the larger of the plane's two bedrooms, her secretary, Liz Hale, sat at a desk near the forward section and typed the third draft of the speech Mary would deliver at London's Royal Festival Hall. Each year in May, in a different world capital, the International Society of Newspaper Publishers and Journalists met to bestow awards on those who had, over the past year, exercised the most responsible standards of professionalism and integrity in disseminating the news. Only twice in the last decade had American newspapers won the society's crowning award. Liz Hale, small and dark and invariably unruffled, considered the delicious irony of any Scofield paper being recognized by the society for its integrity. In Adam Scofield's day the *Outlook*, especially, had been a blatantly raunchy scandal sheet, often vital and exciting and always professional, but impatient with facts that got in the way of a good story.

You showed 'em, boss, Liz said now to the paper in her typewriter. You sure did show 'em.

Jeanne Astor, the plane's pilot, was at the controls. Smilin' Jack Ridley, who served as co-pilot, navigator, galley cook, and occasional court jester, showed Liz the chocolate birthday cake he had baked. "When do we give it to her?" he asked.

"As late as possible," Liz answered. "I made her lie down. She couldn't've had more than a few hours' sleep last night, and it'll be go-go-go from the minute she lands."

Smilin' Jack sat across from her, crossed his long legs, and lighted a cigarette. "You ought to be getting Mama to the Savoy by midnight, London time," he said. "You don't know anybody worth knowing there at midnight; neither do I. But it'll be only seven o'clock our time, the shank of the evening. I'll tell you what: as soon as you can cut loose, I'm at the Park Lane. I'll buy you a cuppa and show you around the Park Lane. They have terrific room service there."

Typing furiously, Liz grinned. "And you also have a terrific ring there on your third finger, left hand," she said.

"I'll keep my left hand in my pocket. I don't use it much, anyway."

"Go outside and play, Smilin' Jack. I have work to do."

"The Park Lane," he repeated. "In Piccadilly. Left hand in pocket."

Her grin broadened. "We'll see."

Liz strove to finish the never finished letters and directives Mary had dictated since early this morning and would want to sign before they landed, and reread tomorrow evening's speech to herself. There would probably be a lot more tinkering between now and then, she was certain, for this was an enormously important speech that would be relayed and translated throughout the world, but the essentials were there and Liz Hale liked them. The speech praised free journalism and journalists and, specifically, *The New York Outlook*'s five hundred employees who were dedicated conduits of information. It praised Joseph Greenwood, the Company's executive vice-president, Mary Scofield's associate and dear friend, who, according to the speech, deserved the lion's share of applause for whatever greatness had been detected in the *Outlook*. It was Mary Scofield's speech, so of course it avoided mention of Mary Scofield.

Liz Hale, who travelled with her, on an average, a half million miles a year and who had almost never been taken into Mary's private confidences in their three busy years together, sipped Smilin' Jack's coffee and stretched. She was thirty-four, a Nebraska farm girl who had set her sights high but had never seriously imagined her career and her life would be as full and fulfilling as it had been over these three years. She loved and admired and protected Mary, who courted no admiration and needed no protection.

At two o'clock and at 39,000 feet, she remembered to turn her wrist watch five hours ahead. In London, she and Mary always stayed at the Savoy, she in her own comfortable but modest quarters, Mary in the 511 Suite. (The London Scofield had been sold before Liz's time, along with a half dozen others in the Company's hotel chain, by Mary, who had gradually unloaded every Company property that wasn't earning its keep.) Late arrival or not, the suite would surely be filled with Mary's London friends, and Liz began to think, not so idly now, of skipping over to Smilin' Jack Ridley's lodgings and ordering room service with him there.

Rick Tovar was finishing a movie in Dublin. Liz knew Mary and he would eventually be ordering their own room service, and wished it were not so. The affair with the cocky, crude instant-success actor was into its fifth month, five months longer than Liz would have predicted.

She's much too good for him, thought Liz. Even if he's the greatest lover on earth, it's incredible that she's not only let it last all these months but seems to want it to go on and on. Remarkable.

But, then, she's larger than life. Everything about her is remarkable. . . .

Mary Scofield lay atop the spread, not bothering to take off her azure blue silk dress—Liz would have a fresh change of clothes ready for her before they landed—and worked to

21

rid her mind of everything but the simple urge to rest.

The day had not begun well. Joe Greenwood had phoned her early at the town house to wish her, in his gravelly yet gentle voice, a happy birthday and a safe journey. But then he'd added, "You can still change your mind about the trip. Yeah, yeah, we've been all over this, but I'm still not crazy about the idea. There're too many loonies dancing around."

"Every inch of the plane's been microscoped for fire-crackers and roman candles, *Yussele*," she had reminded him. "And nobody's going to put a knife in me up in the sky, unless it's the crew. You've *got* to stop mothering me, darling. Anything else? I have to race."

"Well, for what it's worth, I had a call last night from that lady shrink at the Hartford san. It seems your father signed himself out for parts unknown."

Abruptly angry, Mary snapped, "Dammit, that's not worth much at all. Do I have to keep saying it, especially just before I board a plane with a million things on my mind: whether that man lives or dies is of absolutely no consequence to me."

"Okay, okay, I should've kept my handsome mouth shut. You take care of yourself, birthday girl."

Her eyes closed now, she was still annoyed with Joe, normally attuned to her feelings, for having mentioned Harmon Scofield. She shifted about restlessly and decided she resented herself more. That was dumb of Joe, she thought, but downright cantankerous of me. Joe Greenwood means only the best for me. I'm tired and I'm getting too edgy. . .

She sat up, impatient with idleness, then forced herself to lie down again, for the week ahead was indeed going to be busy. Tomorrow she would spend most of the morning and afternoon at Scofield International, whose principal publishing interests were *The International Outlook* and the European edition of the Company's magazine *Scofield's*. Except for the ads, and occasional editorial latitude allowed the magazine, both publications were essentially put

22

together in the States. Both were immensely profitable, and both had been so smoothly developed over the years that they frequently seemed capable of running themselves, but Mary was convinced that the operation required periodic personal visits. She flew to London at least three times a year and swept into the SI building, without advance notice when that was possible, a tactic she had reluctantly learned from Joe. It seemed sneaky, but it nonetheless helped to keep the aging managing director, Geoffrey Metcalf, and his staff on their toes. Metcalf, one of the few Company executives she personally disliked, knew of course that she was on her way this time; the Royal Festival Hall ceremony had been hoopla'ed for weeks.

She browsed again through this morning's edition of *The New York Outlook*, again read the fifth instalment of the series on Ramon Vienna, and again was touched by Joe's mother-hen concern for her safety. Over the weekend, soon after the strong series had started on Vienna, with the charitable heart and the manicured nails and the church-going family and the narcotics empire, disturbing anonymous threats had begun to reach the Scofield Building, by mail and by telephone. And they were against her personally.

They could have been delivered by Ramon Vienna's cohorts, which she doubted, or by any of a number of other citizens singed or scorched by the *Outlook* or the magazine *Scofield's*, which she was convinced was more likely the case.

"The muscle days are over. The Viennas are vermin, of course, but they're too sophisticated for this kind of thing," she had striven to reassure Joe. "The point is that the threats have stopped. And if I'm in danger, if I ever was . . . well, I hope they miss. I can't live with doors locked."

"Wonder Woman," Joe had snorted.

Not much of one, she sighed now, trying to avoid the page one picture of Bill Bradway, who had lied to her and perhaps to himself, young and brilliant United States Senator William Straight-Arrow Bradway, whom Mary had loved and hadn't shielded.

Not a heroine at all, she thought, and regarded Bill's handsome face and asked him, as she had asked over and over, *Why? You were my lover, my friend, my old-fashioned noble hero. What made you do it?* and hated what she remembered: Van Avery, the *Outlook*'s best investigative reporter in Washington, had tracked down a tip that Bill, ten days before, had been arrested on a morals charge involving very young girls. Mary, alarmed and wounded, more easily prepared to believe that a mother superior was turning tricks on Ninth Avenue, had phoned him for explanations. Bill had confirmed only the arrest, denied the rest of it, claimed he would have a clarifying public statement to make if that became necessary, refused to tell her more. Joe had urged her to print the story, arguing, "Sure, it's a bitch. For the past year we've been bandstanding him for the presidency, and now we bombshell him. But it's going to come out, anyway. And if we don't run it, aren't we managing the news just a bit?"

She had forbidden it to be run: "*If* it happened, then it's a personal tragedy. Bill's not the only overworked man—or woman—to get caught up in the pressure cooker and do a single mindless act."

When the provable goods were brought in that there had been other lapses, a series of them, a pattern, when it became obvious that the other papers and news magazines were about to drop their own bombs on Bill Bradway, she had tried to reach him one last time. He was accepting no calls, even from her. In pain, she had nodded to Joe and directed, "Print it."

I'm not flying towards London, she told herself. I'm running away from home.

A few minutes later she buzzed for Liz Hale, who appeared instantly. "As long as you have me shackled here, and all I'm doing is counting my toes," Mary said, "how about bringing me the speech? And some tea?"

"Righto." Liz disappeared. Standing, Mary Scofield pulled her dress over her head, got into a robe, wished she could tell Liz that "righto" was one of her least favourite words, and brushed her rich auburn hair at the mirror and saw in her reflection her daughter Carole, fifteen, her only other living blood relative besides her father. She saw the child, who was at Pearce, her own old boarding school in Westchester, and she felt the guilt engulf her once again, and she said, *I'm sorry about that hurry-up call yesterday, baby. I should've insisted you come to the city so I could kiss you good-bye, even though I'll be gone only a week. Should've, should've, should've. I always seem to be saying "should've" where you're concerned.*

She turned away, and lighted her one cigarette of the day, and said, as she wanted so often to say before, *I wish we could be closer, baby. You didn't ask to be born. Yes, all right, that's a cliché with yards of whiskers, but it's true, nonetheless. While we're at it, have another cute bromide: Someone who hasn't received love, or has in shaky fits and starts, doesn't learn by magic how to give it. I've been a pretty lousy parent to you. I've attempted to do right, with my own brand of fits and starts, but not often enough, sincerely enough but not often enough, and the result is that I've been, I am, a pretty lousy parent. I regret this, dear Carole. That's hardly comfort, but I regret that all I've given you was little more than birth and some assurance that you, or your daughter if women are still having babies a few years from now, will never have to sell matches on winter nights. The same wish wished to me when I was fifteen. The more things change, the more they—*

Liz returned with the speech and tea and scolded, "What I should've done was spike this tea with a Librium. Why do you keep refusing to take a tranquillizer when you're wound up like this?"

"I'm not wound up."

"I disrespectfully disagree. I know you by heart. How about a medicinal slug of whiskey?"

"Out, nurse. Out."

Liz shrugged and said "Righto" on her way out. Mary sat at her desk and began to read the speech aloud: " 'The gathering and distributing of news is, in both its purest and

25

most practical sense, more than a career. It is a commit-
ment, it—' " And stopped, and felt uneasy, and zig-zagged
the unwanted cigarette into a tray, and finally allowed herself to face what she was truly feeling.

Rick.

She sat back, smiling, and saw Rick Tovar, divinely
crazy, divinely loving Rick, twelve years younger than she
but millennia wiser, and heard his cheerful voice: "Tovar,
as in Tovarich, that means 'friend' in Russian—either
'friend' or 'swish cavalry officer,' one of those. Tovar as in
Tovareska, which was Grandpappy's name in Pinsk. Line-
age? Half Ukraine, half Nairobi, half Scottish, half
Samoan-Mexican, all of us the better to hold and kiss you
with, m'dear." Rick, who was in Ireland completing
McGarry!, the film she had strongly recommended he not
make, especially after *Silent Piper*. Rick the jolly, consummate independent. Obstinate, dearest Rick, who would
come to her in London.

"Rick," she said aloud, her arms folded, hugging herself, hugging him. A computer dating machine, accidentally
matching us, would've thrown up its hands and thrown in
the towel—yet how right we are, how good we are for each
other!

He had telephoned her in New York yesterday from his
Dublin suite. "There's a story going around that you have
a birthday tomorrow. I looked up your horoscope. It says
you're romantic, idealistic, attracted to derelict movie
actors, clean and neat and punctual, and you're going to
take a long journey."

"It's all true."

"Are you sure? It says you're going to take a long journey
to Jersey City."

"You nut! How lovely you remembered to call!"

"I'm looking at your picture now and having erotic
thoughts. I think that's against the law in Ireland, so don't
tell anyone. Look, you hold Friday night open. This picture
has about a week's shooting to go, and the producer wanted
us to keep plugging through the weekend, but I made

26

temperamental-movie-star noises, so the set closes down on Friday at five-thirty and stays closed till Monday morning. I've never been to London, and I'm dying to see it. I hear they have great pizza there."

"Friday . . . this is only Tuesday. What I could do, darling, I could stop off in Dublin tomorrow on the way to London. It's been so long—"

Hastily: "No, no, we've waited this long, we can hang in a few days more. I'll bring you a brithday present I bought at Switzer's. If you don't like it, you can return it to the manufacturer in Jersey City."

"A birthday present, at my advanced age? What is it?"

"A record called *Mantovani Plays Roller Derby Classics*. What the hell do you care what it is till I see you? In the meantime, happy birthday, Miss Newfield." (It was always Newfield or Oldfield or Wheatfield, never Scofield.) "Oh, and *Ceád mille failte*. That's Gaelic. I see it on all the walls here. I think it means 'Post no bills.' "

Sipping the tea, she saw Evelyn Hobart, at the Heart Fund Ball last December, a week before she met Rick, once again overheard Evelyn babble to someone, "You know Mary's my closest friend on this earth, and I'd sell my soul for her and she would for me, but let's face it, she's as cold as the proverbial witch's tit. Beautiful, granted, and a gorgeous build, and, one thing about me, I'd kill myself before I'd say a word against her, but why do you suppose she can't keep a man? What you maybe figure is that it's her money, her name, her success, that men are afraid of a woman like that unless they're fortune hunters. Well, that's baloney. Frigid; that's her hang-up. She's been to I-don't-know-how-many psychiatrists to—"

Mary, with a tight smile, joining them: "Why don't you get on the public address system, Evelyn, so you can describe my warts to a maximum audience? Don't bother to document anything. It's all juicier your way."

Evelyn, flushed, hoarsely: "Lord, Mary, I didn't mean—"

Mary, sweetly: "—to be overhead. Obviously." She walked away.

Hurtful, she recalled now. Not only because a supposed friend, or *anyone*, could be that intentionally low, but because it was true. Partly true; not entirely true.

Had been partly true.

Until New Year's Eve, in the New York Scofield's Grand Ballroom.

I wanted ardently not to go to that party, she remembered. A linotypers' strike was brewing. The St Louis paper's circulation and advertising were in serious trouble and nobody could determine why. Father, harmless Harmon (what was it Joe Greenwood said about him? "Harmon Scofield wouldn't hurt a fly, unless it was open"), had just made his periodic rise from the grave, somewhere in Nevada, and was writing spates of rubber checks, his roundabout method of trying to get in touch with me. The White House press secretary was issuing his monthly denunciation of us. The Secretary of Defence was yawping, inaccurately, that we'd misquoted him. Deadline headaches all over the lot. The affair with Bill Bradway, seldom an ode to joy to begin with, was remorsefully over.

Joe talked me into attending my own party, the one we gave each New Year's Eve for every top- and middle-echelon Scofield employee and friend the hotel's ballroom could hold. "It'll do you good," he said. "You should put in an appearance, anyway—you missed the last three in a row. Oh, and this young Tovar's supposed to drop by. You two've never met. You ought to, if only to let him lick your hand for putting him in his current *oy veh* tax bracket."

That was patent nonsense, of course. He was just then beginning to be an enormous success in pictures. I'd suggested early on that our papers and *Scofield's* do some boosting, but all we did was to make his climb a little faster. His booming success was, is, his own.

I went to the New Year's Eve party, but not because Rick Tovar would be there. Not consciously. . . .

He wore a grey leather shirt, open at the throat, and

chocolate leather trousers with a jovial lace-up crotch. Mercifully, there were no clanking chains around his neck. He stood near the ballroom's smaller bar, holding a glass of beer, smiling, cordial, but his gaze just a little bit removed from those talking at him, an impressive-looking young man, a spectacular array of imperfections, of physical inconsistencies. His frame was sturdy, straight shoulders wall to wall; his head was too large and his hands and fingers were disproportionately small, almost feminine. He was clean-shaven, with a bale of jet black curly hair. His skin had the bright, leathery quality of his costume. His eyes were too far apart, and his broken nose had not been properly repaired, and his neck was too short.

He was made all wrong, and there was something almost studiously arrogant about him, and Mary's legs trembled slightly as Joe made the introductions.

"I'll buy you that drink now," Rick Tovar said, and gracefully took her arm and guided her from the cluster around him to the opposite end of the bar. "What's you pleasure?"

"A very light rye, lots of ginger ale."

He nodded. "I see you're a hopeless lush, just like me," he said and placed the order. Once more he looked at her, not quite swallowing her, regarded her with amusement and acceptance. "Thanks for the rescue. A nice lady back there was telling me more than I wanted to know about Christ knows what. Can we get you something to eat? They serve a dandy cannelloni here."

"Nope, I'm fine," Mary answered, afraid her uneasiness was showing, determined to relax. "May *I* tell you more than you may want to hear about something, if I promise not to gush? I finally caught up with *Silent Piper* and you're excellent in it."

"Umm. Fair," he said, shrugging those mammoth shoulders cheerfully. "Well, yeah, better than fair, considering that a year ago, less, I didn't know what the fuck I was doing near a camera."

The word shocked her. With a quickly grasped equilibrium, she said, "That's my point about *Piper*. You've made immense strides. Now you know what the fuck you're doing."

He grinned, catching the putdown. "I'm glad to meet you, Mary Wheatfield, even though you and *Scofield's* ought to compare notes once in a while. They rapped me and the picture. Not that it matters."

"It wasn't a rap," she corrected, and saw by his face that it indeed probably didn't matter. "Not a rave, I'll admit, but then I don't interfere with our writers' copy." Get off that subject fast, she thought. "I did like the letter you sent me just after our first article about you. It was absolutely snotty—wise-guy and sarcastic, as if you forgot that what you started to write was a thank-you note—but I think I got the drift. In your juggernaut way, you *were* saying thanks."

He grinned again. "Yeah, I guess it wasn't bad. You should've seen the ones that got away, though." He gracefully took the bartender's ginger ale and rye and gracefully— all his movements seemed graceful for a man so big—gave it to her, not noticing, or pretending not to notice, that her hand wasn't steady. *Damn*, she thought. *Damn*. "Sure you won't have some cannelloni? Peanuts? Fish eggs? Bubble gum?"

She shook her head, laughing, liking him enormously without entirely trusting him, not at all sure if his good-humoured devouring gaze was insulting or admiring or simply habit.

"Is your next picture set?" she asked.

"Maybe. We haven't decided yet. Look, let's not talk pictures, okay?"

"Why not?"

"Because acting, or whatever the hell it's called, is what I do for a living, and I get bored up to my ass rapping about contributions to the cin-e-maw."

"Okay, let's talk about what you do the rest of the time."

"Better yet, let's talk about what *you* do."

"What I do? I work. All the time."

"No fun?"

"Not often. That's not a pitch for sympathy, by the way."

"How about fellas? Love affairs? Meaningful interpersonal relationships, I'd guess you call them."

Mary frowned.

"What makes you presume that's what I call them? We've known each other for something like three minutes."

"What are you, sore?"

"No, but that was a rather patronizing thing to suggest. You don't know me."

Still smiling, without insolence, he nodded agreement. "I said it because I'm a boor and a thoroughly unsubtle bastard, and because I meant to say it. I size you up as a refined, warm lady who hasn't been balled lately."

Her hand automatically, maybe tellingly, flew to her throat. Suddenly incensed, abruptly turned off by his breezy freedom, certain she had reddened, she said, "What a refined, warm remark."

"Call me Honest Abe."

She set her glass down. "No, I think I prefer to call you Tacky Tovar. Or, let's see . . . Repulsive Rick."

"The lady alliterates well."

"The lady doesn't play these cocktail party chitchat games well, or patiently. Let's end this urbane conversation now."

"Fine with me. How soon can you spring from whoever you're with?"

". . . Why?"

"So we can cut out to somewhere and have a meaningful interpersonal relationship."

She shook her head. "I find a little of your straight-talk charm goes a long way, Mr Tovar. I'm sure you'll have no trouble finding any number of female objects here to accommodate you. Good evening and a successful prowl to you."

"Wait," he said and appeared, for the first time, serious. "Sure, they're objects, some of them. I like them. But who I really like is you."

"And that settles that? There's no time for grace, even a minimal pretence of pursuit? You like a woman and shazam, she's to jump on to your trophy wall? Please step aside. You're in my way."

"Come on, don't go. If you got me wrong, I'm sorry. Sincerely sorry. I want to ball you. That's not a capital crime."

She walked away from him, regally, past guests she supposed she should greet and be greeted by, aware that those guests who had been closest to them and their appalling conversation, perhaps fifteen feet away, might well have had sensitive hearing. She walked to the ladies' room, feeling used and cheapened, and bathed her face in cold water and worked to compose herself.

A fresh contingent of people was around him when she returned. He saw her and she purposely focused smiling, gracious attention on Derek North, Scofield International's chief counsel, who introduced her to his new Korean wife. She desperately wished to leave, and managed to slip out within minutes. Stefan, her chauffeur, drove her the dozen blocks to the Sutton Place town house, now empty except for the servants. She phoned the hotel and was connected with the ballroom. She identified herself to the operators. With cool dignity, she spoke her personal telephone number and asked that Mr Tovar, if he was still there, call her.

The phone rang, an endless twenty minutes later.

"We didn't get to finish our discussion," she said, still coolly.

"Let's."

"How soon can *you* spring from whoever you're with?"

"A couple of minutes. No problem."

She recited her address and replaced the receiver. Then she rang downstairs to Burt, the night man, and directed that a Mr Tovar was expected presently and was to be admitted.

Then she hurriedly showered and marvelled at the speed and ease with which a reasonably normal person can go mad.

The servants were tucked away. Mary, her hair brushed out long, sashed her blue silk robe tightly as she heard the

32

elevator, and she sighed, and hoped he had left his gloats down in the lobby.

He had.

The smile remained, though gentler, devoid of mockery. She closed the door, positive she was Zasu Pitts, and said, "No I-told-you-so jokes, all right?"

"I don't know any."

He did not touch her. He walked down the three steps into the sunken living room and declared, "My, you *are* a rich lady, aren't you? Can I borrow a cup of money?"

Following him but standing yards away, she asked, "Will you settle for a drink?"

"No, thanks. Just browsing." His eye caught the original Dubuffet framed above the east sofa. "That's a Dubuffet I haven't seen. Jesus, the colours!"

"How did you know it's Dubuffet?"

Eyebrow cocked, he said, "Lady, lady, I didn't get beyond two and a half years of high school, and they tore down the neighbourhood where I was born and raised and they put up a slum, but—"

"Ah, I'm sorry, I apologize for that. Chalk up a wrong preconception on *my* side. Are we even now?"

"What was my wrong preconception?"

"That I'm an uptight wreck because it's been forever since I've made love."

"I don't remember putting it exactly that—"

Close to him, she said in a voice that was baby lettuce, weak and unsure of itself, "Let's talk all through the night. We'll speak our evaluations of each other. I can't imagine anything more stimulating."

"Can't you?"

"Well, as a matter of fact, something more stimulating does leap to mind. . ."

Rick Tovar was marvellous.

Marvellous to Mary Scofield, who had had lovers and husbands and lovers, Mary who was Harmon's child, Mary who was thirty-nine and a child, Mary who anxiously wanted this man she did not know. He was in less of a hurry than she. "What's your rush?" he asked. "Will they charge you double for the room if you stay a little past check-out time?" She shook her head. "Good," he said and caressed her. "I don't see how we're going to get to know each other if you're holding me in one hand and a stopwatch in the other."

Marvellous to Mary, whose lovers had been contemptuous of her or felt threatened by her, the same thing, lovers who were ignorant of making love and occasionally even of making sex, certainly never a lover this secure, this very dear lover who was sweetly kissing her, telling her with words unneeded that what they were doing was good. *Rick,* she thought. *Rick.*

The kisses began slowly, growing in promise and meaning, and he wanted the bedroom light on so they could see each other, not with cheap-thrill smirks but with pleasure, playful and honest and increasingly voluptuous pleasure. Then they were building together, building something that became more ardent and more erotic because they knew who they were, what each of them was giving and getting, what they both were sharing—*precisely that, sharing,* she thought, *ah, what a lovely word: sharing.* And soon she was feeling him, Rick, Mary was feeling Rick, feeling Rick not only inside her but throughout her, and the first incredible explosion was near, and she called out, and so did he, so did Rick. . .

"Oh my," she said, seconds or centuries later.

" 'Oh my?' " he teased, relaxed, holding her. "Is that the most lyrical thing you can say?"

"I feel just . . . wonderful. I feel like reciting *Sonnets from the Portuguese.*"

"You try that and the whole thing's off."

I *do* feel wonderful, she thought, lying closer, kissing his eyes. "Please? Just a little part of a stanza?"

"Nope," he said, smiling, looking at her with love. "I know your type. You begin with part of a stanza, then it's the poem, then you sing *Aida,* taking all the parts. Then you get so all worked up with culture that you'll barrel out of bed and you'll want to start debating the classics with me.

Let's keep it simple and genital till we've known each other a little longer. Mercy, we've just met, after all!"

Mary laughed. "You're insane!"

Rick kissed her lips. "And very simple and genital."

"I was saying 'Oh my. . .'"

"All right. Why?"

"Yes, why? Before you so rudely interrupted me, I was going to say, 'Oh my, isn't it interesting, a woman can share something as intimate with a man as sex, and be completely uninhibited, and when it's done, the moment after she begins to think, not just feel, inhibitions start flooding back. What should she talk about if he doesn't talk first? Should she talk about what they did? Should she talk about the wallpaper, should—"

"Umm. Now it's my turn to say 'Oh my.'"

"All right. Why?"

"Our first quarrel, dear. I should've quit when I was winning and let you say a little poetry. What I can't stand more than I can't stand 'How do I love thee?' is a lady analyzing her feelings out loud so fast. Sharrap, awready."

She playfully punched his ridiculously hairy arm. "You're a cretin. And you have ridiculously hairy arms. And a ridiculous body."

"That cut."

"All these muscles are positively ostentatious. Can't you stop them from rippling at least while I'm talking?"

"What's the matter with these muscles? I sent off for them from this catalogue a few weeks ago, right after a bully kicked sand in my face on the beach."

"You still have a ridiculous body."

"Yeah. What else I have is an awfully pleasant, peaceful sense of our being together. You're clucking on like a chorus of magpies."

"But I want to talk! I want to know everything there is to know about you."

He sighed, and shifted his weight to sit up. "Okay, shoot. But keep it to one brief question. I'm double-parked. Are there any cigarettes here?"

"I can get some."

"No, don't leave me. I don't smoke, anyway."

"Did you ever smoke?"

"Never. Which answers your one brief question. Look, I don't dig saying personal things about myself, especially to a nice lady I've just met. I'm a big moom pitcher star. I own a few stocks and some of the San Fernando Valley. Why don't you read that old issue of *Scofield's*? They wrote up everything about me except that I'm gay and I shoot scag every day before and during vespers and I strangle nice ladies who ask me to talk about myself before we've been properly introduced. Are you *sure* you don't have any cigarettes? Or scag? Or someone around who's gay?"

"Can I at least find out if you went to the party tonight with a date?"

Pretending resignation, again smiling, again sighing, he said "You do pry."

"Yes."

"Believe it or not, I can't recall the child's name. Cindy, Sunny, Honey, Money, Funny, something like that. The studio got her for me. I've been in New York exactly three times in my life; I don't have any lady friends of my own here—till now." He kissed Mary's breast lightly, lovingly. "So Honey-Money-Sunny was enlisted for me."

"How does she get home, or wherever it is she goes?"

"How the hell should I know that? What're you, worried about *her*?"

"Only in a general way. I suspect she's a person."

"Uh-oh," he said. "I wander into a town for a little while to sell my Bibles, and I wind up in the feathers with a militant feminist. You go easy, you hear? I'm from the hill country. I once asked Paw what I should call Maw, and he said, 'Call her the woman, that's good enough.' My grannies, Mary Hatfield, but you're a nice lady even if you do confuse a bed with a shrink's couch. . ."

Mary laughed. "Cindy-Mindy," she prompted.

"Cindy-Mindy," he repeated. "The studio may or may not have Cindy-Funny-Money-Rintintinny on retainer; I

36

have no idea and I'm really not all that grabbed. She was hired, presumably at union wages, to perform a service: to show up on the arm of the big moom pitcher star. I'm staying at the Regency. The understanding was that she'd go back to the Regency with me and help me shell lichee nuts. What're you after me about? I may be a slavering Russki pig, but I'm not callous. If I thought Mindy-Funny-Bunny was in the least danger of going on the sidewalk and being raped or whistled at, I'd've made doubly sure that someone from the studio convoyed her safely back to the convent. What're you starting up? You want me to go find her and bring you back an affidavit that her psyche and her hymen are intact?"

He did not stay the night, but he stayed late. Mary brewed coffee, and he scrambled eggs, and the talk was silly and disjointed and, best of all, most warming of all, integrity and sensitivity and goodness glistened under his strong young man's layers of gap-it-up defences. At last, he said, "I better mosey on back to the corral, Miz Oldfield. There's cows to milk and hay to pitch and all."

"Will you come for dinner tomorrow night? *Tonight*, that is."

"Can't. They have me booked to do some handstands for the picture. But I'll call. If you're not in, I'll leave a message at the candy store."

He didn't kiss her. A large, direct smile spread over his face before he left, though, which was almost as good. "Happy New Year, Mary Sunfield," he said warmly. "It looks like very fine weather ahead."

He called three days, an eternity, later. "Would you be free this evening to show me your scrapbook of baby pictures?"

Relieved, testily: "Are you hard up for a date?"

Sharply: "Don't say that."

"I—"

"It doesn't insult me. It insults you. Don't ever be funny that way."

"All right. What shall I wear?"

"Anything that looks nice on the floor."

What began as sex, physical attraction, chemical attraction, happy laughs, grew into something deeper. Though he cautioned her in different ways that each of them was a free bird, that his independence was sacred to him, they arranged to dovetail their hectic schedules as often as possible, Mary sometimes reorganizing appointments to fly to him on the Coast, Rick sometimes unexpectedly popping into New York when the studio wanted him somewhere else. He was not awed by who she was away from the rooms where they met: he called her the Empress, but teasingly. He wished nothing from her except for them to be together; once, when she offered to have her own legal staff advise him on his business affairs, he irritably warned her to do her Empress bit on her own time. And moments afterward kidded her and made love to her.

Joe Greenwood heard about her and Rick Tovar and counselled, "Take it easy. You're occasionally bright in the head, so take it easy. Your mind's not on the store. You're behaving like puberty just hit you."

"It's the most amazing thing, *Yussele!*" she exclaimed. "I know everything even remotely reasonable is against it. I'm pushing forty and he's a baby. We're poles apart in just about everything. But I'm happy, *Yussele!* For the first time in forever, I've met a man, an exceptional man who wouldn't care if my name was Mary Fileclerk. Aren't you always after me to enjoy being alive?"

I love you, she thought now.

I want you.

I love you. I want you.

You brought me awake. Please be there on Friday, dearest crazy Rick, jokes and all, sweetness and all, arms and warmth and body and lips and safety and all, please be there, please be here, now, here so we—

She buzzed the pilot, Jeanne Astor.

"We'll land in Dublin," she said.

A pause. "That could be tricky. The flight plans we filed

said London."

"See what you can manage, Jeanne. Figure out what the Dublin tower will buy. Some malfunction? A sick passenger aboard?"

". . . Dublin."

"Yes. Dublin."

Yes, Dublin, Mary thought, and, excitement building, pressed another button to say to Liz Hale, "Let's have the beige dress instead of the pants suits. I have a birthday date tonight."

She hurried out of her robe. They hadn't seen each other in nearly a month, an unbearably long month. She had done the unforgivable, had spoken of love without smiling. He had frozen, only for a moment, but in that moment she had feared his next move would be to disappear, vanish forever. They had telephoned each other since, sometimes every day. Each call ended with the feeling that they were closer than ever. I'll surprise him, thought Mary. He'll love me for surprising him. Please . . .

TWO

ON THAT LATE, rainy morning of Mary Scofield's fortieth birthday, Judge Aaron Weinzimer sat in Manhattan's Federal Court and concluded his long charge to the jury. The trial of Chris McCabe, Beah Hendrix, and Victor Skinner had taken a month, and the corridor verdict among waiting television crews and reporters was that the jury would vote guilty on all counts for all three within a matter of hours. The defendants, charged with felony murder while in the act of robbing the Bank of America, had smirked at one another and at the jury during much of the often bombastic trial. Now they appeared oddly subdued, almost as if they had finally come to recognize that, while they were still in centre stage, their fate was indeed in the hands of those six women and six men in the box.

And on that day's evening television newscasts were tapes of a ragtag band of protesters in Foley Square, catcalling for the defendants' acquittal, bawling that the press and TV were (bleep) fascist railroaders and (bleep) lynchers. Some carried and hoisted crudely printed signs that read *Free Political Prisoners* and *Hendrix-McCabe-Skinner Innocent, Amerika Press Guilty!!!* A squat, strident young woman, perhaps twenty years old, grabbed the hand mike placed before her and jeered, "No, I won't give my name—that'll get me murdered by the FBI and the CIA all that much quicker. Whyn't choo go after the Scofield press? They're the guilty ones. Go ask rich (bleep) Mary Scofield questions about what's going on in there. She's the (bleep) ought to be strung up. You see me, Mary Scofield? You listening to me in your silks and satins while the poor get poorer and the innocent get fried? You and your (bleep) newspapers deserve all the credit!"

Or so I, Joe Greenwood, heard later. I'd very much wanted

40

to be in my Scofield Building office in New York that day, from where I could be kept in quick touch with developments, such as whether McCabe, Hendrix, and Skinner were indeed sobering up to reality or still saw the trial as some psychedelic circus prank that would exonerate and maybe even coronate them.

I'd very much wanted to be in New York that day, too, because a lot of news was happening or about to break. The reports from and about the Middle East were chilling, more ominous, if that was conceivable, than they'd ever been. Wall Street was having some month of May sweats. Two catastrophes on the very same day, an earthquake in Mexico and a flood in India, were still claiming thousands upon thousands of lives. We—*we* meaning our New York paper, the *Outlook*, and our news magazine, *Scofield's*— were blowing the whistle in print on U.S. Senator William Bradway, Rhode Island's Mr Impeccable whom we'd been plumping as a someday President of the United States until our Washington man, Van Avery, manoeuvred down some back alleys and found that home-and-hearth Bill Bradway was playing with girls. That by itself was scarcely an earthquake. The girls he was playing with, though, happened to be very young girls.

And I'd very much wanted to stay close to home base that day because my twenty-four-hour virus (a word invented by my Greek doctor; it means "Your guess is as good as mine") was entering its second week. Most of me still creaked, my stomach was a disaster area, and I was turning into a Gelusil junkie.

Instead, I spent half of that wet, miserable Wednesday in May—a day that should have carried a warning on the package that it could be hazardous to mental health—flying from JFK to Tampa, tracking down my boss Mary Scofield's fifteen-year-old daughter, Carole, who'd run away with some klutz lover.

The night before, the headmistress of her boarding school in Westchester had phoned me. Carole had been missing all day. The headmistress, a Miss Deane, had privately inter-

41

rogated those girls who might know something. One of them cracked. The school kept strict tabs on its students' incomings and outgoings, but somehow Carole had connected with a gas pump jockey in the village and the two of them had been deathless sweethearts for a week, at least. According to Carole's roommate, the girl who cracked, the couple were fleeing—air fare paid by Carole, naturally—to live and work and pray on a farm estate called the Willows, eighteen miles south of Tampa.

I had my secretary book me on the next morning's first commercial flight, under a phony name. I phoned our best man in Tampa, Charlie Payne, told him to find out all he could about the Willows, and when to meet me at the airport.

And received, barely minutes after I phoned Payne that Tuesday night, a message that I return an urgent personal call to a Dr Halversen, phone number furnished. I needed a moment to remember who a Dr Halversen was, but it came to me, and with no spasm of exhilaration. Anna Halversen was the psychiatrist who ran Hartford House, the private hospital in Connecticut that treated, at approximately eight million dollars a day each, emotionally ill people who happened to be very rich. Harmon Scofield, Mary's father, was there, or at least I had directed that he be checked in there, on Mary's instructions, six weeks before. I did not want to return Dr Halversen's urgent call. But I placed the call, because I've always been a sucker for the word "urgent". And because Halversen, whom I'd never met, and I had a pact: if she absolutely had to contact anyone, it was to be no one but me.

She answered. In soft, Scandinavian accents—I'm often a sucker for those, too—she said that Harmon had carried his belongings out of the hospital at mid-afternoon, over her strenuous protest that he was not nearly well enough to leave. More, she had no idea of where he was bound. "He pronounced himself cured," she said, "and decided there were more important things for him to do."

"So? He's a grown man, isn't he?"

"That's exactly what he isn't. He's fifty-nine years old. He's in incredibly good physical health, and he looks like a youthful forty-five, but he's still a terribly confused adolescent. And terribly self-destructive, for all his undeniable charm and intelligence. If there's any way he can be located—"

"How would I go about that, Doctor?"

"I always imagined the Scofield Company could find anything it cared to find."

"If it cared, possibly yes. Excuse me, Doctor, but that self-destructive label was hardly fastened on him for the first time six weeks ago. And forgive me if I sound tired, which I am, or heartless, which I think I'm not. We had an arrangement. When he was scooped out of that alley a month and a half ago and agreed to have private institutional help, my orders from Miss Scofield were firm, and I relayed them to you: we would pay the bill for as long as he stayed at your place, one day or one year or for the rest of his life. But the moment he left, dismissed or on his own, our obligation immediately stopped."

"Mr Gree—"

"Doctor Halversen, how clear can I make it? You're naturally not interested in my own simplistic evaluation, that that fifty-nine-year-old, terribly confused adolescent should've been forced to look out for himself when he *was* an adolescent. His father and then his mother decided otherwise, but I frankly wonder if at fifty-nine he's ever going to start wearing long pants. If anything, I think Miss Scofield has—"

"Perhaps I should speak with Miss Scofield."

"Miss Scofield's leaving for London. And if you've been listening to me, Miss Scofield has been more than patient, more than generous, considering what a mess he's been not only to himself but to everyone close to him."

"The man is sick."

"The man, Doctor, has been rehearsing suicide for half a century. Maybe what he's entitled to is a plaque for constancy. He's been practising for death all along, with drink,

43

with dirt-road brawls, with kinky sex expeditions, with sloth, with the whole Krafft-Ebing *shmeer*. So now his craft is ebbing. So who really cares, Doctor? You, obviously; he was placed in your charge, and I don't mean to minimize your skills. But there's to be no more of him as far as we're concerned. Send your final bill, and you'll be paid promptly, and thank you for your concern."

Rescuing Scofields, I thought, replacing the receiving. Is that why Mama had me, and Pop skipped the light bill so I could have violin lessons—for me to grow up and rescue Scofields?

Wheezing and not overjoyed, I made the Wednesday morning plane to Tampa minutes before the gate closed. The Company paid a fat annual retainer fee to Pearlin's, the private investigator firm with an office in every major and near major city in the country, specializing in speed and delivery, by fair means or foul. My initial impulse had been to call their central number and have one or two of their boys dispatched to the Willows. I overcame the impulse; this job was mine, not a stranger's. I settled into my seat, resenting the nuisance of the trip, aware it was necessary, all too aware of the serious possibilities. If Carole could be got out of that place peacefully, assuming she *was* there, then no harm done except to my nervous system. If she was there and had to be pried away, that would present problems, though problems that could be handled.

But if she wasn't there, then we had some real rouble. She wasn't just any runaway kid. She was Mary Scofield's kid and, except for a single rebellious act a few years before, the world's most manageable dishrag. The Company, the umbrella name for all the Scofield enterprises, was rich as hell. Kidnapping was a prospect that never failed to keep us alert and guarded, kidnapping for ransom or abduction for just plain psychotic reasons by just plain psychotics. Mary rarely talked to me about the possibility, but of course it had to be a source of concern to her. And to me, Scofield executive vice-president, Mary's friend (and, back in the

44

Stone Age, her lover), and congenital worrier.

I mentioned the kid's one act of rebellion. It happened when she was twelve. Mary was having a quiet affair with young Bill Bradway, whom she'd just then helped get elected to the Senate—I say quiet because much of his public *shtik* was that he was a devoted family man—and somewhere around that time Carole disappeared from school. We found her about five hours later, on a bus heading for Rhode Island. Once the hysterics could be interrupted for a while, she explained what she'd been up to. Bill Bradway had been nice to her, nicer and more understanding than anyone she'd ever met. She wanted to see him and be with him, that was all. Mary came down hard on her, bawled her out for behaving like an inconsiderate, thoroughly selfish and thoughtless child. More hysterics, followed by the kid repeating her surprise that she'd caused such a commotion. She apologized and kept apologizing and swore she would never upset her mother, ever again.

Whatever her reason or reasons for performing that bus act—it was the stupidity that's unique to twelve-year-old girls, or it was her tricky way of sending up some sort of SOS—she kept her promise and went straight. She returned to being the angel child—high honour roll, never a murmur of complaint about anything, steady and obedient.

Until today. Today I remembered our five-hour sweats, three years ago. The kid had pulled a dumb, impulsive stunt. Today, I thought, she's just pulling another one, right? Maybe.

Hurry up, I said in silence. Get this plane in the air.

The nonstop to Tampa took off a half-hour late because of the weather. I tried to tackle some paper work and ignore those rumbling noises the dark sky was making, but I didn't have much luck. I flew a great deal and knew all the heartening statistics about air safety, and yet one of my greatest pleasures in life was staying out of airplanes, even in ideal weather.

I'd spoken with Mary by phone that Wednesday morning

45

before she left for London. I'd mentioned her father but not Carole. All right, I shouldn't have mentioned either one—Carole, whom she loved in her way; Harmon, whom she detested in her way. Why had I brought up one and not the other? Because she would have worried about her daughter, and I didn't want her worrying right then. So why tell her about Horrible Harmon at large again? Maybe because he was capable of absolutely any wild stunt, and some of those stunts had involved the press in the past and could in the future. I thought Mary ought to be prepared for something batty. Or tragic.

In the first-class section, which I stubbornly chose to believe in my mature wisdom was safer than coach in case of emergency, the pincushiony stewardess asked me if I'd like a drink. Normally that would have been a splendid suggestion, but I anticipated a rocky time in Florida, calling for some semblance of a clear head. I asked for Sanka.

And popped another Gelusil and reminded myself again that this was not a seemly way for a man about to be fifty years old to spend a day. I'm large, physically, and when it's necessary or simply simpler, I'm blessed or cursed with a bulldozer manner that often successfully passes for authority, even when I'm not entirely sure what the hell I'm talking about. I have one of those Paul Robeson sub-basement speaking voices that grabs immediate attention with no special help from me. Oh, and I also have only one eye, which isn't the non sequitur it might sound like; it makes me look tough.

But that morning I didn't feel tough, certainly not in the long-ago, heavyweight-contender sense. Sore and controllably agitated, but not tough.

Why was I more anxious than usual? I didn't really think Mary's kid was in danger—not then, anyway—although I didn't cherish that praying organic farm stuff; we'd run an exposé on the rip-offs of a sickie religious cult that called itself God's Love, a series not designed to endear us to those crazies. I'd asked Mary to stay around where I could keep my one eye on her and not go off to England, award or no

46

award, but I didn't really think she was in danger, either—not there, anyway.

So why the jumps?

Because in the past couple of years, on Mary's quiet "Don't you think . . . ?" orders, the *Outlook* and our magazine and our other newspapers had stepped up their investigative reporting. In the best old-fashioned sense, Mary had turned us into muckrakers and crusaders, and there we were, frequently unzipping the flies and exposing the corruptions not only of the professional corrupters like Ramon Vienna but of sacrosancts in big industry and big government. In crass as well as idealistic terms, I was all for it, of course: our circulation shot up and we didn't lose advertisers. And I marvelled more than ever at quiet, soft-spoken Mary, who had the guts of a porch climber. In her guileful "Don't you think . . . ?" and "You may not go along with this idea . . ." way, she was stepping on some mighty toes.

I was all for it, yes, and we worked in happy tandem and generally in complete agreement, but the jitters gradually began to get to me, jitters about Mary. Mary Scofield, publisher, was one thing—a publisher is someone who sits off there somewhere and, in the public mind, probably doesn't even exist.

Mary Scofield, celebrity, was something else. When she caught hold of a cause, when she was convinced that the venalities of this politician and the evils of that untouchable Mafia pasha could be documented, she put it in the papers (always giving her editors, reporters, and columnists plenty of room and independence; the chain's six papers were encouraged to devise their own editorial policies, and the *Outlook* and *Scofield's* were occasionally at snapping editorial odds with each other), and she went on television. She'd started the route with naked nerve ends because she was positive she wasn't a performer, but she began well enough, and got better, and pretty soon she was able to book herself on any talk show she wanted. She had a lot going for her in front: she was luscious to look at, the festive brown eyes, the contagious smile, the graceful figure.

Once she got the hang of making on-camera chatter come out amusing and informed and wordly, she was a dynamite guest and overnight star, pulling in the customers with observations on next season's Paris fashions and giving a great impersonation of Winston Churchill delivering his opinion of American bread, then holding the customers with her proof that Ramon Vienna, the elder statesman of Fort Lee, New Jersey, wasn't a retired gambler but an active director in dope traffic.

I started calling her Wonder Woman, at first with simple sarcasm. Before long, it wasn't so funny. I warned her to go back to the low profile. She wouldn't listen. In April, just a month before, she'd gone on the late-night *Billy Spear Show*, the one on the major network with an estimated thirty million nightly viewers, to talk about something featured on such cotton-candy talk shows called This and That. From This and That, she dove with spirit into Ramon Vienna. "This man isn't a lovable ex-thug who prospered as a boot-legger and then went on to prosper in the Market and real estate and night clubs as he's hired the finest of Madison Avenue to picture him," she maintained. "He's a once and present thug, a here-and-now criminal who controls the syndicate that imports and sells hard drugs. What's this delicate ballet about? The Justice Department calls Vienna the kingpin of crime, yet the Justice Department doesn't go near him. Isn't anyone out there asking why?"

In a controlled voice, completely free of hysteria, she made a peck of charges on the Spear show, charges we'd that day documented in the *Outlook*. Her most damning whammy was that Vienna and the U.S. Attorney General, Alfred Bertrand, were, if not cronies, perhaps not exactly foes. She held up the photograph, the same one we'd run, of both men beaming and shaking hands at a Waldorf charity dinner, and claimed it had been taken a week earlier, which was true. She presented and read her letter to the Attorney General asking how come. The gist of the reply from Bertrand's office was that the nation's number one law enforcer shook many hands, that he certainly hadn't recognized Mr Vienna, and the "unfortunate" incident at the Waldorf in no way suggested that Mr Bertrand looked with favour on any allegedly unsavoury character.

"The operative word here is 'allegedly,'" said Wonder Woman. "If our Attorney General doesn't recognize the face of the quote allegedly unquote unsavoury Mr Vienna, whom our papers and others have been front-paging for a very long while, then I submit the Justice Department could do with some house-cleaning."

Her evidence scrupulously prepared—in her few non-working hours, she sometimes gave you the feeling she'd have trouble ordering breakfast by herself, but the big number about Ms Velvet Claw Mary was that she never went into battle without a full knowledge of her facts and figures—she rounded out her turn on the Spear show with more bull's-eyes on Ramon Vienna. The network was all for killing her taped appearance. Reasonably, firmly, she insisted it run, pointing out that otherwise her papers would have to treat the whole thing as an appalling example of news censorship. The network issued disclaimers before, during, and after the holocaust. But her segment ran.

I was in Denver that day, checking up first hand on why our paper there, the normally shipshape *Register-Forum*, was suddenly having curious personnel problems, but I watched the Spear show from my room in the Brown Palace, and phoned Mary in New York blazing mad. "This is Ramon Vienna's second cousin speaking," I said. "We're very pertoibed, and we're afraid the next time we see you we're going to have to give you two broken legs. There's a gentleman here with us named Joe Greenwood, a handsome man with one eye and gorgeous table manners, he's trying to talk us out of it. He says he wouldn't mind at all if you had skinny legs or fat legs, but he surely does like your pretty legs and he claims we should think it over. A wonderful man, *impeccable* table manners, but we're going to have to break his legs, too."

Mary laughed. "The wonderful man should've been asleep, not watching television."

"You dumb *shiksa!*" I hollered, maybe a bit too loud. "Show me where it's written that you're guaranteed a charmed life. These are *cut*throats you're playing potsy with! We ran the story and the pictures on page one, didn't we? For the sake of your neck, why the hell did you have to by-line it on the tube?"

Her voice was carved in butter. "I adore you, too, *Yussele.* Now you'll have to excuse me. I have a guest."

"Well, make sure you get his name," I said. "If he's Vienna's cousin, tell him he can't hurt you because you have a charmed life." I could guess who the guest was, because Rick Tovar was in New York. They'd been a house afire since they'd met on New Year's Eve; to my everlasting jealous shame, I'd been the one who'd introduced them. "You watch yourself, lady tycoon," I cautioned. "The world's full of Viennas. I finger beads for you, and I'm not even of that faith."

"I know you do, darling, and you know I'm grateful. I really must get off now. Sleep well."

Sleep well.

"We will be landing at Tampa Airport, ladies and gentlemen," said my very own pincushiony stewardess over the loudspeaker. "Captain Miles has asked that you fasten your seat belts, bring your seats to an upright position, and extinguish all smoking materials."

From my window, Tampa didn't look much drier than New York. I stuffed my mostly unread papers back into my briefcase and glanced up to see the pincushiony stewardess sit in the empty seat beside me for the descent. "Do you live in Tampa?" she asked.

I couldn't be sure if she was merely making nothing conversation or if she was hot to have me ask her out. I'd flown alone often enough to spot certain beacons of invitation, and this seemed like one. Unattached stewardesses can get lonely in strange layover cities, too, I'd learned. It's not that they're free lunch, ready to hop in the hay on deplaning, though that's been known to happen. If a man is likewise unattached, if he looks as if he's taken a bath that day and doesn't appear to be inclined toward assault, friendly associations are sometimes born. Nearing fifty and owning a single eye, I told myself she would say yes if I suggested dinner, and I was flattered by her taste. "No," I answered. "I'm going there to pick up a package and fly right back East."

She smiled. "Have a nice flight back."

I watched the roll of her tight, charming rump as she went to the cabin door to wait for the three other passengers in First Class to file past her, and I had to remind myself as I got up that there was no way she and I were going to sing "Hello, Young Lovers" to ourselves. I was a weary old widower with a raspy cold, come south to pick up a package.

I'd been with the Company for seven years. Mary had personally hired me soon after she'd assumed the president's chair, determined to make it a going proposition but less than wildly confident. She'd hired me not because we'd almost married a couple of decades ago—each of us was married by that time, anyway—but because the publishing part of the Company was being operated by bookkeepers and accountants and attorneys who knew not much about business and nothing about newspapers, and I was a newspaperman who could read a profit-and-loss statement. When I joined up, the Company's nonpublishing holdings—the real estate, the mills and mines and the rest of it—were and conceivably always would go on coining money without serious interruption, but the papers and magazines, far too many of them, were limping towards economic disaster.

Mary made some efforts to install and prop up her then husband, Owen Enright, Carole's father, as a corporate wizard. He tried. He was a wipeout. She offered me a free hand. I took it, and looked around and saw that the sagging soufflé called the Scofield Company wasn't simply a matter of old, dead Adam's 1930s brand of journalism still doddering off the presses in the late 1960s. The caretakers were studiously incompetent; the chief counsel was the kind of gallus-snapping lawyer who could get your parking ticket

51

reduced to second-degree manslaughter. What was really criminal wasn't only that the whole host of dozing executive firebrands was blissfully ignorant of budgeting, planning, and coherent growth strategy; they were putting out papers and magazines with all the vitality of a condemned sperm bank. Most of them were relics of retainers, hired by Adam Scofield of sweet charity fame, on lifetime contracts with instructions that they could never be fired—red-faced drunks who took four-hour lunches and talked incessantly about the old days.

I advised Mary, first off, to clear out the deadwood, impose budget discipline, sell or fold the papers and magazines that were coughing blood, and sign up bright new brains with ideas and crackle.

She listened, and asked me to play Torquemada. I "promoted" some of the Scofield dinosaurs into meaningless posts. I gave the others the options of either retiring then and there or being transferred to Podunk. It wasn't a fun way to start a job, but it got us rolling.

It would be gratifying to say that I made the Company the Company.

Gratifying, and drivel. I helped to inject some fresh plasma. What ideas and crackle I brought were brought at the right time, within the right confluences.

But that's all I brought. For more than her first thirty years, Mary Scofield had drifted about in her perpetual ballroom of a professional heiress's life, attended by lovers and husbands and sucker fish, with only foggy notions of why she was there and where she was going, vibrant and brainless.

We should all be so brainless. Once she roused herself out of her superrich slumber and got going, she was unstoppable; she transformed herself into—well, Mary Scofield. She had her emotional screwups, too many, but she left them outside the office. Inside, she performed miracles.

Along the way, she earned herself a standing-room-only list of enemies.

And some friends, too. Not many, maybe, but those few who had been able to get through the princess-in-a-castle barriers of wealth were, some things being equal, fairly close and loyal friends. Not real confidants, that is, but friends. I doubt if Mary had a glimmer of what went into fully confiding in someone; I'm convinced she felt safer with me than with anyone else she knew, and yet I never got a hundred percent of her. No one did, I'm sure, ever. Still, as I say, there were people altogether faithful to her—a neat trick, considering how hard it is to locate delicacy inside steel. . .

On my way out of the plane, I nodded to my pincushiony stewardess and walked down the ramp, catching sight of the waving Charlie Payne, who was standing in the downpour behind the gate.

Tsuris, I thought.

Tsuris is a Yiddish word. It means, *Mary, I hope I can get you out of this jam, and every jam ahead. But let's not bank on it.*

THREE

WEARING DARK GLASSES and a silk head kerchief, Mary walked alone and quickly through Dublin Airport's bustling terminal to immigration, her overnight valise and small attaché case in one hand, her passport in the other, feeling expectant and mildly disoriented, as she invariably did on deplaning. She stood in line, alert to the possibility, one to be avoided, that she might be recognized by passers-by. Liz Hale had radioed the Gresham Hotel and reserved a suite for J. Clark, the checking-in name Mary used when special privacy was required. Liz and the crew would stay at the International, adjacent to the terminal building, and she would phone Liz in the morning when she was ready to go on to London. They likely were unhappy about the stopover here, she knew, though they had given her a chocolate cake with a single lighted candle and sung "Happy Birthday," purposely and outrageously off-key, though clearly with affection.

The immigration officer inquired, "Your purpose for your visit to Ireland?"

To sleep with my lover.

"To visit with some friends. I'll leave for London tomorrow."

He touched his temple. "Do enjoy your stay. Next." The customs inspector barely glanced at the valise and attaché case and also wished her a pleasant stay.

A mammoth taxi driver, grizzled and merry, a jumbo edition of Barry Fitzgerald with little broken veins in his bulbous nose, tugged at his shapeless wool cap in salute, took her articles, and led her to his cab. "The Gresham, please," she said.

"The Gresham Hotel, yes, the grand old Gresham on O'Connell Street, missus. There's just the one of ya?" Mary nodded. "John Hurley at your service, missus. Drivin'

54

thirty year, never neared a drop o' the craythure, never had a motor accident, bless God." He helped her into the taxi, slid himself heavily behind the wheel, and drove, and commenced to talk. Mary knew Dublin, had come to it often with Tommy, her first husband. They had loved it for its reluctance to leave the graces and courtesies of the nineteenth century. She recalled most fondly its taxi drivers, especially the older ones, constantly jabbering, intuitively kind.

"Glorious mist tonight, isn't it, missus?"

"Glorious," she agreed. "The rain was dreadful in New York this morning."

"From America, are ya?"

"Yes."

"I'm hopin' to go to America one day in the not too distant future. I have me a nevvoo, stoodyin' at school in Massachusetts. Wouldn't dream you'd know him. Still, never can tell. . . ."

"What's his name?"

"Padraig Hurley, missus. He's not from here. He was born and bred in County Clare. He's stoodyin' dentistry. Nah, you wouldn't know him."

"I don't know him, but I do know Clare, a little. What part?"

"You do know Clare, do ya? Would ya know the Limerick area now?"

"Oh, yes. And Burren, and Moher, and Ennis."

The driver whistled and whinnied. "Now, now. I'd best quit whilst I'm ahead. Is it Irish you are, then?"

"Somewhere along the line, I'm sure, Mr Hurley."

"How'd ya know me name?"

"You told me."

"Did I now? And ya remembered. Isn't that darlin'!"

He talked. And talked. And Mary warmed to the easy richness of him. She saw a Catholic medal on his dashboard, and noticed that he crossed himself as he drove past a church, and wondered how much he would disapprove of her if he knew her mission tonight.

Please don't be displeased with me, Mr Hurley, she thought as they chatted together, Mary asking him questions about his life and his family, his opinions on the situation in the North, about Ireland's future and Ireland's present, hoarding his answers in the memory bank she would eventually unlock and sift through. Accept me, Mr Hurley, she thought, like me. In my way, I see sex as a holy sacrament, too. I spent the last twenty-one of my first thirty-nine years viewing it with suspicion, plunging into it, sometimes enjoying and even admiring it, almost never trusting it. Because I almost never trusted my lovers, or me.

But it's altogether different with Rick, Mr Hurley. You'd say, *Very well, then, marry up with the lad and make it right with God*. But it *is* right with God now, or whoever or whatever is in charge of the cosmos. I once tried to total the number of lovers over these last twenty-one years. Including the husbands, Tommy, Gil, and Owen, the number came to about ten, give or take a forgettable weekend or two with the half-remembered transients. I may have scared most of the good ones away—I, or the money, or the combination of us both.

Please accept why I'm here, Mr Hurley. I'd do the same for you. . .

"God save us all, it's been a delight, a delight," John Hurley declared at the Gresham, pulling his cap off and running his swollen fingers through scraggly hair. "Would ya be wantin' a driver after tonight, missus?" He gave her a wrinkled card. "Cheap rates, and I never had a motor accident."

"I can't stay as long as I'd like, but thank you," Mary said, wishing she could kiss his cheek simply because of the glow of sweetness from him. She made him take a pound note as a tip, though he protested it was far too extravagant of her. "You said your son Dominick's First Communion is this Sunday. Get him a little something extra with this, and tell him its from an American lady who loves the Hurleys."

The desk clerk indeed had a reservation for J. Clark. A

bellman accompanied her in the lift and asked if she didn't agree there was a magnificent mist out tonight.

In her sitting room, she phoned Rick Tovar's suite.

"Uh-huh?" came a honeyed female voice.

Puzzled: "Mr Tovar, please."

"Mr Gitcheegoomee Tovar, the honest Injun?" A young voice, giggling, either giddy or drunk. "Nobody here but us chickens. Call back Christmas."

Click.

Mary phoned again. It rang a half-dozen times, and then the same voice answered. "Who dat say who dat?"

Firmly, imperiously, Mary announced, "This is Mary Scofield calling Mr Tovar. Tell him Mary Scofield—at once."

There were muffled background sounds, too many tantalizing whispers, too few actual words to be heard, and presently Rick came on the line. "Howdy, Miss Oakfield. Where're you?"

O Jesus, what do I do now?

"I'm here."

"Here? In London? So soon?"

"In the hotel. Your hotel. This hotel."

"Oh. Where, exactly? In the lobby?"

"I'm in the Terrace Suite. I checked in under the name of Clark, but the rest of me is real."

She heard the giggler's tone of rebuke, again in the background, but couldn't distinguish what was said. She heard Rick snap, "Christ sake, shut up a minute!," heard him close to the mouthpiece now. "I said Friday. I said I'd come Friday."

Mary replaced the receiver on its cradle.

She sat for a long while, staring at the open peat-burning fireplace. Her phone rang. She continued to stare at the fire. When the ringing stopped she read the number of the International Hotel and began to call Liz to direct *Get everyone ready. We leave for London in an hour.* She hung up—Liz and Jeanne and Smilin' Jack would be settled in

57

by now—and wearily rose and ran a tub, instead. Television was done for the night, but she found radio music, a beautiful Mendelssohn that filled the suite.

In the master bedroom, as the bath water ran, she undressed and unzipped the valise for a toothbrush. The frilly black Italian nightgown was in the valise, still wrapped in tissue, the gown she had brought to surprise Daddy with. Now it would—

Her head shot up. *Daddy? I meant Rick!*

She zipped the case swiftly, and fled from it. Numb, purposely closing herself off, feeling nothing, she stood at the terrace window for a moment and looked out, naked but on a Gresham floor too high to be observed, and pretended to ignore the telephone that had again begun its insistent rings. The mute street below was empty of passing cars. She saw her father, Harmon, down there, smiling up and waving. Annoyed with the image, she drew the curtain.

What made me suddenly think of him? she wondered as she sank into the vast tub. Yes: Joe mentioned he's on the loose. How cozy. How bloody psychotic-cozy.

She rubbed her fingers back and forth across her throbbing forehead. She heard her doorbell. Think about something else.

She would have to phone the Savoy in London and apologize to her friends—not friends, really, except for Eileen Phillips; acquaintances of value—who were surely now gathering in the Savoy suite. She considered how thoughtless she'd been: I ask people to rearrange their late evening to come see me, and then I rearrange my own schedule to suit myself. Selfish. Self-absorbed. Inexcusable.

I'll call later. Not now, not till I'm certain of my voice.

The sounds persisted, the doorbell and, presently, a pounding fist. Hideous, she thought. Degrading, to us both. Of course I should run and let him in. Not for him to apologize, certainly, not to expect him to don sackcloth and ashes—as if he ever would do that, anyway. But to greet him, to let him know I'm wounded and derailed, because I am. . . God, it hurts!

58

And to see how gracefully we can pick up the pieces?

Doorbell.

He'd made himself clear almost from the beginning: "Neither of us is looking to sing 'Silver Threads among the Gold.' That first time we met, I gave you the needle about 'meaningful interpersonal relationships.' You're right: I *was* being smartass. And what's a smartass? Somebody who kids what he maybe wants most, what he's no good at. If you and I would dig to see each other again, to swing a little and laugh it up a little, that's great. But I'm not the type to hold on to the handlebars. I'm not proud of that, but that's how it is."

Doorbell.

I bought that, Mary reflected. It applied to me, too, it fit without the need to take in the sleeves, and I bought the arrangement, lock, stock, and animal crackers. Never dreaming, dear Abby, that I was becoming obsessed with him.

Pounding at the door.

The aloneness, the indecisiveness grew monstrous. She thought of Eileen, who would be at the Savoy now. Eileen, her single close friend, single lasting friend since the Bryn Mawr, double-date days, upbeat and wise Eileen Phillips of Wyoming, the present Lady Benjamin of Surrey, alive and well and jubilating in the role of wife to an earl. Head-on-straight Eileen, always available by transatlantic telephone and in person with a warm ear when Mary had the special jeebies and needed to talk to a—friend. There weren't many unbuyable friends; there never had been.

A simple call would reach Eileen now. And then what do I say? Mary asked herself: *Nothing's changed in twenty-five years. I'm still the college freshman, ready to die if the crew-cut Adonis doesn't invite me to the prom.* No. That would embarrass us both. After twenty-five years, swooning gets less and less fashionable.

The doorbell once more, and then silence.

She emerged from the tub, dried her body with a heavy, nubby towel, wrapped herself in it, and telephoned the

Savoy and identified herself. She began to ask for Lady Benjamin, and abruptly changed her mind. "Some friends of mine are in my suite or will be shortly," she said. "Would you be so kind as to explain that I've been delayed and can't possibly be there till tomorrow? And see that they're served anything they like? And ask them to come back again tomorrow night if it's at all convenient? Thank you so much."

When her phone rang again, she scooped it up. "Hello."

"Banging on your door like that reminds me of a scene in the kind of movie I hope I'm never hungry enough to do," Rick said sternly. "I'll come back. Let me in."

Yes, yes, yes.

"No."

She heard a deep, exasperated sigh. "There're little-child games and big-child games. I can't figure out which one you're playing."

Quietly she asked, "Who was that giggling answering service?"

"A kid who's in the picture. A kid far away from home, like me, which is about all the explanation I think I have to give here on the horn. You blow into town and you expect what? That the world stops in its tracks? Listen to me: you mean a lot to me—that's what I was going to tell you at that goddam door and what I'm telling you now—but neither of us has a holy claim on the other. This kid's in the other room now. We have a night-time run-of-the-picture friendship that ends when the picture ends. The nights get lonely and she was available. So what's the big deal?"

No trembling-lip tone, Mary warned herself. "The deal is simply this," she replied evenly. "It appears I'm not the sophisticate I thought I was, after all. You and I caused some nice electrical storms, and they'll make colossal memories, and it's done. Over. See how simple?"

"I'll get rid of the kid."

"No. Keep her. She's yours, with the studio's and my compliments."

"London . . . I'll be in London day after tomorrow."

"Really, Rick, I can almost see you perspire. That's all out of character, and its disappointing. Goodbye, sweet prince."

She wandered through the luxurious suite, regarded the sitting room's bowls of candies and fruit and vases of flowers welcoming the occupant, J. Clark, remembered John Hurley's card, for a ludicrous moment considered phoning him and inviting all the Hurleys for an indoor family picnic, considered walking to her favourite nineteenth-century street in Dublin, Moore Street, where gay old ladies stood at their stalls by day and loudly hawked their oranges and pork chops and toffees, wished it were later, wished it were earlier, wished . . .

Enough, she thought suddenly and returned to the bedroom to dress. It hurts, but it will pass. Enough of bumping into myself like helpless Betsypoo Unrequited in one of Gramp's 1929 confession magazines. I'm a big girl now, not bouncing with judgement, but big. This isn't the first time I've begged to be kicked in the teeth. Damn it, it's going to be the last time. Hear ye, hear ye, a momentous proclamation: Mary the masochist announces that from this day forward love is strictly a tennis term. Three husbands and a dozen sweeties later, the contender wisely admits defeat and retires from the ring. Loving right is a skill. Some have it, some don't. Mary-Contrary doesn't, never did, never will, and that's that, so be it and amen, Mary-Contrary herewith gives up the ol' elusive ghost and adjusts to the facts as they are, not damned happily but damned realistically. Henceforth, sappy Scofield straightens up, screws 'em as she meets 'em if that's indicated, and gives them dinner and a goodnight smile if it isn't. Easy as pie. Easier, once you learn the knack.

Hurriedly dressing, Mary noticed the nightgown, still in the tissue in the valise. She took it out and placed it on a bureau, reminding herself to present it to the first chambermaid she would see in the morning. She rode an elevator to the lobby, with no notion of where she was bound, knowing only that her body clock said it was early evening, that it was late night Irish time but Dublin was one of the last of the cities safe for late-night walking, knowing she needed to walk in the bracing air, to walk fast.

In front of the Gresham, her mind's eye caught a fleeting glimpse of her father. She had flatly refused to see him all these years, but there he was, still thirty-five years old, still dashing, with that irrepressible smile.

You bastard, you supremely uninvited, egregious bastard, she said, and resolutely marched to the corner, towards O'Connell Bridge. He followed her. Stop hounding me, Mary demanded. Go away from me. Go away!

He followed her, back to the Saturday in May, her sixteenth birthday. . .

The two of them lunching together in the Plaza's Oak Room, the discreet luncheon orchestra playing "Oh, What a Beautiful Mornin'," she unendurably shy, dazzled by the huge birthday cake the waiters had brought to the table, she sixteen years old today and in from Pearce School to be with Daddy, Daddy thirty-five years old and impeccably tailored and gorgeous, their first meeting in ever so long, seeing his radiant smile, hearing him exclaim, "My, how you've grown! So pretty and mature. Breasts and everything!"

"Well . . ." Squirming, desperate to sink through the floor, both of them awkward, clearing throats. He was no more used to being with a daughter he barely knew than she was with a father she barely knew, maybe he was uncomfortable with all young people because their worlds were foreign to him. That smile, that joyful, welcoming smile. . . He did most of the talking, saying things that sometimes came out wrong though they were meant well, meant to be said right.

"Very lovely breasts, too, I'm sure. Your young swains must go mad. How many lovers have you captured in your web by now, lovely princess?"

Nervous, wishing he wouldn't talk like that, trusting

him, anxious for him to see her as grown-up, anxious to impress him, to please him: "Not many." Let me unfreeze this dopy grin, she prayed. 'I'm sitting here like an imbecile with my very own father, who's urbane and worldly. I'm disappointing him, I'm boring him.

Daddy's smile sunny, animated eyes dancing: "Ah, a full-fledged blush, thank heaven, I'd started to suspect a young lady's blush had whisked out of style. But we're still men and women of the world, aren't we? Sure you won't have a drop of wine? No? Mind if I order a second? Light wine's the strongest thing I'm drinking these days, the strongest thing I'll ever drink again. I'm dying to hear about you and your conquests." He nodded to the waiter and offered her a cigarette. She thanked him, refused it. "Have you seen your mother? Heard from her?"

"No. I hardly remember what she looks like."

"No idea what's happened to her, what she's up to?" Mary shook her head. "Tsk. She seems to've disappeared into the wilderness. A pity: there was always something pathetic about Eunice. She was so pretty and . . . vivacious, I guess you could say, but unfortunately she had so many emotional problems she just couldn't handle. Terribly immature. Pretty as a picture, though; took after her daughter." He brightened. "But enough of the ghosts of the past; birthdays have to be upbeat days, right? Sixteen! I can't get over it! It seems like yester— Would you like to know what *I'm* up to?"

"Of course." The sommelier filled his wineglass. The orchestra was playing "I'll Get By." Glasses clinked at another table and someone coughed. Mary abruptly changed her mind, took a Chesterfield from his pack, her hand unsteady as she put the cigarette between her lips and puffed hard as he lighted it for her.

"I'm bursting to tell you all about it. I've written a play that's bound for Broadway! I met this absolutely perfect girl. Named Mary, if you please—Mary Kemp. You ready for a laugh? Some couples meet on cruises or

63

at dances, correct? We met at an AA meeting." He chortled. "How's that for a setting for romance! Fabulous girl. She's only in her early twenties, and she's been through the wringer, but she certainly bounced back. I've got to have you meet her sometime. She's so much fun, always kidding, you'd be crazy about her.

"Anyway, we fell in love almost on sight. It's still weird to us both, how it happened so fast. We discovered we have a million things in common, not just the AA thing. We're living together now; I hope that doesn't shock you." Pause. "Does it shock you? That a girl that young finds me physically attractive?"

"No." Please, Mary thought, I don't want to hear this, any of it. Please don't.

"Where was I? Yes: the play. How does this title strike you: *Surviving Reality*."

Mary nodded, smile still frozen, began to speak, to say something supportive and surely dumb. "Any writing instructor will tell you: 'Write what you know,' " he burbled, borrowing her unsmoked cigarette to light his. "Well, what we knew best was the life that leads up to joining AA. We wrote the whole play in a week! And now here's the clincher, little princess: guess who's going to produce it? Mike Todd, no less! Only the hottest producer on Broadway, right? He's seriously considering it! A few months from today we'll all be . . ."

and

"Waiter, one brandy, in honour of my young lady's birthday." To Mary: "Back to the wine after this. A celebration's a celebration, right? The important thing, pretty princess, is that all I've ever wanted was for you to love me and be proud of me. You're going to be proud of me. I'm finally on my way. For the first time in my life, I'm really happy. What you'll learn someday if you haven't yet, and I'll bet you have, is that love works all the miracles that matter. Mary—I call her my other Mary —is the Rock of Gibraltar. She's drinking a little too much these days, but I'm helping her to come out of it.

64

We help each other in a hundred different ways, we're perfect for each other, not only sexually, we . . ."

and

"It's all right if I have just this one last brandy for the road, honestly; I'm one of the lucky ones who can handle the stuff when I put my mind to it. Sixteen years old! Six-teen! You still haven't told me about the young stallions that swarm around you. Ah-oh, there she goes, blushing again. Don't you know I wouldn't embarrass the pretty, buxom young maiden for all the rice in China? I want to help you all I can; isn't that why fathers were born?" He held her sweaty hand. "Let's talk straight; I'm no good at beating around the bush. Whether you've gone all the way with a young man yet or not is none of my business. But let's face it, pretty princess: if it hasn't happened yet, it will soon enough. And you'll never hear me put the damper on anything as natural as—well, you know the word I mean. You're human, you're young, you have normal desires, you wouldn't be a Scofield if you didn't, would you? But take my advice: no matter how responsible a boyfriend may seem, don't put your faith in condoms. Get yourself fitted with a good diaphragm, and presto, good-bye worry. Mary—my other Mary—knows all about those matters, what doctor to recommend, and my feeling is there's no time like the present, you're here in the city today, after all, I realize it's Saturday, but I could give Mary a quick call, and she could check if her doctor's available, you wait right here, princess, I'll make the call, order me another brandy, will you, the positively last one, I'll be right back, I think the two famous Marys ought to meet, don't you, let's see, what'd I do with my cigarettes, they were here a minute a—"

He followed her now, through Dublin's dark streets, as e had through the years of her life. . .

She was twenty when Gramp died. A letter to her, not long after, from Daddy in Mexico City: he thought of her often, always with love and pride, lawyers telling him Gramp hadn't left him a cent, no legal way to collect a smidgen of the estate, Gramp had left her a bundle, would she be a doll and come to Daddy's rescue? He was blissfully married to Monique, royal French blood, blissfully happy but in dire need of ten thousand dollars, the sooner the better, or he risked being waltzed to prison on some stupid charge too grotesque to discuss. Urgent need. Repeat: Urgent.

She didn't have ten thousand dollars. At thirty, she would come into her full inheritance, a quarter of Gramp's thirty-million-dollar personal estate, plus the Company, worth twenty times that. Until then she was to receive adequate but modest monthly allowances, on Gramp's conviction that she might spend her whole fortune on fortune hunters if she had it all at once, whereas at age thirty she would be sufficiently mature to respect money's value.

She wrote this to Daddy, asked if fifteen hundred dollars would help. Her letter was returned: Not here, no forwarding address.

There was news about him from time to time. That he was remarrying his third wife, thirty-six hours after their divorce. That he was drinking badly, that he'd entered a detoxification clinic, that he and a brunette nurse had fallen in love there, that he'd been arrested for beating her up. That he was exuberantly into grandiose business ventures, that he couldn't hold a job but had vast charm and a genius for making friends, friends without money and a few with lots of it, men friends who carried him because he was so much fun at parties and even bailed him out of jams, women friends who paid his expensive bills because he was an attentive and doting lover. He would periodically write to Mary for loans, guaranteeing that he was on his way to wrapping up a fantastic business deal. She would refuse him and then invariably give in, until finally her new husband, Gil, caught on and demanded that she stop.

In September, four months after her twenty-third birthday, she hid in the family seafront estate in Bermuda, ill, drained, recuperating from the devastations of mononucleosis, recovering not at all from the certainty that her marriage to Gil was done. She hid in the large house, wandered the pink beach of Sandys Parish, marvelling at the depths of her emptiness, hollow, helpless, pointless.

She wasn't hiding as carefully as she'd thought. Daddy had heard she was in Bermuda, and phoned her.

He was in Bermuda, too, in Warwick, honouring the family attorneys' formal edict that he keep away from any place owned by Scofields. Tomorrow was his birthday, of all gigantic non-events, he said, a non-event he had chosen not to be around to celebrate. "The queerest thing," he said, his voice hushed, almost sepulchral, like a man newly bereaved. "I'm going to die, and it doesn't exhilarate me or depress me or even faze me very much. Peculiar—I'd always thought it would be an adventure worth investing some emotion in. But zero, *nada*. Tsk. Tell me about you, pretty princess—or majestic princess, I should say; I've been watching you grow up through your photographs and you're sensationally beautiful. Tell me: Are you happy?"

"You're frightening me. What's your address in Warwick?"

No, no, he said, she was a darling to sound so concerned, but he'd work matters his way, he wasn't a child.

She insisted he tell his address. She rushed to him.

His door was ajar. The only light came from the bathroom, but she could see him well enough. He sat mandarin-like in a chair, wearing a velvet dressing gown, his legs crossed. He held a tumbler, a quarter filled, his hand trembling. There was a whiskey bottle, a quarter filled, on the table next to him. Incredibly, he looked even younger than he had in the Plaza's Oak Room.

"You're a dear heart. You always were," he said, his voice flat, words slurring. One eyebrow cocked in amusement. "Do you really want to keep that door open? You're not visiting a sailor, after all."

She closed the door, switched on the table's small light. His hair was awry, his feet bare, his pedicured toenails glinting. "You can have anything to drink you like, long's it's Three Feathers." He raised a filled ashtray, grinned. "Cigarette?"

"Nothing."

"You said I frightened you." She nodded. "Why? I'm grateful I'm still able to stir feeling in anyone, but why? Wha'd I do to earn your interest? Pity? Compassion? Passion?" He sat straighter. "Do sit down, dear love. I'm not going to bite you—unless . . . well . . ." A snicker. "That does invite a couple o' gag lines, doesn't it? Here now, let your ol' pappy pull you up a seat."

He began to stand, holding the bottle by its neck, and pitched forward, barely breaking the fall, and lay on the floor, still clutching the bottle's neck, and laughed. " 'Floats through the AIR with the GRAY-des' of ease,' " he sang, and started to roll from side to side, and cackled. She knelt beside him. He held her arm for support, and she lost balance, too, toppled across him, instantly shot to her feet, saw him, heard him, knew she must run, knew she couldn't leave him alone like this. "Come," she said gently and helped him, a slim man suddenly leaden, to the side of the unmade bed, where he slumped heavily, drunk, weak, smelling of whiskey and good cologne. He rambled, talking maudlin, mostly incomprehensible talk. ". . . takin' care o' me . . ." she heard, and he co-operated, like a small, sleepy boy, raising his arms for her to draw the dressing gown off his limp shoulders and then his arms. The shoulders and arms and chest were white. She saw he wore nothing under the gown, had seen men naked before, supposed she oughtn't to be shocked. Leave, she thought, get out of here. Still gently, her fingertips ice, she guided him, helped him to lie back, brought the top sheet and single blanket over his stomach.

She turned to go. "Ol' Man Mose . . . ol' Pappy," he

crooned. "Ol' Pappy, li'l Mary's ol' Pappy's cold, so lonely. Good ol' Mary, she came to comfort ol' Daddy-Pappy. M'ere." She looked. He was spanking the undersheet with the flat of his hand. The top sheet and blanket had been whipped off and her eyes fixed, ever so briefly, on his huge erection. "Here. Lie down 'side me. Keep me warm a li'l while. Five minutes."

As she opened the door: "Where you going?" he bawled.

As she fled down the hall: "Five minutes! Where you going? Why's everybody RUNNING from me? FIVE MINUTES! Oh, God, five MINUTES!"

On O'Connell Bridge, gazing vacantly down at the gloomy Liffey, Mary's shoulders suddenly hunched and jerked and she began to weep, softly at first, soon with racking, convulsive sobs she could not restrain. *You bastard*, she raged at Harmon, at Rick, at Mary Scofield, *you bastard, you bastard, you bastard. . .*

"Are you needin' some assistance?"

She looked up, mortified, to see a man and woman near her, elderly and eager to help. She strove to compose herself, and couldn't. The man and woman held her as she wept and grew smaller, the woman hugged her and patted her and crooned, "There there, girl, there there, it's all right, you wait, it'll all be right as rain before long, what can we be doin' for you?" and the man said, "Maybe she could use a doctor. Are you ill, then, young lady, should we toot a whistle and get you to hospital?"

"No. I'm so ashamed. No. Thank you. I'll be all right," Mary answered and clung to them.

"I'm fine," she said presently, freeing herself, smiling at each of them. "Truly. I was sad for a bit, but I'm perfectly all right now."

FOUR

GREENWOOD.

Charlie Payne and I, Joe Greenwood, shook hands at Tampa Airport and he drove me to the Willows. "No hard drugs there, as far as I could make out," he said on the way. "There's a bunch of these old rundown estates around here. Way I understand it, ex-addicts who're into the religion bit live on them and do a little farming. Some people think they're up to more than that, but who's to say? They call themselves God's Love, something like that. Didn't the *Outlook* run some pieces on them some time back? Seems I recall, yeah; we picked it up down here but I was out with appendicitis and I wasn't reading much. Anyway, the cops pretty much leave them alone because nobody swears out complaints. This Willows, where—ah—Miss Scofield's daughter's supposed to be, I didn't have time to learn much. I hear they're screwballs, but nothing to collar them on."

They call themselves God's Love. I'd been afraid of that.

Yes, we had run a series on God's Love, on Mary's orders, a half year before, almost to the week. We surely had.

Until then, it had been one of dozens of cuckoo religious cults that spring up cross-country, cadging a neat tax-exempt status because they didn't sell snake oil but dished it out free to young losers who were looking to get found. So far, so harmless.

What made God's Love different from the others was that its high priestess was Sister Florence Cody, a rouged and beaded wizard with a spectacular gift for getting dying old ladies and gents of means to will her their earthly goods, money and property that would otherwise have been bequeathed to their surviving cats and parrakeets; in return, the Sister placed person-to-Person calls to the reservation desk Upstairs and arranged for their safe ascent and entrance. Somewhere between five and ten thousand misfits

70

were residing in ancient mansions and farms from coast to coast, having their souls saved by shoutin' hallelujah, planting a carrot once in a while, praising Sister Florence, and getting in good with the Redeemer.

Still so far, so harmless: Sister Florence's disciples were trading one addiction for another, dope or early boozing or promiscuity or whatever their bag for salivating over the Scriptures, but they were off the streets except to shake their cups for dime donations, and Internal Revenue was satisfied that no one was profiteering.

Mary wasn't satisfied. She asked for some quiet reporting to be done, on the understanding that if the Sister's sole mission was to rescue lost lambs, if everything was indeed on the up-and-up, fine. "Call it a hunch, *Yussele*," Mary purred. "Naturally, I could be all wrong." I put Ben Manger on the story, because Mary's purr was a Mount Sinai command, and because her hunches proved all too consistently to have substance.

Manger dug for a month, but he returned with gold. Not only had Sister Florence's proclaimed vows of personal poverty been just for laughs, but she was milking ignorant innocents right and left, growing fatter and fatter pockets, and not sharing a sou with Uncle Sam. Courtesy of the Scofield press, Uncle Sam began to lean on Sister Florence Cody—who was, of course, squealing up and down the land that Mary, who'd initiated the investigation, was the heathen who would be parboiled through Eternity.

So that's where I was heading that Wednesday: to anti-Scofield country, in search of a Scofield. A fifteen-year-old Scofield who, for all I knew, was wearing a badge with her name on it.

As Payne's Rambler drove me over rainy, bumpy ribbons of Florida roads, I tried to dock my attention to the news on the car radio—

The fighting on the Syrian border grows more intense. Rhode Island Senator William Bradway's Washington

office calls the charges a trumped-up conspiracy by his
political enemies and promises a clarifying explanation
soon. The court case of political revolutionary Chris
McCabe and associates ended in New York, and is expected
to go to the jury today—

I stared straight ahead, grunted when Charlie spoke,
solemnly chewed Gelusil, and decided I was in the market
for good news.

"Stick of gum?" he offered. "I quit smoking last
Memorial Day."

I shook my head and said, "That's the day I quit chewing
gum." I liked Charlie Payne and, though part of his paid
job as Tampa stringer on our Florida paper, *The Miami
Standard*, was to be on tap around the clock to chauffeur
Scofielders in from out of town, I wanted to turn to him
and thank him for taking the time. I didn't. To my eternal
annoyance, I'm not very good at things like that.

The rain had settled down to a slow, dismal drizzle as we
approached the estate, which was off a markedly treacher-
ous dirt road. I'm a lifetime city boy, awed that anyone of
his own volition would choose not to live in a city, but I
recognized this place immediately. It was Dresden and
Nagasaki, the morning after. There wasn't any mulch,
whatever mulch is, but I saw, as I told Charlie to sit tight
and got out of the car and looked through the high gate, a
generous array of twisted beer cans, animal turds, wrinkled
rubbers, scattered newspapers and tall thickets of grass and
brush, filth and more filth. At one time the house may have
been Tara, grand, white-columned, elegant. Now it was
Jeeter Lester's vacation hideaway, a symphony of peeling
paint and busted windows, a broken front step, a half roof,
a porch loaded with old radios, books and magazines open
and strewn, bashed-in bird cages, torn and maggoty bed
mattresses, junk and more junk and more filth.

I saw no one but I heard loud voices singing something
with "Mother Jesus" in it. The gate was locked. I pulled
at the lock, tugged at it, shook the metal gate that was still

too much for me, and yelled, "Hey! Hey you, open up!" I yelled it again, and kept yelling. The singing went on. A face appeared at the window, a hairy face. He waved his hand; the message said: Go away, we don't want any. I hollered louder than they sang, and in another minute my next-to-last ounce of strength might have broken the gate's lock. The house's door opened. Another hairy face emerged, belonging to every Fordham tackle of the last five years combined, and came towards me.

Mother Jesus, I thought. What if the kid isn't here, hasn't been and won't be? Mother and *Father* Jesus . . .

He was a beatific-looking gorilla not quite my size but a good twenty-five years younger. "Sorry, brother," he said happily. "No one's allowed in. I'm sure you mean well, but you're disturbin' our prayers."

"You open up or I'm back here in thirty seconds flat with dynamite," I said, or, rather, bellowed.

He opened up. "We don't believe in no acts of violence 'less we're forced, brother," he said. "Who'd you be lookin' for? Maybe I can—"

I strode past him and, quintessence of grace that I am, stumbled on that front step. The singing continued, but someone had closed the door. I kicked it open, breathing heavily, mad and not a little frightened. I made a quick head count, in that mammoth and dirty-spooky parlour, of about a dozen and a half dirty-spooky dregs ranging in age from, say, sixteen to, say, thirty, sitting alone and on laps. Some of them gave me tentative smiles, some looked puzzled, some frowned at the intrusion, some seemed not to have noticed my d'Artagnan entrance. Either mocking me, or spiritually transported, they all kept the hymn going strong, louder than before.

I didn't see Carole.

Oops.

But I did see an Ichabod Crane of a young man who came close enough to the description Carole's roommate had given the school's headmistress—about twenty-one years old, well over six feet, skin and bones, spiky black hair, and

73

a barely visible chin. Leo Trascano, the headmistress had said his name was.

His hand shot to his mouth as I went to him. "Get her," I rumbled. "Get her right now." The singing softened. One of the hairies came near me in that parlour that smelled of mildew and cat pee and bad pot, and warned me, ever so gently, that I was trespassing and courting a few crushed bones. Ignoring him, I asked Trascano, "Do you get her now? And bring her here with her suitcase or whatever she took with her?"

He nodded.

"I'll be outside," I said. "Both of you are to be there in exactly two minutes."

He nodded.

The hairy who'd unlocked the gate was at the door, blocking me.

The thought didn't escape me that, while I could possibly take him, he and I weren't the only gorillas in the stadium-size living room. I glared at him, and put on my best Paul Robeson, and said, "Try some heroics, brother. You throw the first punch. I don't believe in no acts of violence against scumbums unless I'm forced. I leave here easy or your next visitors will be the law, and that should give you extra reasons to pray." Thanks to Mother Jesus, he finally stepped aside.

Two minutes later, on the dot, Carole and Trascano came out. She wore cheap baggy dungarees, an expensive brown Mexican blouse trimmed in white braid, and a look of fearful confusion. "Take your bag to the car. Get in the back seat and sit there," I told her. She went, silently if not on steady feet, and I faced Ichabod Trascano, who appeared petrified, and for a moment, only a moment, I almost felt sorry for him. Close to him, I said, "You pump gas at the Chevron station in Arrow's Hill, is that right?"

He nodded.

"You don't have a brain. Let's see if you have a voice."

He nodded again and murmured, "Yes." He cleared his throat and repeated, "Yes," with not much more volume.

74

"You know that girl's name," I said and pointed to the house. "Do they?"

"Uh—I'm not sure."

"Try. Does anyone in that house know her last name?"

"Well, her first name. . . One of the brothers is a friend of mine, that's how come we came here, we were invited to be babies in Christ together. I mentioned it to her, and she says, 'Let's go.' "

"The last name, baby, the last name."

"That she's a rich girl, is that what you mean? Nobody here cares about money, if that's what you—"

"I'll make this fast," I said. "It doesn't matter whose inspiration it was to waltz off together, yours or hers. What matters is that she's underage and you're not. You took her across a state line for immoral purposes, you—"

"That wasn't—"

"Shut up. You took her across a state line for immoral purposes. You committed statutory rape. No, shut up—a court of law knows what statutory rape is. You contributed to the delinquency of a minor. Those three counts can earn you ten years of making licence plates. How would you like to learn to make licence plates?"

"Please, it wasn't like—"

"I said shut up. Just listen. If you're ever seen or heard from again, *ever*—and this is what I suggest you listen hard to—you may not even get the chance to learn how to make licence plates because these hands of mine will tear you apart first. And you can relay the message to your junk-heap pals that *their* smartest bet is to stay dumb."

"Can—ah—I say someth—"

"No. I think I've said it all, don't you?"

He nodded. I walked to the Rambler.

We rode towards the airport, Charlie at the wheel, I on the passenger side, Carole mute in the back. I didn't glance at her or talk to her about what had happened. Charlie Payne knew, of course, why we'd gone there, and I suspected he was bright enough—and insecure in his job—not to regale his family and friends with an account of this trip,

75

but I didn't want him tested more than necessary. The sky was beginning to darken again with the promise of more heavy rain. The radio was playing a country and western. I changed it to another station and yet another country and western. I'd met Charlie twice before, had talked with him by phone perhaps a half-dozen times, always about Company business. Now I asked him his wife's name, how many children he had and where he was from originally, getting-to-the-airport small talk. I asked him what line *The Miami Standard* was taking on the McCabe-Hendrix-Skinner trial, although I knew. I asked him about the *Standard*'s approach to the Senator Bill Bradway story, although I knew. Charlie answered all the questions, initiating none except about the weather back East, as though he understood perfectly well the reason for the purposely vapid conversation.

At Tampa Airport, he scrambled inside the terminal to check flights. I pretended to concentrate on his copy of the *Standard*, one of Mary's least favourite papers in our chain of six. The only sound from the rear was the kid's sometimes gaspy, irregular breathing. Charlie scrambled back. "You're in luck," he said. "There's a nonstop to La Guardia in forty minutes."

This time I thanked him. Guiding Carole to the ticket desk, I asked her if she had a return ticket. She shook her head. I showed my first-class return ticket to the lady at the desk, bought another, and said to Carole, "I have a phone call to make. We leave from Gate Three. Will you be there waiting for me, or should we plan on some more fun and games?"

Her tiny voice said, "I'll be there."

I phoned my office and told my secretary, Arlene, when to have a Company limo at La Guardia. The kid's overnight bag was on a Gate Three leather couch, but she wasn't. Trusting ol' Greenwood, I thought in disgust, and then she came out of the ladies' john, eyes red-rimmed from crying. She wouldn't meet *my* eyes while or after we boarded the plane, and there still wasn't a sound from her, but a bird in my head advised me to throw an arm around her and somehow relay to her that she'd pulled a stupid stunt but all right, things will work out. I didn't. I was still sore as hell, and even if I weren't, reaching out to people, as I mentioned a while ago, isn't something I'm able to do without ferocious effort.

A second after we were off the runway, she tensed and gripped my wrist. I squeezed her hand until we were airborne; she was nervous at takeoffs as my wife, Sylvia, had always been, and in this case I couldn't honestly fault the kid; it was early afternoon, yet the rainy sky said nighttime and we heard thunder. "It's okay," I soothed. "It's going to be okay." I looked at her gaping at the window, and I squeezed a little harder. She was a pretty kid—if fifteen is a kid, and I'm buggywhip enough to think it is. She had some of her mother's best features, the same large brown eyes, the same healthy skin tone, the incorruptible mouth. She hadn't Mary's striking beauty, but then, that would have been a mighty tough act to follow, for Mary was a genuine stunner. I'd had only a few brief encounters with Owen Enright, Carole's father and Mary's third husband, but there was a resemblance there, too, especially in the frightened expression. She wore glasses. I'd watched her laugh a few times in the past, a nice laugh though without Mary's deep-gut sincerity and animation. A pleasant enough figure, though not as splendid as Mary's.

The other thing of Mary's she didn't have enough of was sense.

When the *Fasten Seat Belts* sign switched off, I asked her, "How long would you have stayed with that high society if I or someone hadn't come to collect you?"

"I don't know. . ."

"Did you really go for that long drink of water?"

"Leo? No."

"Were you itching to find God? And in that plush Riviera retreat?"

"No."

"So what was worth giving me fifty kinds of heart attacks for?"

"Does my mother know—what I did?"

"Your mother's in England. She and I talked on the phone early this morning before she left. I knew you were off and running somewhere—your headmistress rang me up last night—but I didn't say anything to your mother."

Weakly, distantly: "Thank you, Uncle Joe."

" 'Thank you, Uncle Joe' doesn't pay me for my services. Why in the hell did you do that?"

"I'd rather not go into it right now."

"I'd rather you did."

She paused and sighed and kept staring at the window. "I wish I knew why I do ninety percent of what I do. I see Dr Marco five sessions a week in Arrow's Hill, and I can't explain it. Sometimes I'm there the whole forty minutes and I can't think of a word to say."

Marco was a word that made me naturally, maybe unnaturally, uncomfortable, like *arthritis* and *bedbug*. Dr Alan Marco charged sixty bills a session. Five sessions a week at sixty bills a crack comes to three hundred bills a week. Why did that upset me? The money was Mary's, not mine, not the Company's. The Company was paying me a hundred and twenty thousand a year, plus options to buy Company stock, privately owned—not bad for a Jewish boy from the Brooklyn badlands whose first pair of shoes worn by nobody else first were his when he went into the Army at eighteen and whose tailor father was lucky to bring home three hundred dollars, at his luckiest, over a period of a month.

Yet, that's what I was and would always be: *Yussele* Greenwood from the sunless back apartment, five flights up, on Venders Avenue, no toilet, half frozen in winter but heat generously supplied in July and August, run down the milk bottle and get the nickel deposit, Joe the made-it-on-his own Scofield executive, *Yussele* the passenger on the *Titanic*. Three—excuse the expression—hundred dollars a

78

week for Dr Alan Marco of Arrow's Hill?

Anyway.

"This Leo was kind to me," Carole said. "He told me about this place in Florida, where everybody was kind to everybody else and you didn't have to follow dumb rules unless you wanted to. So we went."

"Like that."

"Like that." Softly and with strain she said, "Don't hate me, Uncle Joe. Everybody else hates me. My mother despises me. Don't you hate me, too."

"Whoa, there. When did your mother start hating you—a minute ago and nobody let me in on it?"

"Well, not *hate*. It's just . . . she'd just rather have me out of her way . . . make good grades and not bother her. It's like I'm a dress she had made for her and when it was delivered to her she decided it didn't fit." And suddenly, imploringly: "Do I have to go back to school? I'm so miserable there. Can I—Maybe I could stay with you. For just a while, till I get myself together. . ."

"What's going on with you, all of a sudden? Your life isn't automatically cream and silk every minute, so it's the end of the world? If something's bothering you, you have to start facing it and solving it. Running's no answer," I said, sounding like my mother if my mother had sounded like Paul Robeson. Of course the kid was bleeding and of course I wasn't helping her. But there are tortured teenagers and there are spoiled brats, and a brat was how I saw her at that moment. I had two daughters of my own—stepdaughters, but mine—one then only a few years older than she, and Sylvia and I had loved and cared for them without giving in to their every whim, and both of them had turned out fine.

She didn't talk much for the rest of the flight because maybe she realized she wasn't going to be spoon-fed. I didn't talk much because my patience had run low. I wanted to bawl her out. I wanted to hold her. I couldn't.

We landed at La Guardia, a rainy hour late. A Company limousine was waiting. I put her in it, told the driver to take

79

her straight to the Westchester boarding school, and said to her, before I shut the rear door after her, "You start shaping up, miss. The world doesn't revolve around you. You caused a lot of commotion. I want no more SOS calls from Miss Whatzername."

She averted her eyes, as if I were an insensitive, unhearing brute—which, in a way, I guess I was.

I bought newspapers, and caught a cab to the new Scofield Building on Lexington. My official title was still executive vice-president of the Scofield Company, though I no longer had my fingers in all the media pies, thanks to last year's very mild and lavishly uninvited coronary, barely a week after my wife, Sylvia, died. Mary was my friend—we could fight over editorial and policy decisions without lasting cuts and abrasions—but she was also my boss. She'd demanded that I cut back on work. I'd told her to mind her own presidency. She'd pulled rank in a most bosslike way and warned me I could be eased out of my chair or bounced altogether, for my own good, arguing, "A dead Greenwood gathers moss. What's your hurry, *Yussele*?"

She'd won that match, because she was right; I *had* been overly spreading myself, not pacing my energies, not rolling with the pressures, and so I was doing my health no favours, and probably not doing the Company many favours, either. For a time I slimmed my eighteen-hour workday to a slug-abed six or eight hours, limiting myself to the job of general overseer of *The New York Outlook* and *Scofield's*. It wasn't a backbreaker, considering that until my heart and I had our disagreement, I'd been in charge of everything that happened in and to the Company, answerable only to Mary.

I'd eaten on the plane. Arlene, my secretary, brought me a cup of broth and a raft of paperwork and messages that had come in while I was off sallying around in the back regions of Tampa. The first call I returned was to Howard Bradway, the senator's brother. "I got in from Rome just last night," he said, he voice pained. "How in God's name could you let those stories run, Joe? Doesn't friendship mean anything anymore?"

It was an unfair question to put to a newspaperman, but an understandable one. "We run papers and a news magazine here, Howard," I said, loosening my tie, "not a booster club. Have you talked with Bill?" Yes, Howard conceded, he and his brother had talked, but—"Did he tell you that when our Washington guy began to uncover the story, Mary went to him not once but over and over again to get his side of it? And that Bill kept denying the whole thing, even though the evidence was clear as crystal?"

"Bill still denies it. It's all a smear."

"Then why's he hiding?"

"He's not *hid*ing. He's going to speak up. He says there are reasons why he can't just yet, and I believe him. My God, you and Mary of all people know he's not some *per*vert! But that's not even the point—Christ Almighty, Joe, Mary built that boy and now you and she are ruining him! The other papers, *Time*, *Newsweek*, that's one thing. But *your* papers! And *Scofield's*!"

I listened to him rave on. He was so exercised that his facts weren't coming out straight. We were seeking out and reporting the facts, not conducting a vendetta against William Bradway, as he seemed so certain was the case. He finished finally and I said, "All I can do is repeat Mary's position, Howard. If and when it turns out that Bill is innocent, or that he was involved for some innocent motive that hasn't surfaced yet, we play that up big, we don't bury it back in the truss ads. Till then, we're scrupulously keeping him off the editorial page. We can't be any fairer than that."

"But I hear two of your columnists, Louis Wilmot and that torpedo MacNair—"

"Are commenting. Yes. We call this a free press, even when it roughs up good men. Wilmot and MacNair have the right to write. Mary and I may not like their copy, and you bet it can hurt to print it, but that's the only way we know how to run the store. I'm sorry, Howard. I suppose I can't expect you to believe that, but I'm sorry. Mary's in London on business, but if Bill has anything to tell, she can be reached very easily at the Savoy."

"Terrible. It's downright terrible," Howard Bradway said. "With friends like you, we don't need the dependable hatchet press."

I polished off the broth with a scotch chaser. There were times when I didn't like my job. This was distinctly one of them.

By nine o'clock that night, two staff meetings and a grillion phone calls later, I was into the day's third bottle of Gelusil and my head was exploding. The McCabe-Hendrix-Skinner jury had been locked up for about eight hours, indicating that a guilty verdict for all three on all counts wasn't shooting fish in a barrel, as it had promised to be all along. Dow Jones had closed up shop in tears. The latest report from Israel and Syria was that they were barking but, as of nine o'clock, our time, they weren't firing. The casualties in the Indian and Mexican catastrophes were still being counted. The wife of an unemployed Detroit steelworker had given birth to healthy sextuplets, just what they needed. At his televised press conference, the President of the United States had been asked to comment on the apparently indisputable proof that William Bradway, the cross-country spokesman for integrity in government and moral order in the family unit, had been arrested on a morals charge involving several teen-age girls. The President, who surely knew as well as everyone else that the only serious contender to unseat his party an election or two away was Bradway, spoke about human charity and waiting till all the evidence was in, but you could almost see him licking his lips. A mine cave-in in Wales. After forty-nine years of blissful marriage, the acrimonious divorce of Hollywood's most happily married couple. Another homicide, another coup, another insurrection, another jump in food prices, another shivering kitten safely brought down from a tree. Another day, another dollar.

I yawned. I'd had it.

What I most wanted, besides a long vacation or maybe

82

just to watch a chair become an antique, was to have my first real drink of the day; I'd drunk only coffee on the plane and that snort after Howard Bradway's call didn't count. I rolled my shirtsleeves down and decided to wait till I got home, where I could hit some leisurely scotch with my shoes and socks off. Getting up, I remembered Carole. I certainly had no desire to use a telephone again—I'd been on them continually through the afternoon and early evening—but I got guilty about Carole. I assumed the Pearce School number would be handy. It wasn't. I put my wrinkled jacket on, switched off the lights, left the office, called good night down the hall to Terry Franks, the *Outlook*'s night editor, and took the private elevator up one flight to Mary's suite of offices.

Even without Mary, her cavernous office bustled with her. It faced east and north and it was, like her, uncluttered and disciplined. Except for Teletype and wire service machines, there were few signs that the business of communications was conducted here. There were framed plaques and awards celebrating her service to journalism and the public weal, though discreetly on a remote wall, suggesting she was pleased by recognition of her achievements but that she was too sure of herself to be a horn tooter. She knew most of the movers and shakers of the world, yet there were only a half-dozen autographed pictures on the west wall, all of personal friends. There were formal chairs and easy chairs, and Braque and Manet originals and a striking Giacometti sculpture. The central piece of furniture was a round leather-topped desk (always fastidious) that had once been a Barbary Coast gaming table. There were no photographs on the desk, but there was a woodcut I'd mailed her from Wyoming a few years before; it was a seventy-year-old original and its legend read *Cheer up, Bob, they ain't no Hell*.

I found her book of private telephone numbers and dialled the headmistress at Pearce School. Yes, Miss Deane said, Carole had arrived safe and sound, tail between her legs but quite all right. I asked that she take it easy with the kid, and said that Carole wouldn't run off again, that she had some problems and confusions that wouldn't be helped by punishment. Miss Deane didn't agree. "I'm afraid that forgiving and forgetting simply won't do, Mr Greenwood. Pearce had been a school for proper young ladies for nearly ninety years. We appreciate that times change, but character or the lack of it doesn't. For the sake of our other girls as well as Carole, an example must be set. We feel that detention and demerits are absolutely necessary."

"Very well, as long as she's all right," I said.

Half-past nine. Mary would of course be sound asleep now at the Savoy, would have to be because in the morning she would begin a full day of reviewing the troops at Scofield International on Fleet Street—and then participate in the Royal Festival Hall ceremony in the evening. I'd told her she was nuts to plan to cram so much activity into one day. One word from me. For better or worse, the lady was always on the go.

Not that our British division didn't need to be personally checked at intervals; we called *The International Outlook* and overseas *Scofield's* shots from here, but running a tight ship from a distance of three thousand miles is impossible unless you have a manager at the other end who's on the button. Geoffrey Metcalf, our managing director there, wasn't exactly Lord Beaverbrook.

I phoned for Brian, the side lobby's night doorman, to have a cab ready; after Sylvia's death and after our kids had gone their own ways, I'd put our chauffeur, Harry, on part time. In the elevator to the lobby, I was taken suddenly, unaccountably horny—unaccountably because I was close to falling off my feet with virus aches and exhaustion. I thought of Wendy, whose flat was precisely halfway between the Scofield Building on Lexington and my apartment on East River Drive. Wendy was a comparatively golden-age call girl, about forty, but she had something for me young girls didn't have: patience.

Brian opened the taxi door for me and said, "Take care, Mr Greenwood." I gave the driver Wendy's address—she and I had a fiscal agreement that she would save Wednesday nights for me—and sat back and realized after several blocks that sex wasn't at all what I was looking for; what I was looking for was an excuse to postpone going home to an empty apartment and loneliness. "Change that, driver," I called, and gave my address. I glanced out. The rain was bucketing down.

FIVE

CAROLE ENRIGHT PLEADED with Miss Deane.

"Please," she said quietly, desperately, not able to meet the woman's icy eyes. "Please listen to me."

"Listen to why you left the grounds, without permission, and with riffraff?"

"Yes."

"And dishonoured Pearce as well as yourself?"

"Please . . ."

"Sit up and *look* at me, Carole. I won't have that shoulder-hunching nonsense. When your mother was a student here, a fair number of years ago, she always looked everyone in the eye. However insecure or guilty she may have felt, she always—"

Suddenly, incomprehensibly, Carole cried, "To hell with my mother!" and stood up from her chair, and moved towards the door.

"Carole! Carole Scofield!"

The girl turned. "No! My name is Carole Enright!" she said, hearing her own unheard-of-defiance with something akin to awe, certain of more punishments in store because no one defied Miss Deane successfully. She stopped at the door and returned to her chair because Miss Deane ordered her to, and nodded in agreement that she had displayed and was displaying shocking behaviour, and was silent.

And wanted to say, *Forgive me for all the trouble I've caused, forgive me, everyone. I don't know what's happening to me. I'm so scared, so very scared, I need for you, for someone, to be patient with me, to let me talk even though I don't have the vaguest idea of what it is I need so much to say.*

There's this tremendous ball of tears that's inside me, that's hurting me so, oh, please comfort me, please love me, someone please comfort me and love me. I didn't mean to go to

Florida. I didn't want to go, not with Leo, not to spend a minute with those awful people out there, those people even more helpless than I.

Please please please don't look and speak so coldly to me, Miss Deane. I'm not wilfully bad. Why can't anyone understand that? Why can't I say that what I want more than anything is for my mother to hold me and comfort me and love me. . .

"You're excused now, Carole. You're to go straight to your quarters and concentrate as hard as you possibly can on the demerits and detentions you've ahead of you and of how much you deserve them, of how little that snivelling is like a Pearce girl."

I'm drowning. You're telling me to swim. I'm saying I can't swim, I'm flailing, I'm sinking deeper. Don't let me drown. . .

"Good night, Carole."

"Good night, Miss Deane. Thank you."

"Are you thanking me by rote or because you believe there's a reason to thank me? The moment I was informed you ran away, I had the authority—and, I'll admit, the impulse—to have you expelled from the Pearce student body."

"Thank you for everything, Miss Deane. Truly."

In a long, wide corridor, halfway to the dormitory room she shared with Phyllis Meacham, Carole Enright tripped on the bunched edge of a rug and plunged forward, so startled and humiliated by her gracelessness that the palms of her hands barely cushioned the fall. A hellish cry escaped from her. She heard footsteps. From her awkward position, she saw Miss Lindauer, her freshman social studies teacher, smile at her as if to say, *I'm glad to see that nothing hurts you except the embarrassment*, saw Miss Lindauer trot on. Carole got to her feet, insulted by the fall. Her breathing stopped. Attempting to right herself, waiting for her breathing to resume, she found herself dizzy, pressed her shoulder tight against a wall. Voicelessly she called, *Miss Lindauer, come back, please don't race on like that, come*

back, come hear me, come see me, be my mother for just a
little while. . .

In her dormitory room, Carole Enright sat and stood and
paced and sat again and talked foolishness, frantic foolishness, to Phyllis. What she deplored when she was alone later,
much later, as she showered after Phyllis was asleep, were
her gaps of memory. She could remember talking of love
and hate, of hate and love, of some fusion there, she could
remember chattering on, could remember seeing Phyllis
vainly suppress a yawn, but she could remember only
pauses of what she had said. She stood under the shower's
prickling needles, stood inert and let them rain on her. Her
shoulders sank and her hair was drenched and she weakly
rubbed her breasts with a bar of soap, her breasts that
someone else had touched, today or yesterday, it didn't
matter, touched these nipples, fondled these breasts, it
didn't matter, there was no reason for it to matter. Distantly
she recalled her second swimming lesson, when she was
eight. She was encouraged to swim out farther. Swept up
by her instructor's praise, she did swim out farther and
then, abruptly, discovered herself unable to touch bottom.
She refused to swim again.

The water's engulfing me, Mommy. My shin hurts,
from falling. I let Leo, or someone, touch me here, and
here, and maybe here I don't know I don't know anything now, and I'm sorry my head is so wet, Mommy,
don't be ashamed of me. Please.
Please.
Please engulf me. Please hug me. I'm so scared. I've
done everything in the world I know to make you proud
of me, love me, know me, come to me. I can't know what
more I can do, say, act out, act upon. Please help me. . .

At her desk, Carole Enright saw what she had written:

and some of the hostility turned in upon herself. But

88

that bloated whitish face with the wet, loose mouth-chewing, pulling, sucking at the most intimate and would be, should be, most inviolate me. Bloated and sickly smooth with the flesh and substance of my dreams and hopes. No wonder, vampire-sucked by insatiable hate, I walked palely, haltingly, poor bloodless bones.

Slimy, dark, dirty monster, wearing then your sleazy cape of self-loathing which, as in the past, you would have fit over my shoulders—monster of evil—I saw you naked, shiny with slime like the excrement of ruined, bought-out gods—I saw you naked, strong and almost beautiful in the dynamic wholeness, oneness of your horror. . . Evil, I salute you and enjoin you. Neither of us wears the cape.

Carole Enright slept, ever so fitfully. She dreamed:

Running. She dreamed of running, running on an elongated treadmill, running naked from the whole monster, its belly strong and sweaty and tubular as the bull neck of a man, its belly wrinkled and twitching like a witch's afterbirth. She stopped and turned. Her arms spread. Her breasts tautened. Held, she was held, without love, but held.

Carole Enright, small and apologetic and never wilfully bad, saw the day break from her window. She dressed without sound, left her dormitory and school, and walked down the winding road to town, to find a telephone where she could place calls for help without being spied on by Pearce busybodies.

Shops there had not yet opened. A diner was open, but it had no phone. Its waitress pointed to a public phone booth outside, several hundred yards away. Carole meekly asked if she could be given ten dimes for a dollar. The waitress shook her head, then seemed to sense how important it was, and gave her five dimes and two quarters in exchange for the dollar bill. Carole thanked the waitress, went to the telephone booth, and could not think of a single person to call.

SIX

ALL 3,047 SEATS at the Royal Festival Hall were occupied on Thursday evening as Nils Thorssen, that year's president of the International Society of Newspaper Publishers and Journalists, spoke lavishly, and much too long, of *The New York Outlook*'s invaluable contributions to responsible journalism.

Mary, in a gossamer-light gown the colour of champagne, sat on the stage with other colleagues from other countries who had already accepted their awards, and partially listened to Herr Thorssen's praise, feeling no sparkling confidence yet not particularly nervous. The speech she would deliver had been prepared with care. The time for reworking it, worrying over it, touching it up, was past. Satisfied that she'd given it her best, she sat back and tried to relax.

And couldn't, quite. This *is* a fantastic honour, she thought. I'm experiencing the significance of it, I'm not, I am, I'm not, I'm a neon sign with a short circuit, switching on and off and on. When does the weight of it all hit?

"The society," Herr Thorssen was saying, "recognizes *The New York Outlook* as a vigorous example of journalistic investigation at its most reliable and fearless best."

The day had been long, beginning with the forlorn early morning flight from Dublin. A flood of messages descended on her as she and Liz Hale arrived at the Savoy, none from Rick, none expected, messages from long-time London acquaintances and associates sorry she couldn't have attended her own party last night and hopeful they could be rung up at her leisure, some of them assuring her they would be at her rain-check party tonight after the ceremony; invitations to cocktails and dinners, sincerely offered but far too many to be fulfilled; messages from the heads of various bureaus and departments of the Company in London; a message from Downing Street, respectfully requesting that

91

she and the Prime Minister have their meeting tomorrow morning at eleven rather than noon, as originally arranged; flowers and messages, too many messages, none from Rick.

By half-past nine, she had been ready to be driven to Scofield International on Fleet Street, fairly satisfied that she appeared rested and contained, reasonably certain that the simple emerald green dress piped in navy made her look consciously seductive ("Cawn't navigate with us men as a person, has to prove she had blinking headlights and a round bottom") nor neuter ("Cold mutton, that one; devilish hard for us to deal with someone without a gender").

In the lift to the lobby, she had striven to erase all remnants of the Mary Scofield who had shuddered in the Terrace Suite of the Gresham. When the cage door opened and she was guided to the Company's waiting limousine and chauffeur, she was Mary Scofield, president and chairwoman and controlling stockholder of the Scofield Company, employer and mover, a woman fully aware of her abilities and influence.

"This tribute to a great newspaper," Herr Thorssen was saying, *"is a tribute as well to one remarkable woman, a woman of tenacious courage and foresight who—"*

Geoffrey Metcalf, Scofield International's overseas managing director and a closet sexist, welcomed her expansively into his office. She was pleasant in return, thanked him for his congratulations on tonight's award, answered that she'd had a good flight across, asked about his wife's health, and subtly cut short his threat to go on with chitchat by directing, in the form of a courteous suggestion, that they get to work. She picked up the current issue of *Scofield's* European edition and said, "I see there's no mention of Senator Bradway here. We gave it a full page this week in the States."

Metcalf's bushes of eyebrows raised. Joe Greenwood, who couldn't stand him, conceded he was a competent enough administrator as long as he followed orders, but despised him as a totally self-serving Etonian cartoon, still conquering Injuh, an anachronism who ought to be told it's no longer necessary to wear a starched collar while swimming. Mary, privately agreeing with the evaluation, had reminded Joe that performance, not personality, remained the name of the Company's game, and that Metcalf did perform. This day, Metcalf's eyebrows raised because a policy decision of his was being criticized. The understanding had always been that he and London's editorial department had the right to delete any news story from the American *Scofield's* they felt was inappropriate for their European readers.

"Quite," Geofffrey Metcalf replied with bristly dignity. "It isn't in for the simple reason that the senator is something of a folk hero over here. In some places in Britain and on the Continent, he's a bigger figure than your President. These remarkable accusations against him. . . I felt the poor boy ought to be left alone, at least until he's had the opportunity to make his own answer."

Quietly, Mary said, "Mr Metcalf, it's just possible that you've misunderstood your authority to leave out certain stories. A Utah mayor may be of no interest over here. The very fact that William Bradway *is* the figure he is here is every reason to run it. This story isn't rumour and it's certainly not trivial; the charge is serious, and important, and documented. I usually admire your judgement, Mr Metcalf—that's why you're in that chair. I'll be happy if I never again have to explain to you what stories matter and what stories don't."

"Indeed," he said stiffly. "May I speak frankly?"

She nodded, loathing that question.

"Quite to the—ah—point, Miss Scofield, I chose not to run it because I suspected you'd be relieved if it were left alone. I mean . . . I've known for some time that you have, or you'd once had, a rather—um—personal relationship with Bradway. . ."

She blinked. "May we follow that through? If I did prefer suppression, then why on earth would I have allowed the Bradway story to run in our edition?"

His shrug was lordly. "I took it on myself, in your interests, to presume it was carried without your knowledge, that some eager soul hurried it in before you were consulted. I'm sorry. I meant only the best."

Mary fought to control her anger. "Until our publications become the Western arm of *Izvestia*, Mr Metcalf—and you'll be advised well in advance if they do—you're to presume nothing about my sensibilities," she said sharply. "Is that entirely clear?"

Geoffrey Metcalf, surely boiling, regarded her. "Ah—quite."

"Thank you. I think I'd like to visit Advertising first." Then, to restore a shred of his dignity: "Unless you'd rather I start somewhere else?"

"*The Scofield newspaper empire*," Nils Thorssen was saying, "*once castigated and condemned as . . .*"

Through the day she'd moved from department to department, office to office, remembering the names of sub-executives and even some of their secretaries, friendly and interested yet inviting no chumminess. She remembered Joe's early admonition: "You have several thousand people working for you. You have to be civil, sure, but you start getting chummy with them, you get too democratic, and you're a gone goose. They'll be dropping by the house to drink your gin." She had purposely memorized many key employees' names, in and out of the States, and with Liz Hale's help, she usually remembered to have personal gifts sent when a baby was born and to write personal condolence letters when someone's loved one died. But except for Joe, and at various times a few others, she suspected she really was constitutionally unable to be one of the gang. The culprit, she was sure, was an innate shyness, a lifetime of isolation from all but a restricted circle.

Through this day she met with Scofield International executives and with Scofield bureau chiefs from Amsterdam and Brussels and Berlin who were in London to attend tonight's ceremony, gave each of them charm and a measured dose of amiable conversation, put perceptive questions to them and indicated that she expected thoughtful answers, listened attentively, altogether aware that she was called the

94

Velvet Claw and determined to leave each of them equally aware that the name was justified. She asked questions about the Company, and she asked questions about the West End theatre and the solvency of the German mark and Britain's new government and Cyprus troubles and Europe's observations of the President of the United States, essentially the same questions she would ask others while in London, to gather soundings, to feed them all into her mind's hopper and take them home to the *Outlook*. Though she would be here again tomorrow and part of the following week, she rationed small talk, insisted that as many minutes as possible count. At five o'clock, when she was ready to leave, she made a point of entering Geoffrey Metcalf's office to smile and inquire, "We're still friends, I hope? The Bradway discussion notwithstanding?"

"Quite," he said, his tone both chilly and somewhat relieved.

"I'm glad," Mary said, her smile broader. "And I'm glad we both agree that with the next issue of *Scofield's* you'll carry all the stories except the Utah mayor stories. Perhaps we'll see each other at the Festival Hall reception. I'd love to say hello to Mrs Metcalf."

Clement Hodge from Circulation saw her to the limousine. "I've been watching you since ten this morning," he marvelled. "You didn't stop working for a moment. And in a few hours you're off to Festival Hall! Just thinking of all that energy makes me want to lie down with a cold cloth over my face."

"It's all in the genes, Mr Hodge," Mary responded. "All I do is go along for the ride. Thank you so much for your courtesies today, and thank you for seeing me down. I know you meant to have the new circulation figures better organized than they were at our meeting today. You'll keep in mind our three o'clock appointment tomorrow, won't you? Thanks *so* much!"

In the car, as she was driven back to the hotel, she gazed blankly through the window at the late afternoon's heavy pedestrian traffic. Odd, she thought, how some people often look like old friends at a distance, then as they get closer the resemblance vanishes—like that tall man, turning the Strand corner, who looks like someone I once knew. . . Who?

Gil? Yes, Gil Stafford, her second husband. Of course. . .

Suddenly Gil's face and lean, flawless, sexually insatiable body were in her mind like neon, though the pedestrian was nothing like Gil. Lord, how long has it been since I've seen him, or even thought about him, she wondered, feeling the shameful, familiar prickle of heat creep up her thighs, the stiffening of her nipples.

Insane, she thought, that the very image of him can throw this absurd passion switch after so long. Insane that I should flush like a schoolgirl at a dirty movie, just visualizing him. Gil Stafford, who had been her whole life and being for a time, who had taught her that there was no end to the erotic miracles her body could perform and feel, that life was a nonstop seduction of the senses.

Stop it, she insisted, crossing her legs and squeezing her thighs together. And like a movie projector gone berserk, the pictures flashed: the parties, the endless parties, the beds and beaches of a hundred jet-set spas. The day, on that St Tropez beach, when they strolled through a haze of champagne, nude and nut-brown, and met that other nude and lovely couple, and flowed, melted together, all of them, on that blanket in the searing sun. . .

Breathing hard, she snapped off the vile projector, shut the scene from her mind. Crazy time, she thought. . . That was truly the year of fruitcake Mary the Gil-worshipper, Mary the accommodating sex machine. . .

The projector was on again, running another scene from that year, a few months later. And this time she could not shut it off, this scene when it had all begun to turn bad, sour, so grimly sad.

They were in the villa at Florence, and that night was their farewell cocktail party for the dozens of equally aimless people they'd sailed and swum and drunk with. It was a zany notion when Gil first laughingly suggested it, and she agreed that yes, the guests would surely remember the night if she greeted them, poker-faced and quite socially correct, wearing every single piece of jewellery she owned—and nothing else. She wouldn't do it, certainly, but she laughed at the idea, appreciating its madness, and Gil talked some more, and somehow they finished a magnum of Mumms while she decked herself out with strand upon strand of pearls, with bracelets and tiaras and earrings and bangles of every kind, smirking and posing in front of the mirror. And then, tipsy yet oh-so-formal, she glided down to welcome the guests, and for a couple of minutes it seemed like a great lark, the silliness of it, the freedom of it. And then there were the snickers, and one couple stalked out, and a drunken woman made a showily vulgar suggestion about where she could carry her cigarettes, and the woman's escort leered and grabbed for Mary. And then abruptly she was blushing furiously, and running from the room, hearing the loud laughter and, worst of all, most demeaning of all, seeing the amusement on Gil's face and hearing him urge the escort to see if he could catch her before she locked the bedroom door.

The scene ran down and the projector stopped, and Mary sat in the huge back seat of the huge limousine, hugging her throbbing breasts and cursing Gil Stafford, over and over, all the way to the Savoy.

The hairdresser and manicurist from Erika's were waiting for her in her Savoy suite. "I'll be right along," she called and swiftly leafed through the new batch of messages, none from Dublin. She showered hastily, felt depleted and unstuck as she dressed in a robe, nodded as Liz commanded her to take a rest as soon as the Erika ladies were done, and went to the Erika ladies and apologized to them for being late. As they worked, she listened to Liz read the Festival Hall speech to her, replaced a weak word with a stronger one, changed a sentence, revised a paragraph. She intended to obey Liz and rest till the last minute; Eileen and Stan, Lady and Lord Benjamin, would arrive at half-past seven to whisk her to the hall.

At seven, Eileen phoned from the lobby, and Mary asked her to come up.

"Stan, too?"

"No, just us college kids."

"Done. I'll park Stan in the bar here. Order me up some Kentucky bourbon." Mary had telephoned her four nights before from New York with the promise of two hen's-teeth tickets to tonight's awards, and the apology that there mightn't be nearly enough time in London for the two Bryn Mawr alumnae to spend with each other. Waiting for Eileen now, she again debated the wisdom of confiding her wound.

Eileen strode into the suite's sitting room, engaging and effusive as ever, heavier than last year, animated and cheerful and, as ever, wonderfully warm. They embraced, and kidded, and the Kentucky bourbon was delivered, and they brought each other up to date. Carole, Eileen's goddaughter, was at Pearce School, happy and doing beautifully, Mary said. Eileen had bumped into Owen Enright, Carole's father, in Brighton; he still custard-bland and imperturbable, living near the beach and into Buddhism and still semi-gorgeous. "Some fun without you here last night," Eileen chided, her accent an amusing tug-of-war between Wyoming and Britain. "Do you realize Stan and I had to talk to each *other?*"

Mary grinned. "I'll make it up to you somehow if I can ask a favour. If you and Stan are free, will you invite me to Surrey for the weekend?"

"No sweat, kiddo, as we in the upper clawsses put it. The joint's yours, as long as you don't keep showing off your fancy-pantsy award and go around putting on airs. But wait a minute—didn't I get some glimmer that you and the muscle actor were going to do a weekend shack-up?"

"Your delicacy is right out of Browning," Mary said, and told her of Dublin, told her everything.

"Well, what's all the hand-wringing about—that he plays the field?"

Mary nodded.

"And he said all along that the both of you were to be free as birds, and you said 'Okay, okay?' " Mary nodded again. "Why are you mooning, then? A pact is a pact. When did you turn into Mrs Andy Hardy?"

"I guess I always have been. I—the sex is marvellous, we ... I guess I've always envied you, Eileen. You were the one girl I knew who could go on a first date and—ah—"

" 'Put out,' it was called."

"—and wake up feeling fine, no regrets, no remorse. I— oh, damn. You know what? I've been asking questions all day, and this is the biggest question of all: How can I tear myself up and start all over?"

"—*dies and gentlemen,*" said Nils Thorssen, "*we present to you Mary Scofield, of the United States of America.*"

At the lectern, before her peers from five continents, heart thumping, caught up at last in the excitement of the event, Mary appreciatively acknowledged the unqualified and prolonged applause, thanked Herr Thorssen, and kept her acceptance speech to a respectable quarter of an hour. Every word was hers, all a compilation of *The New York Outlook*'s principles and convictions of dedication to truth in bearing the news. She spoke persuasively and well, aware that some of those out there who listened and some who would later read the speech were or would be critical of the *Outlook* and therefore of her, but she continued to its end without faltering and at the conclusion she heard a thunderous ovation, saw three thousand people stand to cheer her, Adam's granddaughter, Harmon's girl.

Then the stage was mobbed with photographers and well-wishers, and she smiled, a bit frightened, and spoke her gratitude, and contained tears and forgot for a moment that she was alone. With the beaming Nils Thorssen at her side, she attended the Royal Festival Hall reception, exchanging snippets of conversations with sweet and gracious people, still giddy yet once again inwardly flat and suspended, numbed by the noise and force of too many people.

"This is a pretty dull party, Miss Cornfield," she heard, from directly behind her. "Even the ice cubes are warm."

Rick's voice. Rick.

She wheeled. Rick, who was in Dublin, was here, inches from her.

Wearing a grey wig, dark glasses, grey whiskers, and a shapeless grey suit.

Control was impossible. Mary laughed. He shook his head in mock reprimand and said, "Stop that at once, young lady. You may be old someday, too. Say something respectful."

"Such as what—'Fancy meeting you here?' It's all a little *déjà-vu*-ish."

'Funny, you don't look *déjà-vu*-ish."

Again she tried to control herself, again she laughed in spite of herself. "But Halloween won't be for months! What *is* that absurd getup all about?"

"Trick or treat, you young whippersnapper. Let's go home and ball for apples. And be quick about it: I have a plane waiting outside."

"How did you get in here? I'm supposedly the star of the show, and I had wretched troubles wrangling tickets for friends."

Soberly shaking his aged head: "If I've told you once, I've told you a thousand times: what you lack is imagination. There I was, in the foyer, reading the sign—'*Admittance by written invitation only*.' I showed the guard my Master Charge and chicken inspector card. No dice, so I went and milled around and really got classy. I pulled a jostle."

"I think I know what that means, but it might be the better part of valour not to ask."

"To pull a jostle, Empress mine, is to accidentally bump into an elderly gent who's holding a ticket. Treat me with utmost deference. I own the Parrott newspaper chain in Australia. Not bad for an American kid who grew up in bleak poverty, wearing my big sister's dresses to school, is it? Listen, let's cut out of here and go to your place."

"My place, in less than an hour, will have between thirty and fifty guests."

"Let's walk, then."

"I couldn't possibly just leave here and—"

He described the location of the exit door where they could meet.

". . . Ten minutes," she said.

He was at that door in ten minutes, still wearing the costume. He opened the door for her and they walked in the night's bracing air.

"What's this about a plane?" she asked.

"That's for real," Rick said. "Flying here on a commercial line wasn't going to be a problem, but the last flight back to Dublin tonight is around eleven, too early, and the first one in the morning is around eight, too late—they want me on the set at eight—so what the hell, I chartered me a silver bird."

"That has to cost at least nine dollars."

"Yeah. It goes on the studio's tab. They don't know it yet. Want to talk dirty?"

Near a corner, on a dimly lighted street, Rick suddenly stopped, pulled the whiskers off, and held her in his arms.

"No," Mary said weakly. "Miss Cornfield is hurt and feeling disagreeable. She's going to expect to be pursued with the equivalent of loads of long-stemmed red roses."

"For how long?"

"I've no idea. Days. Maybe weeks. Maybe longer."

"What're we doing, playing Take a Giant Step because of that nothing peanut-butter sandwich in the Gresham? I have to be on the set at eight in the morning."

"My hunch is that that's something between you and your studio. Let's walk me back. I'm serious. You're very important to me, but I need time to get over competing with a peanut-butter sandwich. It's as cornfield-simple as that."

He looked over her shoulder. "There's a hotel, with a sign lit up," he said. "I'll bet you a pound and a half they take customers."

Firmly: "No. How often must I—"

He took her arm. "Let's just go and check. Somebody once told me London hotels don't take customers. Just for

101

the sake of research, let's go see."

The lobby of the Point Hotel was tiny, smelling of disinfectant. Mary stood nearby, feeling both detached and deliciously sinful as Rick, whiskers replaced, registered as *Mr and Mrs Paul Parrott, Melbourne.* Discreetly, the clerk asked about luggage. "The madam and I will be leaving for home a bit on, at the airport," Rick explained in a shaky Australian dialect. "Want to rest awhile. Deuced English climate, don't you know. I'll pay in advance, of course."

The room, bathless and immaculate, wasn't quite a cell but minuscule, nonetheless. "You really must get rid of that beard," Mary murmured. I have awesome problems relating to spirit gum."

"Let's see," he said, touching her. "Where were we? I left the bookmark here someplace."

Without meaning to, without having planned to, she abruptly drew away, as though burned.

Rick frowned.

"No," she said.

"I'm not altogether sure I get the motivation of this scene," Rick said.

"My fault. I ought to learn how to project better. I'd try, but the acoustics aren't good here. The more I think of it, they've been fading for weeks now."

"Whoa. Suppose you quit talking like a textbook and tell me what's going on. Quit this eye-jabbing. Quit scratching your back with your hind leg. Talk. I'm brighter than I look. If you speak slowly and simply, maybe I—"

"Stop it!" she cried in misery, appalled that she was clapping her hands to her ears. "How dare you stick your superstud machismo in some hole—not even a person but a hole—and then belly up to the next available bar, Chez Mary the faithful happy hour, and expect me to roll over and pant!"

"I said whoa!"

"Awfully sorry, your superstudship, but the shop's closed. I've forgotten everything I was taught in obedience school. It's my turn to say whoa now. These infantile hit-and-run games we've been playing are done—or we're done. We start to grow up and face what we mean to each other—and that begins with your dropping every peanut-butter sandwich—or you and I close out the account."

Silence.

"I mean that," she said falteringly. "I expect it of you. You owe it to me."

The look of disgust was hard on Rick Tovar's face.

He left the hotel room, without a word, and shut the door after him.

Mary waited. Presently, she left, too.

SEVEN

Greenwood.

On that Wednesday night I'd let myself into my apartment, feeling as if I'd been away from it for weeks, feeling more than my nearly fifty years, at once seeing Sylvia who wasn't there. I saw no light under my houseman Luis's bedroom door as I shambled to my study, where the scotch, the first order of business, was kept. The long walk stressed the leviathan size of the apartment. My two daughters, the one in Montreal and the one in Vermont, were still urging me, by mail and by telephone, to give up the memory-drenched flat. What did I need eight rooms for? They were right, of course. I slept there, and drank morning coffee there, and once in a blue moon ate my suppers there. I'd recently begun again to court some non-hustler ladies, nothing serious but I didn't even use the place to conduct my occasional transient affairs; for probably a complex of psychoneurotic reasons, I still couldn't bring myself to take the willing ladies there, not where Sylvia had moved and sat and slept and loved. And yet the simplest remedy—unload the behemoth and move into the Pierre or even the New York Scofield—was something I wasn't ready for yet.

Luis had filled the ice bucket. Good old Luis.

I poured, even before I checked with my answering service or took off my coat and tie. And I'll be damned. The phone rang and sunlight was coming through the window. I'd fallen asleep right there at my desk, and it was morning.

And it was Miss Deane on the line. Carole had been disciplined yesterday. She wasn't in her bed this morning, or anywhere on campus, nor did anyone have a notion of where she could have gone. "I thought you should be alerted, Mr Greenwood," Miss Deane said.

Yeah.

I buzzed for Luis to bring me coffee, and showered.

Groaning with irritation and feeling no better physically, my first thought was that of course the kid would have to be found again and this time have her bottom or its equivalent swatted for this totally irresponsible behaviour. My second thought was that maybe she'd gone off some deeper edge, that she was suffering more than she'd let on.

My third thought was the one that made me scrub my back all the faster. It went, *Mary has enemies, enemies looking to get back at her. And what better, crueller way than . . .*

I stood in my study, in my shorts, staring imbecile-fashion at my coffee cup, and for a few moments, no more, contemplated phoning Alex Andreas' office for an appointment. Alex was the doctor who'd diagnosed my pint-sized coronary a year before and my virus two weeks before, a pleasant enough guy on the infrequent occasions we got together for gin rummy, a common scold when on duty. I briefly contemplated an appointment because it wasn't possible but I was feeling lousier than I had when the bug had first taken up residence in this noble carcass. As an extra added attraction, I also had a titanic hang-over—the classic headache, nausea, and inside sweats—the neatest trick of the week, inasmuch as the glass of scotch I'd poured last night was there on the study desk, nearly full. I began to assemble the priorities of the day ahead and decided against on-duty Alex. First things first.

I found the number of Dr Alan Marco, Carole's shrink, and dialled it, and told the recording that answered to have him ring me back the instant he got the message. I looked up the central number for Pearlin's, the fifty-states private investigators we kept on retainer, found it, and had myself connected with the Tampa branch; Carole surely wasn't at the Willows in Florida, but there was the chance of a chance that her gas-pump lothario, Leo Trascano, might be. "If you hear from me within the hour," I said to a Pearlin's man who identified himself as Don Claffey, "that means two of your best men are to be ready to hustle eighteen miles south of Tampa and locate someone."

"That's a tall order, Mr Greenwood. Tampa's a bit shorthanded at the—"

"The Company pays Pearlin's fifty grand a year to perform tall orders," I reasoned. "You want to reconsider?"

"We'll be ready, sir."

Still trying to come to, I checked my AP Teletype to see what had happened in this vale of mirth while I'd slept. For openers, the McCabe jury had come in. All three felony-murder defendants, McCabe, Hendrix, and Skinner: guilty, guilty, guilty, with no jury recommendation. Fair enough. On the direct line to my Scofield Building office, I told my secretary, Arlene, to come up with the Arrow's Hill, Westchester, number for the Chevron service station, preferably with the name of the man who ran it. I waited while she repeated the instruction to her secretary, and then she, Arlene, asked me, "Are you feeling any better? You looked awful yesterday. I was worried."

"A good night's sleep works miracles," I growled, the sarcasm meant for myself; chair-sleeping is no Caribbean cruise. "I just read the McCabe verdict on the wire. Why the hell didn't somebody call me?"

"We kept calling. You needed the sleep, Luis said. Do you want me to get Berney on the line?"

Berney Kristall, the *Outlook*'s managing editor, orchestrated the big quick-breaking stories when I wasn't on deck, as I certainly hadn't been for nine hours. I answered that Berney could wait; the *Outlook* was an afternoon paper, which meant that the McCabe story had been filed and printed, for the first edition, anyway. "By the way," said Arlene, "the pickets started early this morning; there were about a dozen, last time I looked." That was hardly a scoop; from the time of the Bank of America broad-daylight robbery and gunplay, nuts faithful to McCabe and Hendrix and Skinner, who called themselves the People's Resistance Army, dedicated to destroying our corrupt system, were loudly blaming the *Outlook*—other papers, too, but mostly the *Outlook*—for editorially convicting their heroic trio before and during the trial. That was nonsense, of course; our editorial beef was with violence, especially mindless violence posing as idealism.

What was a scoop, and one that got my adrenalin galloping, was Arlene's next number: "The switchboard's been lighting up with crank calls since the verdict last night. It's not just the fascist Scofield press stuff anymore. There's been that, but there've been some ugly threats, too."

"Like what kind?"

"Like telling the *Outlook* to warn Miss Scofield and her family that they'd better always look behind them from now on. It's all sort of vague and veiled, but it sounds organized. Maybe it's nothing, but Berney Kristall got the police in. All incoming calls are being monitored."

"Did any of these clowns mention the People's Whatzis Army by name?"

"As far as I know, no. And that's part of what's so funny: some of them said they're going to get the Scofields—one said something about God smiting them—because the *Outlook* was too friendly to the defendants." Reading my mind, she said, "It could be just a matter of a lot of kooks coming out to play—but do you think Miss Scofield ought to be alerted, even though she's in England? And her daughter?"

"Yeah. I'll be in the office in—"

"Oh, wait. Here's your Chevron number." I wrote it down. "The manager's name is Ike Hollis."

"Okay. I'll see you in a while. The other phone's ringing."

It was Alan Marco. He didn't have a clue about Carole. "She missed her last two sessions, but she sometimes does that," he said. "What's wrong?"

I told him about the Tampas trip, about this morning's call from Pearce School and the calls to the *Outlook*. "I don't like the sound of that," said the three-hundred-dollar-a-week seer and healer.

"I'm not too crazy about it, either, Doctor," I advised him. "If she's proving something right now by hiding under a tree because the world is too much with her, that's your department. But if she's in any physical danger, that's mine.

107

Maybe she just stepped out for a long Coke, but let's go on the hysterical assumption she's run off or she's been taken. I appreciate I'm asking you to divulge confidences. You have my word that all I'm interested in is her safety."

"I'm not sure how helpful I can be, Mr Greenwood. Carole's a labile personality; she's simultaneously too suspicious of people and too trusting. She began to talk about the Trascano boy, oh, five or six sessions ago. From what I could gather, he appears to have a frail ego too. He evidently started to try to persuade her to run off to that religious retreat with him shortly after they met. No, I didn't try to dissuade her in so many words; my function has to be more indirect than that. The last time she was here, she said she'd made up her mind that she wasn't going to see him anymore. That's about it. I'm sorry it's the best I can do. Carole's an extremely sensitive and vulnerable girl. She hasn't been able yet to bring herself to say she's always felt abandoned, unwanted by her mother and her father, but it's all there. And until she's made some practical adjustment with herself, she's likely going to make a number of wrong judgements. Would you let me know as soon as your hear something? It goes without saying that I'm concerned."

I phoned the gas station in Westchester and asked for Mr Hollis.

"Speaking. Who's this?"

I was reasonably honest.

"Trascano, that dago bastard," Ike Hollis hissed. "After all I did for him, he helps himself to fifty-some dollars in the cash register, day before yesterday, and disappears," Hollis had rung for the cops, with no real hope of seeing the bum or the money again. Leo Trascano had wandered in from nowhere a month or so earlier, and Hollis had taken him on and treated him fine, even though he was one of those Christer weirdos, yakketing too much. The man believed he had a room in Arrow's Hill, but that was the end of the information. No, he'd never seen a teen-age girl, or anyone, around the bum. "Like I always say," Hollis observed, "you can't trust nobody."

My next call was to Don Claffey in Tampa. I gave him exact directions to the Willows from Tampa and a top-grade description of Trascano. "I don't know if he's still there," I said. "If anyone mentions trespassing, your men can mention kidnapping, and that their boy Leo is wanted, and that it would be very easy to come back with eight hundred cops and roust the joint. Trascano weighs five pounds dripping wet, but I want two of your toughest boys there just in case somebody wants to get cute. If he's found, I want him to know that Ike Hollis, his old boss, is thinking about a larceny charge. He won't be happy about it, but I want one of your two boys to escort him on the first available flight to New York. And I want to be called." I read him my office number.

Luis cooked me some eggs as I dressed. I was or I wasn't doing the right thing, check one, by not contacting the New York Police Department. That would've, might've, been Mary's up-front decision.

For all I knew, the girl would turn up by nightfall, perfectly all right.

Elephants have wings.

You go to the police and you say the name Scofield. Not Smith or Jones; Scofield. The report seeps out, then torrents out. Keep the lid on for a while, I thought.

And wondered how long is a while.

In a taxi to the office, the cabby was jabbering about the McCabe verdict, mourning the loss of New York's electric chair, and hoping the keys would be tossed in the garbage once the trio was locked up. "*If* they're locked up," he snorted. "Their shysters is for sure gonna appeal, and if that Jew judge plays ball, the whole thing could drag on another hunnert years, and they could end up driving home in a Fleetwood. Animals. Especially the woman, the nigger; you ever seen meaner eyes'n that this side of Africa? The system's not fast enough for them, they never worked in their life, so they got to go gun down innocent people. And brag about it, yet—whadda they call it, 'justified'! Animals like them, they oughtta be in a cage. Made out of electric. I right?"

I pondered.

What gave this case its unique flavour was that the participants were disturbingly familiar names from the past. Hendrix and McCabe were minor celebrities in the late 1960s, a comparatively simpler time when they were frequently arrested and booked, not for protesting Vietnam and ancillary social insanities but for their continual Come-and-Get-Us dares to the Establishment. They were an intelligent and feeling pair. In their lust for public attention, though, the baby too often got thrown out with the bath water: Bring American boys home at once or don't be surprised if the water supply across the nation is spiked with LSD; the Haves who exploit the Haven'ts deserve to be shot down like flies—the kinds of calls for anarchy that served mostly to stiffen the Establishment's back. Chris McCabe wasn't dirty fingernails scratching an armpit; he was a spectacularly handsome young fellow with clean-cut features and an engaging personality, articulate and know-ledgeable when he wasn't heralding the coming Apocalypse. Beah Hendrix, a mighty fetching young black woman who talked in interviews like Beulah as her way of saying up-yours to the honkies, owned a Ph.D. in Greek and Roman history. They were revolutionaries who read a lot, listened a lot, knew a lot, and they might have been solid social activists if they hadn't insisted on opening all doors with axes.

They were brought down and into eclipse in the early and middle seventies, partly because the *Outlook* helped to put them to pasture but mostly because their brand of barn-burning went out of vogue.

So from pasture to bank robbery was some juicy jump. They and four others were caught as they fled, caught because the caper had been planned by Baby Snooks; it was a muck-up from start to finish. The job's pure amateurishness almost made it funny. The fact that the shootout killed eight people—two cops, three robbers, one bank

110

teller, and two customers—wasn't so funny.

McCabe, Hendrix, and a fat youngster named Victor Skinner pleaded not guilty, in awesome spite of the witnesses who positively identified them and the bank's cameras that photographed them. They never changed their plea but they did work to spread the word before and during their trial, through their super-gung-ho attorney, Frances Holmes, that there would be no peace on earth until the fat cats were made to feed the hungry. Ms Holmes, an extremely sharp lawyer, periodically turned the felony-murder trial into a ringing defence of three latter-day Dreyfuses—aided and abetted by the assistant D.A., a consummate dumdum who blustered and flubbed, even with all the facts nailed down beautifully. Holmes's basic thrust was that the true enemies of society were the Mellons, Rockefellers, Du Ponts, and Scofields.

Scofields.

It was a diversionary success, while it lasted, but why did she—and, out of court, the trio's sweaty and very vocal legions—pick on the Scofields? Simple, kind of simple: politically and philosophically, the *Outlook* was middle of the road, not a nice thing to say to any throbbing radical. While our news coverage had been eminently fair—Mary's Law was that, as much as humanly possible, news and opinion weren't to get in each other's way—we came down hard editorially on the McCabes, who were no friends to the needy. In one of her rare publisher's editorials, which she signed, Mary endorsed most of the McCabes' idealistic aims, cited, chapter and verse, the support the *Outlook* had given progressive causes over the past seven years, listed specific laws enacted by Congress as a direct or indirect consequence of the *Outlook*'s exposés, and concluded that the McCabes' ways of fostering change were and always would be dangerously counterproductive. To the People's Resistance Army and their followers, that meant war. Also, the Scofields were very rich. Who the hell were they—they, meaning Mary Scofield—to pretend to comprehend hunger? That single signed editorial, said Frances Holmes, exempli-

111

fied everything that was sleazy and two-faced about capitalist exploitation.

The taxi let me off in front of the Scofield Building. Cops were containing pickets, but not their banshee noise. They were a scabrous-looking lot, though none of them seemed menacing. I could imagine the Ramon Vienna folks, for instance, grabbing Mary's kid; I couldn't visualize one of these yawping losers figuring how to begin any trouble more sinister than yawping.

I hoped I wouldn't have to be in touch with Mary.

I went up to my office, hoping for a message that I return a call to Miss Deane.

No message.

A Pearlin's man named Dick Horton phoned me early in the afternoon from Tampa Airport. "I have Trascano right here with me," he said. "There's a plane at three fifty-five, arriving in New York at six."

"Which should get you here at around seven if the traffic's not too heavy. You have this address?" Yes. "Any trouble from that end?"

"Not much."

"When you get to the lobby, ask for Sam. Sam'll scoot you right up."

I tried to keep my head, befogged by virus and Carole, on getting out a newspaper. The three cops who were running taps on all incoming suspicious calls were set up in a ground-floor supply room, close to the switchboards; the operators had been instructed to divert all such calls to the monitors' special line. I knew as well as these cops that it's nearly impossible to trace crank calls, but I kept checking with them, anyway. I sat in on a budget meeting, first telling Arlene to interrupt if there were *any* personal calls for me.

One came, from Dr Marco. He hadn't heard anything, but he said, "This may or may not be useful; I suddenly thought of it just a little while ago. Carole's talked from time to time about Parnassus. She associates it with pleasant memories—apparently it's the only place where she and her parents got together for happy times. I don't have any solid reason to believe that's where she'd go, but there is a certain logic to it."

"It's certainly worth looking into, Doctor," I said. I wasn't sure it was, but I placed a call to the Long Island barony old Adam had built for himself. Parnassus was a castle with some subsidiary castles and guest houses, given to New York as a state park by Mary, who, wealthy as she was, couldn't swing the astronomical taxes. The proviso had been that the Scofields would keep part of it—a sizable chunk of acreage, one of the smaller castles, a pool, a tennis court, a beachfront and a few other of life's necessities— for occasional family use and for putting up friends and visiting VIPs. A skeleton staff was maintained, year round.

Mrs Parry, the head housekeeper there, said no, Carole hadn't been seen or heard from in ages. "Contact me immediately if you see her," I said. Was anything the matter? "No."

I seldom had cause to talk with Mrs Parry, but once I hung up it occurred to me that she'd sounded a little odd, almost as if she wanted to stay on the line and bring up something else, but she was waiting for me to extend the invitation. I'd cut her off because my only interest had been the kid. I thought about ringing her back. And didn't. What would I say—"You sounded odd?"

I was getting awfully itchy.

At a little past seven, Sam, the evening desk man, buzzed me. "A Mr Horton's here."

"Someone with him?"

"Yes."

"Okay. Send them up."

Leo Trascano, wan and looking in need of a bowl of warm milk, half cowered behind Dick Horton, thirty and blocky, without contest the toughest kid in the neighbourhood. My finger pointed Trascano into my private office, I walked Horton to the elevator and slipped him two fifty-dollar bills, though Pearlin's would of course bill me for the plane fares and expenses. "This ought to be enough for cigar money," I said.

I lumbered back into my office and closed the door. Young Trascano, a maze of fright and apprehension, said, "All I want is to be left alone."

"That's all most of us want, son," I said. "Sometimes it can't be all that easily arranged. You answer me one question and maybe you'll live to walk out of here. Where's Carole?"

He seemed surprised. "You took her."

"And lost her. I'm going to ask it one more time. And I hope you're going to be smart, because you stand to lose a considerable amount of blood. Where's Carole?"

"I'm not sure I'd tell you, even if I knew."

"Is that so? Why not?"

" 'He that scoffeth at the Lord and not repent, he shall be punished. He that is godless—' "

Godless, maybe; patient, no. I sent him flying across my desk.

And followed him and bunched his shirt collar in my fist and roared, "That finishes your preaching, you thieving little shmuck! You're up to your ass in trouble. I want straight answers or you'll have the crap kicked out of you. How many of your pals out in Florida know Carole's a Scofield?"

"Please don't hit me. . ."

"How many?"

". . . I told Lon. Because he asked me, after you took her away yesterday."

"Who's Lon? The chief of that gang?"

"There aren't any chiefs among—"

"Once more. Who's Lon?"

"Well, he's sort of in charge there. But if you think any of them's interested in worldly possessions—"

"Christ," I said reverently and belted him again, this time in the belly, harder than I meant to. He doubled up on the floor, probably in fear as well as pain. I went for him once again, feeling brutal and feeling foolish, ready to kill the

114

skinny crud, and then, as he began to blubber and gasp for breath, madder at myself for acting like every muscle-brained bully I despised. I pulled him up. His one hand clutched at his stomach, and his other hand covered his face, and I roared for answers, and he pleaded, "Don't hit me anymore. I swear to Lord Jesus I don't know where she's at. Honest. Please. Please!"

Finally I released him, still suspicious and yet satisfied that even if his Florida buddies knew where the girl was, this poor klutz didn't. What *I* knew, as I moved back, was that hammering a marshmallow was no shining example of my finest hour.

"All right, get out of here."

Saucer-eyed: "You mean that?"

"No, I like to hear my voice. Get out."

He showed a hint of class. Near the door, far enough away from me, he said, "Look, I care about what happens to Carole as much as you do. More. I care about her ever-lasting soul, I—"

"Don't beg me to break you in half. Start running. Keep running."

Tsuris, I thought, sitting alone; we have us some real *tsuris.* I checked again with the monitors down in the ground-floor supply room. "They're slowing up, averaging about a half dozen an hour," one said. "No, we don't detect any real pattern, except they sound like a bunch of kids on a harassment binge, like they don't have anything better to do than act like big shots to one another."

"What're these harmless pranksters saying?" I asked. "Are they still warning the Scofields to look where they walk?"

"Well, there's still a little of that," he admitted. "Mostly, it's loud speeches—the same speeches, almost word for word—about the punishment of a vengeful God. That kind of thing."

"And there's no way to collar a single one of them?"

"They're too fast. They talk for fifteen, twenty seconds,

tops, and then they hang up."

"You have my home number," I said. "Call me if there's anything. Anything."

Sighing, having put off the inevitable long enough, I picked up another phone and asked for the overseas operator. I was still unclear about calling in the police. I was quite clear, though, about calling Mary. The last thing I wanted was for harm to come to her daughter. The other last thing I wanted was for Mary to learn about it late.

All overseas lines were engaged. "Ring me back the moment one's free," I said.

I waited, and rubbed my chest. Crazy, draining day. I'd begun to suspect everybody, not only the People's Resistance Army, but everybody: Ramon Vienna, God's Love, the Bill Bradwayites, the Girl Scouts of America, The Masons, Harmon Scofield, my Aunt Hattie, everybody . . .

Waiting, I puzzled over how it had all come to this. The Company and the Scofields, I mean. Especially the Scofields . . .

EIGHT

IN THE LATE 1880s, while he was effortlessly flunking courses at Yale, Adam Scofield inherited from his uncle a family-owned insurance firm, a timber mine, and two newspapers. The insurance firm and the timber mine were flourishing businesses; the newspapers, with conservative, aged men running them, were not. Before he was twenty-one, Adam quit Yale, ignored insurance and timber, about which he knew and cared nothing, fired the mossbacks, and hired people to teach him how to be a publisher.

At twenty-five, he was indeed a publisher—an imperfect businessman, as he would remain for the rest of his intensely active life, but indeed a publisher. *The New York Outlook* and *The Newark Sentinel*, vulgar and vapid, frequently crusading, always readable, teemed with immediacy. If he was not yet Pulitzer, not yet Hearst, not yet Scripps, his name and what and whom he represented were, in New York and Newark, indisputably better known than any of his competitors'. He cared deeply and raged about exploitation of the oppressed, and he understood, more daringly than his competitors, the public's disapproval of and fascination with sin.

He lured the best journalists and business managers he could find from other papers, paying exorbitant salaries. At twenty-six, he hired Caleb Buckminster—a bright, chubby, professorial-looking young administrator he liked at once—to scout the West Coast as a possible Scofield newspaper city. In his lower Broadway office, he served Buckminster a bourbon and a cigar, and he explained publishing.

"We're successful today," he began, "and within a few years we're going to be at the very head of the parade, Caleb, because we sell a good product that people want: The three C's. And we're more vigorous at it than anyone else."

"The three C's?"

"Crime, cunt, and children."

"Oh."

"Crime is lawlessness, whether it's a darkie stealing a chicken or Wall Street stealing a darkie. It's corruption, it's violence, it's stories exposing predators large or small, preferably large, with names and dates and places in the boldest print possible.

"Children is sentiment. It's the sanctity of the religious family unit. It's pigtailed Jane and freckle-faced Johnny honouring their father and their mother.

"The other ingredient, Caleb, is what knits the whole shooting match together. People are frightened of the very word *sex*, but give it to them in the right package, with the right moral alarm, and you have them hooked. Atheistic vice dens never fail: print the juicy details and get ministers of the Gospel to write editorials denouncing them. Fathers want to know how to save their daughters from being raped by blacks or Orientals or that supposedly nice young boy next door. And we never forget the wealthy and the mighty, Caleb: the working man and his wife are intrigued by the adulteries of the rich.

"Most of all, Caleb, we're the working man's spokesman and guardian. And the quickest way to reach him is to shout."

At twenty-nine, shortly after the turn of the century, Adam fell in love with Eugenia Harmon, seven years his junior and daughter of the prestigious New Haven Harmons. He had bought or founded three more newspapers, all on the East Coast, *The Albany Call*, *The Philadelphia Banner-Clarion*, and *The Harrisburg Citizen*, each a duplicate of the other except for local news and advertisements and causes, all reflecting the restless, dynamic personality of Adam Hurd Scofield. Tall, vitally handsome, powerfully built, without an ounce of fat or self-doubt, he zipped from city to city, state to state, coast to coast, moving swiftly and with grace, moving with total confidence. He enjoyed people, often democratically, those who deplored his principles and

118

liked him personally, those who drank and slept with him, those who talked back to him, those who stood in quiet awe of him. Marriage had no place in his unobstructed ambitions until he met Eugenia.

Her parents were pleased, reservedly, with Adam. They became satisfied that Eugenia was fond of him and that he was of good family stock, but, as he came to call more and more frequently, they questioned themselves about him. They regarded life primarily as a God-given opportunity to perform noble deeds and shoulder mature responsibilities, and they did not quite understand newspapers except those that promoted spiritual uplift. Adam Scofield's journals seemed to deal all too often with squalor and seamy people —all the more astonishing because Adam, extremely charming and with impeccable manners, continued to impress them as a man of sterling character.

The sixth time he and Eugenia were together, Adam proposed marriage. Eugenia, lovely Eugenia, asked that he wait at least a month, until her father knew him better, and then ask again. "Waiting is what old folks do at the post office and the barbershop," he scoffed. "Do you love me?"

"Oh, yes, Adam!"

"Do you want to marry me?"

"Oh, yes!"

"Don't move," he ordered, and strode to the adjacent parlour where Nathaniel Harmon was reading, and said, "Sir, Eugenia and I love each other and want to marry. I realize it's a short courtship, but I worship her, sir, and I'll devote my life to caring for her and making her happy."

Her father raised his eyeglasses and raised many questions. An hour later, he consented. In the Harmon bedroom, Mrs Harmon said she hoped the decision was right. "I have some doubts about him, certainly, but then so did your father about me," Mr Harmon worriedly assured her. "I think he's basically sound. Eugenia will help clear the way for Jesus to reach him and help him turn those vulgar papers into something worthwhile."

To Adam, ecstatic with the certainty that he *would* care

for her and make her happy forever, Eugenia was a marvel of delicious inconsistencies. She had not gone to college because her parents were convinced that colleges encouraged too much curiosity in the minds of refined young ladies, yet there was more than cotton in that mind; she had read Shakespeare and the Scriptures, but she had read other books as well and she wasn't embarrassed to say things that were intelligent. She had let him kiss her early, at only their third meeting, and though she naturally pretended that the act was all his fault, she indicated that she liked to be kissed. He was uneasy with that religious clap-trap of hers, but he was sure that her churchly chatter was largely a pose, the safe language of a decent but secretly lusty young woman eager for a lusty but secretly decent young man. Two nights before their wedding, as they sat on the back-porch swing of her Whalley Avenue house, she was startled when his hand rested on the front of her blouse, but she didn't pull away. Jittery and smelling of jasmine, she said in a shaky voice, "Do wait, dearest. We'll be husband and wife soon enough, and then your hand may go there and anywhere else it pleases. Your hand and . . . you."

On Adam's instructions, the Scofield papers carried news, discreetly but on the front page, of the nuptials, and, over Eugenia's shy objection, a picture of her. They were married in the Harmons' parlour, with a Presbyterian minister, the Reverend Paul Hastings, presiding. Eugenia's mother and sister and grandmother and aunts wept. Eugenia's father kept glancing at his pocket watch and, when he spoke, after the wedding, his voice was husky. "Take good care of my little girl, young fellow," he said. "You're taking away the salt of the earth, the gem of the ocean."

"I know that better than anyone, sir," said Adam. "You have my word: I'll treat her the way I would a princess."

"A queen," Mr Harmon corrected. "A queen."

Their wedding night was spent at the Woodmont, in a hotel suite facing down on Long Island Sound. The bell-boy brought champagne, at Adam's instructions beforehand, although Eugenia's parents would have been scandalized, would certainly not have permitted strong drink. At the wall-length window looking out on to the water, Adam stood behind Eugenia, who gazed at the sea, and enveloped her with his arms. "Love," he said. "Love. Love. Love. Love."

"Do you love me, Adam?"

Sighing, he said, "Love. I love you."

"May I have your baby?"

Sighing, he asked, "Why did you bring this Omar the Tent-Maker robe, Eugenia? It must have seventy-seven curtains, and we're booked here for only a couple of nights. . ."

"You sound cross."

"No. Just let me turn you around, will you? I have to be at least fifty pounds heavier than you, but you're standing there as if your feet are stuck in cement. Will you for Christ's sake let me turn you around so I can at least kiss you?"

"Don't be profane. I can't bear it when you're profane."

"Very well. I won't be profane. Help me turn you around, Eugenia."

"Don't be brutal."

"I won't be. I promise I won't be. You're standing like an iron statue. Help me turn you around."

"No."

Good Lord. "Why not?"

"Because I hate you. Because I miss my father, I want to be with my parents. Please go away."

She shivered.

She pushed him, actually pushed him, and fled to the bathroom, but Adam caught her before she could lock the door.

"You're hurting me," she whimpered.

"You know perfectly well I'm not. Eugenia, if you prefer, we could . . . we needn't . . . you shouldn't be this frightened, but you are. Would you rather wait till tomorrow?"

"Yes. Thank you. I love you so much, Adam."

"A moment ago—"

121

"Will there be terrible pain? My mother told me if I hold my breath and think of something else, the pain won't be as excruciating. . ."

When the time came, hours later, after she had sobbed and rambled, now coherent, now unreasonable, after the nearly exhausted Adam had assured her over and over that the act was normal and that she wasn't going mad, the act was incredibly simple; Eugenia gasped, spoke of being tortured, and then her arms enfolded him.

Before they slept, Adam asked her teasingly if she still wanted to go to her parents' home. "I'm in my own home now, where I belong," she murmured, and then said, "Oh, dear. I forgot to say my prayers." She began to move away from him to rise, evidently thought better of it, and returned to him in the warm four-poster bed and said, "He won't punish me if I skip this one night. Every single one of my prayers has been answered, anyway."

When Adam was thirty-five, and owned eight newspapers and three magazines, Eugenia suffered her third miscarriage. The possibility that he was in any way responsible for her inability to maintain a pregnancy never crossed his mind. He was keenly disappointed, for he wanted a son, to further certify his masculinity and to one day be given the Scofield Company, as it was now called.

The Company was growing and prospering. Money was making more money, in publishing and out of publishing. To the papers and magazines and the insurance firm and the timber mine were added lumber mills and real estate, full-time operations that required the attention of experts. He maintained those experts to work hard and keep him uninformed, concentrating his own energies on publishing.

Everything was successful, wildest-dreams successful. Everything except his marriage.

Several days after the third miscarriage, Eugenia's mother went to be with her at the Manhattan town house, and Adam's carriage drove him and Caleb Buckminster, just in from Los Angeles, to the Long Island estate he was building for Eugenia. He was fonder than ever of Caleb, who had worked wonders with *The Los Angeles Criterion*, three years old and often the most profitable paper in the chain.

"I'm anxious for you to see the place, Caleb," he said enthusiastically. "I'm calling it Parnassus."

"After Apollo's mountain?"

Chuckling, Adam answered, "The idea, in time, is for that Parnassus to be thought of as an imitation of my Parnassus. We started building just a few months ago. I have fifty-five men at work there full time, but they've just begun."

"When will it be done?"

"Oh, I'd say about ten years. Maybe twenty."

"That's supposed to be a joke."

Adam shook his head. "Not at all. It'll take all the time it needs. I call it an estate, but it's going to be a castle. It's going to be the biggest, the greatest castle in history."

They arrived, and he showed the goggling Buckminster about. "The indoor swimming pool will be there," he said. "The zoo will be outside, next to it."

"The *zoo*?"

"Whoever heard of a home without a zoo? I expect to give weekend parties here. I have this image of fat ladies in the dressing rooms, changing into their bathing suits, and a hyena gawking at them through the window and laughing. Would you happen to know if hyenas laugh a lot naturally? Or if they can be trained to laugh on cue?"

"I could look it up," Buckminster said, shaking his head in wonderment. "I suppose if anyone could get them to laugh on demand, you could."

Adam enjoyed that, liked Caleb, who was a clear blend of romantic idealism and no-nonsense pragmatism, who was realistic enough to know he was an employee yet individual enough, secure enough in his position, to take issue with Adam when he believed it warranted. "Come along," Adam directed, and showed him the frontage on the Sound. "What we'll have," he said, "is a place so large, so vast, that

123

that you'll need a week just to find your way through the front coatroom. Over there will be the main house and six guesthouses. I figure more than two hundred rooms—not just rooms but individually designed and constructed rooms for our guests. And that's where we'll have the tennis courts and the outdoor swimming pools. And the gardens begin there. We'll have ballrooms, and theatres, and—well, as I say, there's no hurry."

On the just-begun patio outside his nearly completed study, Adam called for drinks. "My wife is fervently against liquor, for everyone, not only herself," he said. "She's already laid the law down to me—any spirits here and she won't come—but what she doesn't know won't hurt her." He waited. "Well? What do you think?"

"I'd better have that drink first," Caleb said, again shaking his head. "I'm dazzled."

Adam grinned broadly. "Undazzle. I want a reaction."

"Very well. I think you're clean out of your mind."

Mildly, Adam said, "Granted, that's a reaction."

"With all due respect—"

"Forget that 'all due respect.' I trust your judgement. Sometimes it's all wet, but I didn't bring you here to butter me up."

"It looks as though the horse has been stolen. It's too late to lock the barn door. If you'd asked my advice before you got this under way, I'd've said absolutely not. I can read ledgers. I know the Company's earnings, and I know what the future prospects can be, knock wood. But this represents millions of millions of dollars, and no one has millions of millions of dollars to be indulgent with, not even the Company." Drinks were brought. "You asked me, I told you." The servant left, and Caleb lifted his glass. "You're not smiling."

"You're not, either, and you should be," said Adam. "The Company's just opening shop. Five years from today, sooner, we'll be bigger than anyone you can name. You're part of it and you'll get bigger with it. Parnassus is confidence. Where the hell is *your* confidence, Caleb? Boldness

124

is what built the Company, boldness and daring, not timid tiptoeing. I don't want to listen to quibbles."

Shrugging, Caleb said, "You're the wizard."

Damn you, thought Adam Scofield. Damn you, and damn me. I didn't call you here to tell me I make mistakes. I called you here for a reason. And you work for me, it's not the other way around, and now that you're sitting across from me, I can't bring myself to say out loud: Caleb, you're a crackerjack in your job. Outside of that, I don't know much of anything about you. I don't know what delights you, what wounds you. I don't know if you love your wife while you're making love to her. I want to ask you what touches you, what frightens you, what you think of me, what you think of yourself, because I need something now I've never needed before—a friend. A friend who would listen to me while I say.

The reckless extravagance that's going into this place is for Eugenia, whom I love and run to and can't stand to be with. How did the warmth and the love we had so sincerely slip away? Where did it go? I get into strange beds with strange women, and I come away empty, empty of sperm and empty of myself. I want Eugenia to love me. I despise adultery. I detest dishonouring myself, and Eugenia.

What's happening, Caleb? Why am I so unhappy?

Soon after his forty-fifth birthday, his fourteenth year of marriage, Adam surprised Eugenia with two steamship tickets to Europe. "We could both use a long vacation," he said. "I promise not to do a lick of work on the ship. We'll loll and doze and enjoy ourselves. We leave this Friday. Everything's arranged."

"That's impossible, Adam. You know my mother's ill."

"When hasn't she been, or thought she was? I want to check our London and Rome bureaus first hand, maybe a few others, but that won't take up all our time. I want to get away—with you, just the two of us. I've had my nose to the grindstone so long I've forgotten what a holiday is like.

You have my permission to shop me into bankruptcy."

"Can't you ever listen to me?" Eugenia protested. "I couldn't dream of leaving her alone, certainly not with Father gone only a few months."

"Your sister can take care of her."

"What we could do . . . We could take Mother with us. The sea air just might do her a world of—"

"No."

"Really, Adam. . ."

" 'Really, Adam.' 'Really, Adam.' I'm goddamn sick to death of that 'really, Adam.' When I look for you you're either with your mother or you're in some goddamn church. Do I have no rights at all? I've built thirteen newspapers and five magazines for you. They don't interest you. I built Parnassus for you. You're almost never there. Where are you? With your goddamn mother or in a goddamn church!"

Her hands at her ears: "I will not hear blasphemy."

"You'll hear all I goddamn want you to hear! You've given me plenty of cause to let my eye rove, but I've been faithful to you all these years," he lied. "You were affectionate once, you were warm. I want that again. It can happen again if we go off by ourselves."

"Only if Mother can come, too."

"You and your mother can both go to hell. I'm leaving on Friday, with you or without you."

He sailed on Cunard with his black valet, Enoch.

The passive crossing was misery for Adam, who had always been at a loss to understand idleness, misery because he knew that only childish stubbornness had forced him to make a trip he did not want to make without his wife. He determined to meet people, to be outgoing. By the evening of the third day at sea, he decided that the passengers' average age was ninety. Shuffleboard appalled him, reading for pleasure held his attention for only brief periods, those antique passengers who trapped him into deck-chair conversation were abysmal bores, and so he took to having his meals in his stateroom with Enoch. There he worked, as well, and found to his intense displeasure that he was working as hard as he did on land. "Write a book for me, will you, Enoch?" he asked. "A book that can teach a man how to relax."

Enoch chuckled. "I'll do that for you, Mr Scofield."

On the third night at sea, he stood alone at a rail, inhaling the night's crisp salt air, staring at the dark waters. He heard high heels clicking and then stop, and he turned to see a woman at the rail, no more than a dozen feet away. "Good evening," he said after a watchful moment, unable to see her clearly. For all I know, he thought, she's one of those ninety-year-old passengers, quick steps and all.

"Good evening," she replied in a low, lovely voice.

He was silent again and then he asked, "Aren't you freezing?"

"Not particularly," she said, still not facing him fully. "I like late night air."

They met.

She was a tall, handsome woman, stately though not icy, probably in her early forties. Her name was Margaret Brooke and she was returning to London after a month's stay with her American friends in Boston. Adam had introduced himself, but his name didn't seem to register with her until a minute or so later. "Oh, yes," she acknowledged. "Someone mentioned you were on board. I glanced through one of your newspapers while I was in Boston. What's it called—the *Beacon*?"

"The *Leader*. Close enough. I'm sure you didn't approve."

"Not tremendously, no, but we produce shoddy journalism in England, too."

He laughed. "You speak your mind."

"Mmm. I learned to in the States. That's one thing I admire about Americans. They're straight out with it, they have very few inhibitions about saying what they feel. It saves a great deal of time; one knows where one stands. Britons are petrified at the idea of getting to the point."

"Was it your first trip to America?"

"Mmm."

"May I ask why you were there for only a month?"

"Certainly you may ask. Beware, though, my friend. The answer's tedious and it could take till Southampton."

"I'd be happy to listen till Southampton. Are you sure you're not cold? I'll give you my coat."

She shook her head. "My husband died eight months ago—nine, actually, in a week and a half from now. A lovely man, cheerful to the end. His mother was born in Pennsylvania, if that adds a hill of beans to the story. After I lost him, several months after I lost him, I thought I was beginning to mend rather nicely. I wasn't, actually. I kept walking into myself—disgusting, tiresome business. Have you fallen asleep yet?"

Adam laughed again. "Go on."

"Our Boston friends kept writing and insisting I come visit with them for as long as I liked. It became more and more attractive in time—the change of scenery, sweet friends to be with, that sort of thing—and so one day I simply closed up the flat and sailed. Have you read that a sea voyage can help one come to terms with herself? Rot and rubbish. I was in silly agony on the way over, as lonely and numb as I was back on Bayswater Road. I planned to spend at least a year in the States, perhaps even live there for the rest of my life." She paused, examining the ocean. "And Boston was lovely, and Bobby's friends couldn't have been more divine, and I realized straight on that I was solving nothing. So back I go."

She looked at Adam. "I say. You *are* still awake, aren't you?"

"Very much so."

"I'd best get on to my cabin now." She extended her hand and, smiling with a brightness that dazzled Adam, said, "Thank you, my friend, for both those ears."

"Ears?" he repeated, gripping her hand.

"They listen so patiently." She waited a beat and then asked, "May I have my hand? It's the only one of its kind I own, until I get to London."

"May I see you to your cabin?"

"I . . ."

"What is it, Mrs Brooke?"

"I have a confession to make. I read the passenger list at some loathsome tea yesterday, and under 'S' it said A. H. Scofield, Esquire. No missus."

"That's hardly a shocking confession."

"Oh yes it is. I asked a steward to learn if A. H. Scofield, Esquire, was indeed travelling alone. Are you aware, A. H. Scofield, that you've only a manservant travelling with you?"

Tingling and apprehensive, Adam escorted her down narrow stairs and through narrow passageways to the door of her stateroom and asked if they might meet for breakfast in the morning.

"What would happen to your good name?" she asked. "Everyone on board knows who you are. If you were seen dining with a widow under the age of eighty, wouldn't word scatter back home in a wink?"

"Let me see you again. Please."

Margaret Brooke, in the passageway's candlelight, was not as striking as she had been in the deck's dimness, but he was deeply attracted to her, to a woman he could not have imagined possible, a lady of immaculate dignity, yet freshly forward, even saucy.

"My friend . . ." she began.

"Yes?"

"Against every article of maritime law, would you like to come in?"

The door was bolted and she asked, "What are the wages of sin, my friend?"

"Life."

"Jolly good. My word, you *are* clawing at me, aren't you? This can be lovely, truly, if you don't claw."

"I'm sorry. I don't know how to act with—ladies."

She raised her head to him. "Shall we be friendly, my friend? Not savage. I do detest savagery, don't you? I've missed making love. I adored Bobby, but I don't think I'm being faithless to him."

A couple of days before the liner was to dock at Southampton, the news of an illicit and highly improper relationship between the wealthy American newspaper publisher and the coquettish English widow had spread throughout the ship, in spite of Adam's clumsy efforts, during their additional days and nights abroad, to be as circumspect as possible. Exposure sometimes concerned him, and often did not. All he was completely certain of was that he had been moved to pure exhilaration for the first time in his life, that he had been reborn, that he and Margaret would marry. She would not concede that she loved him.

"I've no hesitation about breaking rules I don't find sensible, my friend, but I'm bloody well not going to tell you I feel something I don't. For now, I like you, I'm cosy with you. Unless you're horrified that two people can be this close and intimate without pledging bloody troth every moment, why can't we leave it at that?"

But she did love him, Adam knew; it was unimaginable that she could be so loving without love. They agreed not to be seen in each other's company in the public rooms, not even on deck or at tea when the passengers and crew would have small reason to take gossipy notice of them. They would meet on deck only late at night, after the dinosaurs had retired. On the night before Southampton, Margaret said, "I have begun to love you, I think. It's been a rather extraordinary shipboard romance, and that's where we'll end it—tonight, on shipboard."

He protested.

"Neither of us is twenty," she said. "Even if we were to keep company for a time, as that stodgy saying goes, and marriage did come around to seem agreeable, it would be terribly difficult. I'm not at all as brave as I may pretend. I'm not at all sure I could endure being pointed at as the vampire who broke up a man's home. No, no, no, my darling," she hurried on, pressing her fingertips to his lips.

130

"Do listen to me. It would be ruinous, it would be—degrading. Please believe me. Don't see me in London. I expect I'll miss you, but that'll go away. Everything does, eventually, you know."

On the second day he was at Brown's Hotel, a messenger brought a note to his suite: *May a bold vampire of limited propriety invite an American of unlimited sweetness to tea? M.* He flew to Bayswater Road. Margaret framed his flushed cheeks between her palms, stood on tiptoes very close to him, and whispered, "I'd no clue you were so fond of tea."

Later, he said, "You're going to marry me."

"You're quite mad, you know."

"Of course. About you."

He telegraphed Eugenia, with the truth: he would forever honour her, but he loved and intended to marry a woman who had brought him wholly alive, who loved him and cherished him. He wished a divorce, as free of hurt and recriminations as possible. Eugenia would be assured not only of more than enough money to last her through her life, but as much financial interest in the Company as she deemed suitable to her needs and wishes.

The war made travel to the Continent difficult for most civilians, though not for Adam, who had only to lift a receiver to be assured immediate accommodations on a train or boat. Margaret travelled with him, always just a trace detached and observant yet never removed from him. She was continuously marvellous to be with, to be near, to talk with, to be teased by, to love. In the cabin suite they shared on the ship to Rome, she asked, left eyebrow cocked and right breast exposed, "Do you realize, you insensitive beggar's boy, that this is our anniversary? We met precisely one month ago today. The very least you could give me as a remembrance is a chummy hug."

Laughing, extending his arms, he asked, "What's the most I can give you?"

"Guess. Don't force me to call on the services of our steward. A glorious Spaniard—you would've been furious at the merciless way his eyes flirted with me."

At the Grand, in Rome, Eugenia's letter awaited him:

My dearest husband,
There can be no life without you. I implore you to not punish me further, to come home where I shall take the greatest of pains to prove myself to be the woman you married. We shall never speak of your infatuation. I have been selfish & unworthy of you. This I do know now.

Dearest husband, I vow to you that I will change & be your eternal beloved. I beseech you, dearest husband, for I otherwise will die. It is my shame that I have not borne the child we have so desired. Let us adopt a strapping boy. We shall nurture & love it together, & whither thou goest I will go. Please do not fail me, do not pain me more. I conclude this missive as I commenced it. I cannot survive without the dearest man any woman ever had.

"I'm deeply sorry, Margaret. She does need me, after all."

"Yes. Splendid."

"It's scarcely splendid . . ."

"But it is, my friend. Which is what you are: my friend. I didn't seriously expect you'd ever begin to take Bobby's place."

"You sound—"

"I sound exactly what I am—annoyed that I considered for a moment that I was in love with you. No, you mustn't there-there me. It's quite all right, you know. All I ask is that you go away. Now. Perhaps I'll pop up in your States one day. We'll all have a grand time, shall we?"

He sailed home.

Eugenia looked lovely. Her only requests, timidly offered, were that the boy be born in wedlock, that he be healthy, and that his blood lines be British. The boy was born in a Brooklyn hospital to a Scottish girl whose Welsh husband had died months before the birth. Adam wanted to name the boy Adam Junior. Eugenia asked, "Would you care terribly if we named him Harmon, to perpetuate my father's family's name?"

Adam regarded the beautiful, sturdy boy whose tiny fists groped for battle. "Very well. Harmon," he agreed. "Harmon Adam Scofield. We have a son, dear Eugenia." He opened the window wide and roared, "Stand aside, all you mountains! Harmon Adam Scofield is going to move the bejesus out of you!"

NINE

I'LL LEAVE here at once," Mary said to Joe Greenwood from her bedroom telephone at the Savoy, and buzzed for her secretary, Liz Hale.

"Hey, I wasn't suggesting you hop right home," Joe said from Manhattan. "This could be nothing at all. . ."

She looked at her watch: 1 A.M.; that meant 8 P.M. in New York. "With any luck, I should be in the air in an hour. I don't know what the winds are like, but with a little more luck the flight shouldn't take more than six hours. When we hang up, I want you to contact Martin Hargill and Leonard Slater personally and have each of them call me on the plane." Martin Hargill was in charge of the FBI in New York; Leonard Slater was New York's police commissioner. "I don't want you to tell them why they're to call; just get the word through to them that it's urgent. And I want Hargill and Slater, not lieutenants."

Liz came into the bedroom. "Then," Mary continued, "I want you to arrange for Stefan to meet me at the airport. I'll phone you as soon as I've landed and I'm in the car. If you have anything to report—anything—call the plane."

"I'll say this one more time," Joe cautioned. "You could go through all this and come home and find she's safe in bed."

"That's exactly where I hope she'll be."

Replacing the receiver, she turned to Liz. "Round up Jeanne and Smilin' Jack. They're to pack and have the plane ready to take us to New York immediately."

"May I ask why?"

"Later. Then ring down for a porter to hurry up here—to this bedroom door, not the drawing room door—and pack for you and me. And then ask Lady Benjamin—see that none of the other guests hears you—to come in and see me."

Eileen Benjamin, high but not drunk, entered the second

134

bedroom as Mary changed from her evening dress to a travelling suit. As briefly as possible, Mary explained the sudden departure. "Back at school, you were always good at making up believable lies on the spur of the moment. Invent a nifty when you go back inside, will you, Eileen, for my leaving so fast? This is rude of me, but if *I* go in and start talking, it'll get all complicated."

"Would you like some advice?"

"Not really."

"Here's some, anyway. If you fly back and Carole's fine, you're travelling for nothing. If something is wrong, God forbid—"

"—then it's better for me to be there than here."

"What about Owen?"

"Well, what about him?"

"Should he be told? I could ring him up."

Mary shook her head. "The last time Carole saw her father, he was as polite and charming as ever but he barely remembered her name. No. Let Owen go on communing with Buddha. As they say in the song, I'll do it my way."

The friends embraced. "I'll be back, Eily," Mary said. "We'll have that Surrey weekend yet."

"With Carole. With my godchild."

"That's a firm date," Mary answered, and looked away from the dread in Eileen Benjamin's eyes.

Airborne, having confided the reason for the trip to Liz, having sworn her to confide nothing to the crew, Mary Scofield sipped a claret and allowed herself, for the first time since Joe's call, to feel the sharp edge of anxiety.

Joe hadn't uttered the word *kidnap*. Joe hadn't needed to.

"If you ever have to worry about anything," *Gramp had counselled her when she was fifteen, Carole's age,* "do your worrying in private. Control is what matters, all that matters. Let people see you're not in command of a situation, even for a minute, and you've lost the bout; you might as well hoist a sign begging people to push you

135

around. No one has any use for anyone else's indecision. No one."

You taught me just fine, Gramp. I was, and am, the best pupil in the class.

I lapse. Once. I stand in the London hotel room with Rick Tovar, hoisting my begging sign, and I bleat, "*I expect it of you. You owe it to me.*" Mostly, though, folks come to the carnival from miles around to go *ooh* and *ah* as I tear telephone books in half.

And I sit here now, searching for sincere anxiety, so frozen with control that even with every conceivable cataclysm darting in front of me, I don't know what I feel towards my daughter.

That I want her unharmed. Of course.

But beyond that?

Maybe nothing, almost nothing. . . Is that really why I'm crying?

Three quarters of an hour in the air, she took a call from New York's police commissioner, Leonard Slater, a man who had cause to detest the Scofield press but a man who would be out of a job in November if his party was defeated at the polls—the party frequently favoured by the Scofield press.

She asked if he could possibly come to her town house, alone, at 6 A.M. New York time.

"I realize what I'm asking, Leonard," she said, "and I'm sure you know I wouldn't bother you except for something terribly important."

"I'll—do my best, Miss Scofield. Can you give me some indication of how I can help you?"

Not on a transatlantic line, she decided. "I'll tell you at six. Thank you, Leonard." She replaced the receiver, and poured another inch of wine into her glass, and wondered if she had been wise in not telling him about Carole just yet. He could have got started immediately, she thought, could have begun the wheels spinning, could bring me news when

I land. Maybe by waiting, I'm endangering Carole all the more.

No. This needs extremely delicate handling. It has to be as secretive as possible.

I hope.

Aching for sleep, aching to buzz Liz to come and comfort her, aware that there was no way to invite that, Mary walked the length of the plane's larger bedroom and involuntarily watched a kaleidoscope of Carole, now thirteen and wailing to Mother, "Your skin was never broken out like mine! I hate it, I hate it! I want to die!"; now eight and cuddly and hugging Mary and exclaiming, "Oh, Mummy, I love you so much, don't ever go away!"; now three and squealing with delight and mock fright as Owen gently propped her on an equally gentle old pony at Parnassus.

Eileen: *"What about Owen? Should he be told? I could ring him up."*

"I don't want a baby! All I want is the world's best dia-phragm!" Mary Moran Stafford Enright Scofield heard herself insist to Owen.

Now? she thought.

Years, sped-up years ago. . .

She was twenty-three years old, at Sandys Parish in Bermuda, and her father, Harmon, phoned her from Warwick to say he would be dead by morning. She had divorced Tommy Moran. Gil Stafford was about to divorce her. Her naked father spanked the undersheet of his bed with the flat of his hand and asked her to lie down beside him.

After Tommy and Gil, and after the mindless, loveless, hanging-around-for-Meaning affairs that followed Gil, Owen Enright was a rest cure. They were introduced at an Edinburgh dinner party by Eileen Phillips, not yet Lady Benjamin, who prattled to Mary, "I'm not altogether sure what he does for a living—I think he's with some securities firm in Philadelphia—but what he does

137

best is serve as the extra guy at a party. Good-looking, terrific manners, from some Main Line family that went broke, sweet-tempered, and dull as hell. He's thirty-four, a bachelor. I haven't seen the affidavit, but I strongly suspect he's—well, I'm ashamed to use such language."

"Homosexual?"

"No. A virgin. Still unwrapped. Anyway, as long as you're here and there aren't any particular cats howling on your back porch, you could do worse than a date with Goody Two Shoes Owen. Just don't make a pass at him on the first date or he might slap your face."

Mary liked Owen Enright, felt comfortable with him if not electrically stimulated, dined with him in Scotland, took long walks with him in Hyde Park, slept with him in New York, and married him in San Francisco. Like her and like Harmon, he'd had little education or training to "be" anything, but to his credit, he worked, although he might indeed have survived as the extra guy at a party. True, he worked at desks that didn't press him with challenge, and he changed jobs frequently, but he worked —and he was far too intelligent, with too vast a range of interests, however superficial, to be, in Eileen's too often true words, dull as hell.

Unlike Tommy and Gil, though, he was poised and relaxed, neither shying from the Scofield money nor grasping at it, a pliant and sometimes unexpectedly witty man with most of the better Cub Scout virtues. Curiously, the sex with Owen was, for a time, intensely pleasurable. Tommy had persuaded her she was a frigid hen. Gil, His Kinkyship, had taught her that love and sex were to be viewed like church and state, one totally unrelated to the other. Owen Enright's talent as a lover lay in his serene and infinite patience, his complete willingness to stay clear when she wasn't in the mood, to be resourceful and generous when she wished him. Their first seven months of marriage were spent principally in sailing to Europe and back, lolling in Cannes and Como as the desire struck them, in bed, in parties they attended, in parties

138

given by Mary for friends occasionally puzzled by Owen. Owen repeated that soon he would have to knuckle down and stop using her money, Mary continually squeezed more allowance out of Gramp's lawyer than Gramp's will called for.

At a party in Hove, Eileen brought Mary a drink and marvelled, "I don't figure it. I size him up as a fella who'd be satisfied to sit and count his fingers and toes for the rest of his life. And yet you seem more—what's the word I'm after—con*tent* than I've ever seen you. 'Splain me dat, Kingfish."

"What's to 'splain? The men who excited me were the men who always turned out to be bad news. Owen pampers me."

"With whose bread?"

"Oh, beat it, Eily! You know better than to talk like that. I'm content, yes; that's all there is to it. I enjoy what's happening. It'll go on, and I'll be even more content."

In that seventh month of marriage, Mary, clockwork-Mary, missed her period, and a doctor in Milan confirmed her pregnancy.

"I'm not going to have it," she told Owen that night. "What I have now is everything I want. A baby would change everything."

Owen nodded.

"I wouldn't have a clue of what to do with a baby. Am I shocking you?"

"Of course not."

"There's a streak of the Puritan in you, you know."

"Is there? I've been so busy being a sybarite, I hadn't noticed."

"Oh, you're a Puritan, all right. Well, inside here is one foetus that isn't going to have to grow up and tell his analyst, 'I didn't ask to be born.' Look at all the analyst fees we'll save." Owen nodded agreeably, and Mary went on. "The jury may still be out about God, but there's one thing I know doesn't exist, and that's the maternal instinct. I have no intention of doing anything I don't have to do. No baby!"

"Fine, fine, but why are you shouting?"

"I'm not shouting!"

In Zurich, Owen was given the name of the best doctor for the procedure. He made the appointment and then asked Mary, "Are you sure this is what you want?"

"I thought you were with me a hundred percent."

". . . I'm not."

"Now you tell me?"

"Yes."

"When did abortion suddenly become murder?"

"No, no, no," Owen said. "It's even cornier than that. I'd like for us to have the child. It couldn't be more purely selfish. We could get old and grey going from one maraschino cherry to the next, and I can think of worse things but I can think of better things, too. Like solidity, stability. Lord, how's this for the corniest of all: responsibility. What I want, love, is responsibility. Being responsible for another human being besides ourselves to enhance us, make us fuller."

"I married the goddam *Reader's Digest!*"

Carole, six pounds, eight ounces, and perfectly formed, was born at Lenox Hill Hospital in New York City. Owen was ecstatic. Mary wasn't entirely sure what she felt, other than a fuzzy pride in having produced something more durable than a cocktail party, some hairdressers' appointments, and two disastrous marriages.

This marriage would go right. Carole was the stickum.

They settled into the Scofield town house in Manhattan. Owen, who had majored in business administration at college, went to work daily for the Company, its main offices still on lower Broadway, as Consultant. The Company, these five years after Gramp's death, continued rich enough to afford executive slots with essentially silly titles like Consultant. To his credit—there was always something to his credit—Owen took his job seriously; he was out of the house by ten every morning and rarely returned before mid-afternoon, to kiss Mary, to have his three and, presently, four pre-dinner martinis, and to worship the baby. Mary worked, too, at seeking fulfilment in the baby, at appreciating Owen's unswerving sweetness, at wondering occasionally if she would be as useless, as purposeless, at sixty as she was now at twenty-six and twenty-seven and twenty-eight.

As she came to resent Owen, who kept smiling and who was beginning to continue the martinis after dinner, so she came to resent her own long list of inadequacies: her expensive education that had prepared her for absolutely nothing, her fear of venturing beyond the shallow waters in relationships, her failure to become somebody. Loving Carole, being loved by Carole, was only intermittently satisfying. She could display affection as a mother, as she sometimes could display facsimiles of affection as a wife, but in the clinches it was Mrs Boswell, the baby's nurse and governess, who really knew how to care for the child, who could handle the child's illnesses without panic, who could lavish warmth on the child consistently and make it come out genuine. When Mary saw a shade of lipstick not her own on Owen's handkerchief during a Christmas holiday in Nice, she could not become enraged by the betrayal. She did not ask him who owned the lipstick, for the question would have been mere passing curiosity and therefore insulting.

Not in retaliation but rather in an effort to come alive, she considered playing the game herself. On the morning of her twenty-ninth birthday, she wakened with a ghastly hangover in a New York Scofield hotel room in the naked arms of a sleeping, fiftyish man who mildly resembled her father. She remembered the charity bazaar in the hotel's Grand Ballroom the night before, remembered going without Owen, who was in Philadelphia to see his ailing mother, remembered auctioning a sailboat for a pot of money, remembered being amusing, remembered gay and increasingly seductive chitchat with this man, remembered inviting him here, remembered laughing a lot. What she could not remember now was what had been so funny, whether there had been sex or if the champagne had put one of them to sleep first. What she could not remember, the ultimate obscenity, was the man's name.

She strove to invest herself in charities, in motherhood; she thought of commanding Owen to get out of the martini jar; she found herself slipping into other unfocused romances, battleships that passed in the night. On the morning of her thirtieth birthday, the day she came into her full inheritance, Owen swore off liquor forever. That night, morosely drunk, he told her far more than she wished to hear about his year-old affair with Ginny Courtland, their neighbour and the exemplary wife of his drinking friend Buster, Ginny who was Mary's tennis partner and sometimes lunch companion and sometimes confidante, stainless Ginny who could always be guaranteed to know and gossip, with a mixture of breathlessness and Christian distaste, about who was sleeping with whom.

"Why are you telling me this?" Mary asked Owen.

"Guilty conscience."

"Like bloody hell," she corrected softly. "What am I expected to do with this touching confession that you've been going in the bushes with my friend and your friend's wife? Give you heavenly blessings? Kick you out? I guess I never bothered to recognize till this minute how hatefully hostile you've always been, Owen. You needed for me to know about Ginny. With all that insufferable Old Dog Tray goodness of yours, what you've really been doing all along has been to rub my nose in your small regard for me. All right, let's deal with this, right now and head on. What is it you truly want? Your freedom, so you can pledge your troth to another? Forgive the Gothic novel talk, but all this is straight out of a Gothic novel, anyway. As of today, I'm worth a considerable amount of money. You picked today to sing your aria, not yesterday, so you must have something monumental up that

142

Kilgour, French, and Stanbury sleeve I bought you. Let's hear it."

Owen was shaking his head, and drinking, and incredibly, weeping.

"Stop that!" she shouted. "Talk to me or yell at me or throw something at me, but stop that snivelling! My life's been up to here with so-called men who cry!"

He wept all the more, and Mary, despising him, shouted all the more, called him vicious names viciously, and the noise brought Carole, frightened, into the bedroom. Mary was suddenly silent. Owen saw the child, reached out for her, and wept wildly and squeezed her tightly and rocked her from side to side.

"What's wrong, Daddy?" Carole asked, surely more frightened. "What's wrong? What's *wrong*?" Her huge eyes looked up at the mute, mortified Mary. "What's the *matter*?"

Four days later, although Carole's kindergarten year was not yet ended, Mary took her to the family home in Bermuda, expecting, for no plausible reason, that there on the Sandys Parish beach she could sort herself out and come to some decision. Never entirely comfortable with the child, conceding to herself that Owen was a better father than she was a mother, she swam with Carole, raced with her on the long stretch of pink sand, read to her, and lied to her by promising that she and Daddy and Mummy would be together again, and happy, very soon. She watched Carole splash about in the water, and warmed to her sweet, rich giggles, and thought. Where does she go from here, with two gummed-up parents who are twin towers of Jell-O? Wasn't I her age— a bit older, a bit younger—when I looked at *my* Jell-O parents and sensed trouble on the way?

What do I have to give you that's genuine, innocent baby? Not nearly enough. A few fortune cookie quotes: Love gives out of fullness and needs little. The emptier the barrel, the more to be filled. Let a smile be your

143

umbrella. There's a Rimbaud 'round my shoulder. You were conceived not in love but in boredom, and how can I make it up to you, or any of us? If wishes were horses, beggars would ride. . .

Mr and Mrs Hobbs, the Sandys Parish housekeepers, clucked and fussed over the five-year-old Carole, much as they had clucked and fussed over the five-year-old Mary, and Mary left her with them and their seven-year-old granddaughter, on the first sunless day, to go into Hamilton to shop. On Front Street, unsure for a moment but then very sure, she recognized Joe Greenwood sitting on the iron bench outside Trimingham's—Joe from twelve years before, darling Joe, gruff and to-the-point Joe Greenwood, whom Gramp had been carefully grooming as the Company's next white-haired boy until the discovery that Mary was in love with him and had every deliberate intention of marrying him.

His craggy face lighted up and he shot up on seeing her, and they embraced and kissed, and each rushed the other with questions and repeated greetings, Joe bear-hugging her again, looking more filled out and prosperous than he had at twenty-eight. "God, I feel a cheap gag coming on: You're a sight for sore eye!" he exclaimed. "What're you doing here?"

"I live here, sort of. What's a city boy like *you* doing here?"

"The city boy's turned squarer than you could've imagined. My wife and I are on a *cruise*, yet. It's what's called a systematized vacation. We sailed from New York three days ago, and our first land stop is here . . . this is Monday, isn't it? Then we're either in Belgium or Bermuda. We have to be back on board at six o'clock to set sail for the next call. The whole thing's a shameless excuse to loaf and eat like a pig."

"Where's your wife, Joe? I'd love to meet her."

"She's in there," he said, his chin nudging towards Trimingham's, "doing some incidental shopping, meaning

144

she's probably buying up every incidental that isn't nailed down. We're to meet at Smith's down the street at four on the dot, meaning she'll materialize at four-thirty."

It was not quite three. "Will you buy me some coffee?"

"You bet, Mrs—what *is* your last name these days? I kept reading about you, but I'm here without my score-card."

The lunch trade at Hoppin' John's was thinning, and they were left alone. Mary, genuinely delighted to see this good man, had coffee, Joe had a beer, and they brought each other up to date. He was managing editor of a Cleveland paper in the Headley chain, minor competition to the Scofield press. He had gone to work for Headley soon after his war games with Gramp and his refusal to marry Mary, had married Sylvia Saks, a young widow with two daughters. Sylvia wrote and illustrated children's books; he said the cruise was barely four days old but Sylvia was putting on weight already, and she was never on time, and went on periodic buying binges as if they had money, and every criticism of Sylvia somehow certified that he was crazy about her. He was doing well enough, he said; Cleveland wasn't a city, but it had some decent eating places and a nice symphony orchestra if you went in for symphony orchestras.

"But you'd rather be in New York," Mary quietly baited.

"Now *that* town has a *nice* symphony orchestra," he agreed.

"Then why don't you move there? And join the Company?"

Joe's forefinger played with the edges of the ashtray. The corners of his mouth went down and he shook his large head. "Yeah, I know, I thought a couple of hundred times—I have the exact number marked on my calendar— of contacting you. And decided to stick with the nice orchestra in Cleveland."

"You're still the proud Turk."

He nodded. "Something like that. Look, my saga's run

out of steam. Let me hear about you. What is it now, four husbands and one child, or one husb— No, it's more than one husband."

"Well, the first one doesn't really count, but it's three husbands and one very definite child." They drank more coffee and more beer, and Mary told him of the posh briar patch that had been her life from the day he had walked away from her to the rise and fall of Owen Enright. And asked, "Do you remember saying to me, 'Don't sit on your ass'?"

"*I* said that?"

"You said that. On those long weekends at Parnassus, we'd walk and we'd walk and we'd walk, and you were irate that I was settling to be a featherhead. You kept growling, 'Read! Learn things! Ask people what they meant by what they said! Ride a subway, buy groceries at the supermarket, involve yourself, don't be afraid of all strange toilet seats . . .'"

"No, what you said I said was, Don't sit on your ass. How could I've said the one if—"

Mary smiled. "You were the only man of any meaning I every knew who sincerely wanted me to stretch myself." Surely too nakedly now, too transparently desperate, she leaned forward and covered his hand with hers and hoarsely implored, "Leave Cleveland, Joe," fearful of adding *and Sylvia*. "I own the Company now. I separate myself from it, the way I separate myself from everything, but I know it needs steadier hands than it has." A beat. "You will, Joe, won't you?"

Another beat. "'You will, Joe, won't you?'" he mimicked angrily. "The poor little rich girl takes a stroll on the lake and shepherds automatically quake." The fury of his single eye seared into her. "The answer, Mrs Enright, is no. I wasn't a hooker 'way back when, and I haven't learned the knack since. I'll tell you something. That thing you own that's laughingly called the Scofield Company is tobogganing to rack and ruin. I'm not even close to it, all I can do is read and hear and feel, and I

146

know it's on its way to becoming a candy store because it's been run smack into the ground by overpaid stupids who should've been turned out to pasture back in the Year One. But no, ma'am, thank you, ma'am, but I'm not about to come in and clean up your slop.

"I'll tell you something else. I was the first man to make love to you—"

"The first. The very first."

"—and I loved you, and nothing's going to change that. But no, this ageing boy is not about to mow your lawn."

Without breathing: "Your subtlety never fails to amaze me."

"Christ' sake, what I loathe most, what I hope I'll always loathe, is waste. You've been disappointing to me as all hell. Anybody who's born with a gold spoon and never makes any stir with it is a five-star disappointment to me. You can't connect with husbands and lovers? Tough. You can't have a full relationship with your daughter? Double tough. But Christ' sake and Christ' sake, you've had the Scofield Company at your kneecap all this time, you could've broken the sound barrier and passed a gang of wonders with it if you *had* stood up off that ass and tried to learn something. Okay, you've been busy. You've been conversing with your belly button all these years and whining that you haven't had a rewarding come with a single Prince Valiant. Okay. The point is, ma'am, thanks for the offer, but no thanks. It's getting on towards four. Want to meet Sylvia?"

Sylvia Greenwood was in her early forties, a trace older than Joe, a plain intelligent-looking woman with heavy legs and a true-radiant smile that made her beautiful. "Of course I know who you are," she said effusively, welcoming Mary. "It's lovely to meet you. There's our ship docked over there. I'm dying to get out of these shoes and, frankly, out of this girdle. Will you come with us and have something to eat or drink with Herr Doktor here and me?"

The shared love between them made Mary feel almost

147

in the way.

"You're awfully kind. Thank you so much, but I have errands. Another time?"

She taxied home to Sandys Parish, planning an elaborate hopscotch game in the sand. Carole was playing with the Hobbs' granddaughter, Rachel. "Do I have to come now, Mummy?" Carole pleaded. "Rachel and I are having so much fun."

By the time she was ready to devote herself to Carole, not many years after, Carole had somehow become reclusive, hard to reach.

"Why do you call me Mother? Whatever happened to Mummy?"

"You're very lovely, Mother. You have perfect skin."

"What does that have to do with the price of—what does that have to do with anything at all? Come here, let me hold you."

"Do you have to use skin cream, Mother? I always meant to ask, the next time I saw you."

Soon after the plane flew over Newfoundland, the sky thick with fog, the call that Mary was waiting for came from Martin Hargill, New York's FBI bureau chief. Mary took the call, certain that Hargill, whom she had met only once or twice, despised her, and probably with justification: she had publicly accused his boss, Alfred Bertrand, the United States Attorney General, of spragging investigations of Ramon Vienna.

But Hargill was calling, nonetheless. There were times, she thought, when it very much helped to be Mary Scofield.

Crustier, less malleable than Leonard Slater, Martin Hargill let her know that he was an extremely busy man. "I appreciate that," she said, and told him essentially what she had told Slater, without mentioning that she had talked with Slater.

"Six o'clock in the morning is quite impossible. If whatever it is is as serious as you suggest, I can arrange to have one of our best men, Earl Baine or Scott Fowler, to—"

"No. Really, Martin, I know it's an ungodly hour, but I do need to talk with *you*, personally."

Annoyance clear in his voice, he said, "Miss Scofield, I'm accustomed to unpredictable hours. What I'm *not* accustomed to is being summoned to a private citizen's home without an explanation."

Mary kept her voice low, but an edge crept into it. "*Mister* Hargill, I've explained that it's a matter of importance, and I can only add that it's something I can't discuss on the telephone. Again, I'm sorry about the hour, but I must *insist* that you give me a few minutes of your time."

"*Insist?* By what authori—"

"By the authority of a taxpayer, and a voter, and a citizen who pays your salary. And not so incidentally, a citizen who can see that your refusal to answer a bona fide request for help is given full attention in quite a number of newspapers."

"Oh, yes, the bureau's aware of those newspapers, and of the jibes and reckless allegations they toss around. If you think—"

"What I think, Mr Hargill, is that we'd better discuss matters at my house at six. I'll expect you there."

He was still talking when she replaced the receiver.

The plane touched down. Customs inspection was perfunctory, and Mary, every nerve and muscle clattering for the need to rest, was careful to thank Stefan, her chauffeur, for coming to fetch her at this awful hour.

In the limousine's rear seat, she telephoned Joe, who answered before the first ring was done. Her watch, reset to New York time, read 3:40 A.M.

"Anything?" she questioned.

"Not yet. Did you hear from Hargill and Slater?"

"Yes. They'll be at my place at six. Will you come, too, *Yussele*—earlier, if that's at all possible? To drink some coffee together?"

She heard him cough, knew all too well that he was neither young nor healthy, knew what she was asking. "Where're we now? A quarter to four," he said. "Look, let's do it this way: pick me up. I'm sort of into my clothes. If I'm not out in front, have Stefan ring the night man here to ring me. Okay?"

"Very okay. Thank you."

"No thanks necessary. I charge time and a half for all services performed after midnight."

Joe was in front of his East River Drive house, looking rumpled and puffy. Stefan opened the car door for him and he lumbered in, noisily, sat beside Mary and, unexpectedly, kissed her cheek.

"You all put together?" he asked.

Stefan roared the car towards the town house. "Flawless," Mary said with a tight smile, squeezing his hand. "You're not, though. You're exhausted."

"Me? I just graduated from Frankie Avalon High." She instinctively moved closer to him. "So how'd it go with the speech? You get your feet kissed?"

"Joe, how serious is this?"

He scratched his cheek and cleared his throat. "Too serious, if it doesn't break quick. You know I always level with you, Empress."

"I know."

In his call to London, he hadn't detailed his trip to Florida, or the boy named Leo Trascano. Now he did. He spoke of several possibilities besides God's Love, of the People's Resistance Army and its overheated, too often hysterical camp followers, of the hatchets employed by Ramon Vienna. He even included Senator Bill Bradway.

Mary frowned. "Aren't you overdoing the menu?"

"May be, may be. I'm just playing Charlie Chan. In all the Charlie Chan movies I saw when I was a kid, the least likely suspect was always the guilty party. Hell, nothing's logical right now. We may've torpedoed Bradway's career. Is that reason enough for someone close to him to want to get back at you? I don't know. Vienna doesn't make sense, because you put him in the spotlight, but then that Whatzisname Cruz ratted in public on some Vienna operation a few years ago and the next week Cruz's legs and one arm got washed up out of Long Island Sound." He paused. "Sorry."

"When you and Carole flew home from Tampa, is that the only reason she gave you for running away, that she was unhappy? Not why?"

"No. I wish I'd grilled her more, or at least better. I wish I'd done lots of things, like seeing to it that she was always in somebody's sight. All right, that's locking-the-barn-door talk, which you're not itching to hear."

"*Yussele*, have you told me everything?"

"Come again?"

"About Carole, on that plane ride. She didn't say anything about *me*, about resentment?"

Joe sighed. "Watch it, Empress lady. Don't go building a case that isn't there."

The day was still dark when they reached the town house. Stefan followed them up to Mary's living quarters with her luggage, and departed. She apologized to Agnes, the housekeeper, for disturbing and probably frightening her, and gently ordered her to go back to sleep. "What can I get you?" she asked Joe.

"Nothing. I'll make the coffee. You make lousy coffee."

"Agnes can do it."

"Agnes makes lousy coffee, too. You want some toast, or an egg, or something?"

"Just coffee. Instant would be fine," she answered, and showered quickly and donned a red, full-length dressing robe, consciously moving fast to keep the growing anxieties at bay. Joe had mentioned phoning Dr Marco, Carole's analyst. Dissatisfied with Joe's report, sensing he had left something out to spare her, she looked at her bedroom telephone and considered calling Marco. And supposed that hearing her failures catalogued could wait. Joe had also mentioned having talked with the head housekeeper at Parnassus, and that Mrs Parry had promised to contact him if there was any reason at all.

Joe was asleep in the sitting room's winged chair when she returned to him. He came awake with a start. She could always tell when he hadn't rested enough; one eye—the one that wasn't glass—looked more tired than the other. "Are you up to this meeting, *Yussele*?" she questioned. "Be truthful. My mind's fairly clear about what I want to say to those men. I wanted you along for your strong shoulder, and you gave it to me, and I'm in good shape now. You must be feeling wretched. If you—"

"Shut up and drink your coffee."

Mary stood at the patio windows and regarded the pensively quiet early morning. The fog that had smothered her plane was gone now, having given way to a vast expanse of blue sky and the jewelled city below her. She watched the moving lights and presently let herself think of Carole, of the too-young and too-fragile girl who surely deserved more of a mother than she had ever had. She saw the girl, so unsure of herself and so easily hurt, and at last she faced the full sweep of real peril.

Leonard Slater arrived at five minutes before six, alone, followed ten minutes later by Martin Hargill, also alone. They nodded stiffly to each other, in surprise and mutual embarrassment, as if each were thinking, *This officious broad didn't let on you'd be here. I'd as soon you didn't know I jump when she beckons.*

Coffee was offered. Slater accepted. Hargill, stonefaced, refused. Mary sat in silence, covertly appraising each man and his reactions, or lack of reaction, as Joe went over everything from the moment of his flight to Tampa. Questions were asked, and Joe answered those that he could, and then finally Martin Hargill, a broad-shouldered, bull-necked ex-patrolman in a well-tailored brown suit, stood as Slater, a wiry, smooth-skinned ex-patrolman, sat gazing into his cup.

"I don't mean to talk for Len here," Hargill said to Mary, "but a minute or two of homework would have shown that, at this juncture, the case is more properly his than the FBI's." He pointed at Slater.

"Why is that?" Mary asked quietly.

"Simply because we have no mandate to investigate until twenty-four hours after a kidnapping has been *established*."

Joe began to interrupt. Mary waved him to be still.

"I recognize and sympathize with your concern, Miss Scofield," Hargill went on. "I have children of my own. But I see no way in the world we could bend the rules for you, and not for all the other mothers with missing children. I can assure you there are a great many of them."

"Would you care to say something?" Mary asked Slater.

Slater blinked, sat up, glanced at Hargill as though reaching for a cue, cleared his throat. "I'm afraid I must agree with Mr Hargill," Slater said. "There's no evidence of any crime here. The girl's been missing for a very short time. I suggest you start with filing a missing-persons report, getting a description out that—"

Shaking her head, Mary interrupted. "That's an exercise in time-wasting futility, as I'm sure you know better than I do. Isn't this city filled with missing kids, and aren't those reports basically ignored unless some specific crime is involved?"

" 'Specific crime' is, I think, what Mr Hargill is talking about," Slater answered, again glancing at the stern Hargill. "There's been no ransom demand, no indication of a kidnapping or of any foul play. For now, beyond a missing-persons report and perhaps an all-points bulletin—"

"No, no APB," Mary countered, more forcefully now, "not until or unless that's absolutely necessary. What I'm asking you both for is immediate action, official or unofficial, and without fanfare.

A contemptuous grin spread over Hargill's chubby face. "What you're asking for," he said, crushing out his cigarette, "is for jiffy personal service because, if I may say so, the missing person's name happens to be Scofield. I've listened to every word spoken in this room. And my own observation, Miss Scofield—*and* Mr Greenwood—is that what you actually want is fifty thousand free private eyes to drop everything and resolve your family problem."

Joe remained still, except for an active glare that suggested he was nearly ready to crack Hargill's head against Slater's.

Hargill examined his wristwatch. "I have to be leaving soon," he said. "Speaking for the Bureau, I would think it goes without saying that once we come into this case, if it *is* a case for us, every effort will be made to solve it—with speed, and with the most modern procedures and techniques. And we'll solve it, too, if I may say so, without the attempted strong-arming by a well-intentioned parent. Am I speaking for you, too, Slater?"

Slater nodded.

Daylight had come. A boat horn sounded from the river. Joe rubbed his head. The other men stood. Mary, her voice silky soft, commanded, "I'll appreciate your staying, gentlemen. Sit down. Please." They did.

Still softly, she went on, "I've listened to every word spoken in this room, too, gentlemen, and now I'll ask you to listen. I'm not even remotely interested in hearing about legal mandates or how hard it is to mobilize the police. I've heard you tell me, each in your own way, that you dislike me, and I'm not very interested in that, either."

Her hand raised to quiet their protests. "I didn't call you here to have you scold me or pat my head, and I don't need to know that you'll get to this case eventually, in your own good time. We all know you have quick access to nets of informants and undercover people. I want them reached and instantly. Mr Greenwood's furnished you with some specific leads. I want surveillances begun, and information gathered. I want you to start at once; in other words, gentlemen, to do precisely what you would do if the missing person's name happened to be Hargill or Slater."

Rising, walking to the centre of the room, she continued, "I want Ramon Vienna to be got to, and I want him informed of the fact that I consider him a prime suspect in my daughter's disappearance. Even if he's only indirectly responsible—if any of his soldiers chose to avenge his

154

worthy name—I want Mr Vienna to know that the Scofield press hasn't even begun to dig into every evil act he's done or thought of doing. And once we seriously look into his operations, there's no telling how many of his hand-maidens we'll come up with, on either side of the law."

Slater lit a cigarette with trembling hands. Hargill was seething. "Just one moment! This implication that the Bureau has any friendly pipeline to Vienna is an extremely dangerous accusation for you, or anyone, to make! I won't tolerate it, and I don't know about Slater but I've indulged your impertinence long enough! I'm not one of your flunkies, Miss Scofield." He glared at Joe Greenwood. "*If* the girl has been kidnapped, we'll find her as we'd find anyone else—in our way and with *our* skills."

"Do sit down, Mr Hargill. I'm not finished," Mary said quietly. She waited, not for long. "Now I'm going to tell you both what happens if you *don't* give this case your full and personal attention. If I discover that you've impeded the investigation by more than a second, I'll give *my* full and personal attention to ruining you. Both of you. It's as unpleasant and simple as that." To Slater: "You don't worry me at all, Leonard. I know you're planning to go right to work on this because you're a dedicated enforcer of the law, and because you'd like to remain Commissioner after the elections. And because both of us know the *Outlook* has a Leonard Townsend Slater file in the basement with pounds of so-far unproved allegations that your hands aren't altogether clean, at your desk and away from it. Not unproved so much as uninvestigated. If we anticipated a few slow news days, I'm sure Mr Greenwood wouldn't need more than seconds to round up our best city reporters to check out every comma in your file."

It was Joe's turn to nod.

To Hargill: "You worry me slightly, Mr Hargill, with those lofty airs about not bending rules. You've bent a few when they were advantageous: you've bent more than a few. The *Outlook* has a basement file on Martin Franklin Hargill, too. There was that little incident in that public

155

toilet in Wichita, with your son and a sailor—or was it a marine? Somehow the complaint was dropped, the sailor was reassigned, and the booking records were destroyed. Remember? And there's the hush-up of your daughter's several arrests—was it five or four? on pot possession. Small things, Mr Hargill. Your daughter's name is Wanda, right? She's twenty-three now, or twenty-four, and she's in your home town, Wichita, or nearby, and married to a fundamentalist preacher whose name escapes me for the moment. Are we connecting, Mr Hargill?"

Thickly: "These veiled threats—"

"Oh, they're not veiled at all. They're here on the table, out in the open. What I see now, gentlemen, is that you're taking up *my* time, and not out doing your job. Will I destroy you both if I have to? The answer is an unqualified yes. Good morning, gentlemen. I'll expect to hear from you shortly."

"You stole my act," Joe said when they were alone.

"Where do we go from here?"

"Where you go is to the sack, and you stay there till the red phone lights up."

"You need rest more than anyone," Mary said, wanting Joe, not sex certainly but wanting Joe beside her, in bed, legs and arms entwined, loyal Joe, safe Joe, strong Joe.

"You want me to stick around awhile? Sing to you? Read you a story?"

"I do love you, *Yussele*," she affirmed, kissing his mouth swiftly, a conscientiously chaste kiss. "Don't sit on your ass."

"Huh?"

"You told me that once. You don't remember. Go home, dear *Yussele*. I'm not making any sense. Call me."

Seven o'clock, Friday morning.

Agnes offered to run a hot tub. "Sleep is what I want; not much, just a little sleep," Mary drawled, feeling more drunk than troubled, though she had drunk nothing since the plane. She stripped off her robe and sprawled on the

156

long, hard bed.

And sleep eluded her. She waited. She heard Joe: "That Whatzisname Cruz ratted in public on some Vienna operation a few years ago and the next week Cruz's legs and one arm got washed up out of Long Island Sound."

No, she thought, trembling.

No.

She saw Carole, Carole alone, saw the swirling images of that helpless young body, face down, saw—

No. God, oh, God no. . .

Her fists pressed into the bed. Her eyes opened and closed. She listened to the sounds of her stertorous breathing. She forced a picture of Carole here, safe, of Carole well.

She waited. She heard Rick Tovar snap, "Quit scratching your back with your hind leg." And saw her father, naked, spank the undersheet of his bed with the flat of his hand and heard him ask her to lie down beside him.

And waited for sleep. And saw Gramp, her grandfather, Adam Scofield, and unaccountably began to think about Gramp, and waited. . .

TEN

FOR A TIME after Harmon was adopted, Adam and Eugenia strove to make their marriage work again.

They now had five homes—the Manhattan town house, the Palm Springs beach house, the Hallandale and Scottsdale retreats, and the still-building Parnassus—and Eugenia was a splendid, enthusiastic decorator and director of house staffs. Her religion and the demands of mother and sister often seemed to consume her, but she did make periodic, conscientious efforts to be an attentive wife. In each of the various bedrooms they sometimes shared, she continued either to resist Adam or to lie still and martyred, yet there were those unexpected, delicious times when she sincerely tried to respond, even times when she enjoyed him and told him so.

She entertained his associates and advertisers at dinner parties she organized, and she headed charity drives, identifying the Scofield name with worthy causes and good deeds. She learned to be Adam's listening post when he talked about what he was publishing, and, though not always approving, she could draw him out and occasionally offer suggestions. Most suggestions were impractical, but Adam came to relish those times together, for she was listening, genuinely trying to be part of his world and his life. At one point she recommended that he start a religious magazine, perhaps called, simply, *Prayer*, and showed him ideas she had scribbled. Beaming, he began it for her and put her in charge, anticipating no profit other than the joy of giving her a plaything. *Prayer*, silly and innocuous, was an instantaneous success, especially in the towns and villages of America.

And Harmon was theirs. Eugenia babied the boy too much for Adam's taste, displayed disproportionate anxiety at a skinned knee or the sign of sniffles, but there was no questioning her devotion to him. Adam idolized Harmon, a lively, sturdy child with quick intelligence and curiosity, and in those early years the boy idolized him, too. Adam proudly called the family "Papa, Mama, and Baby Bear," and, though he worked long and hard hours, he spent every possible moment with his family, showering gifts and love, feasting in the love returned. He had always deplored his adulteries, considered them both justified and thoroughly wrong. He remained attractive and attracted to women. He avoided them, now, and basked in his family.

As Harmon had drawn Adam and Eugenia together, so he served, unwittingly, to drive them apart.

"My God, Eugenia, I spent four weekends in a row teaching him to ride horseback. You're teaching him that it's dangerous, that he could get hurt or killed. You're teaching him he should be guilty for enjoying himself instead of sitting in those dry Bible classes. You've been undermining me to that boy, you've been undoing all the values I've worked to instill in him."

"Values? Did you or didn't you tell him that the Scriptures are for idiots? Are those the kinds of values you're instilling? He's my son, Adam. I won't let you turn him into a foul-mouthed, crude, roughneck heathen."

"Like me? Is that what you mean?"

"You said that. Harmon will be a gentleman, like my father, a gentleman in every sense of the word—gentle, considerate of others, pious. I'll see that his character blossoms."

The summer Harmon was nine, Adam took him to Europe. Eugenia had promised to go along, even had her luggage packed to go, but her sister, Cornelia, had a sudden heart seizure, or at least a suspicion of one. "You know as well as I that I couldn't take a free breath as long as Cornelia's life hangs in the balance," Eugenia said. In London, Adam showed Harmon Buckingham Palace, the Changing of the Guard, and Parliament, and gave him money to taxi, alone and as a grownup, to Madame Tussaud's and back to Brown's Hotel. Adam sent a Scofield messenger around to Margaret Brooke's flat on Bayswater Road, inviting her to supper. The messenger returned within the hour. No one by the name of Brooke lived there. No one by the name of Brooke had lived there in years.

In Europe, Adam attended to the burgeoning Company's overseas business, met with employees and heads of governments, and bought two tons of antique furniture, paintings and tapestries to be shipped to Parnassus, which would one day be completed. He began to observe peculiar, troubling things about Harmon. The boy would be happy when they were together and then suddenly moody and withdrawn; he would sometimes go with Adam and appear excited about the next adventure, but more often he would ask if he could just stay in the hotel and read. A week before they were scheduled to return to the States, he woke in the night, screaming for his mother. He became more reclusive, less talkative, and Adam, worried and unable to reach him, cut the trip short.

All the more perplexing was that, once home, the boy showed no particular interest in Eugenia, who saw the difference, too, who lavished concern and demanded to know what Adam had done to create such striking changes in her child.

In Adam's fifty-fifth year, the Company owned and controlled, along with the score of enterprises unrelated to the business of communications, forty newspapers that spanned the United States, twelve national magazines, a Sunday newspaper supplement that ran in the Scofield press and in a number of other newspapers throughout the country, a news service, a features syndicate, and a news photo service; and he had the total certainty that, with radio as the coming thing and motion pictures not to be overlooked, he was only just beginning.

He was in robust health. Buoyed by Cal Coolidge's unparalleled economy, he and his empire could only grow.

He had loved to travel, simply to travel and meet people and learn from them. Most of Eugenia's time and energies were now invested in Harmon, ten, who was laughing and carefree one day and in bed with a cold the next, who seemed to be continually struggling to please his father and obey his mother, though never simultaneously.

Increasingly, Parnassus became Adam's escape.

Several weeks before his fifty-fifth birthday, he directed that eighty selected people receive gold-engraved invitations to a long Fourth of July weekend birthday party at Parnassus.

Casual dress was recommended. Those who wished to swim or play tennis or ride horses would be furnished with appropriate clothing upon their arrival. Those who liked the sea were offered an outing on Adam's new, fully manned, three-hundred-foot cruiser, the *Eugenia*. Because he had found that large gatherings at Parnassus were most stimulating when there were dramatic differences in the guests' backgrounds and pursuits, he had prepared a guest list that ranged from the Company's key executives and their wives and some of the Company's competitors and their wives to industrialists, politicians, motion picture executives, screen actors, sports figures, authors, and even a well-mannered, bona fide gangster.

Only a scattered few of the eighty people invited advised Vivien Madden, Adam's personal secretary, that they would be "unable" to attend. Some of them, puzzled or even offended by the invitation, regarded Adam Hurd Scofield as a marauding animal, a ruthless demagogue who blithely used his undeniably influential journals as instruments to break strikes, to foment wars, to brand those with whom he disagreed as Bolsheviks, to report complex issues in vivid but outrageously simplistic terms insulting to the human spirit. His most malicious crime, his critics charged, was that he viewed his readers as peasants and was contemptuous of them, that his intent was to keep them ignorant and poor, with just enough wages left over to buy his papers.

("We don't direct ourselves to the overschooled and the privileged, that's true," Adam defended. "I know precisely who my reader is. He works hard for his family and he trusts in God. He doesn't trust the fat cats and he certainly has no use for foreign ideologies. He has simple tastes but he's not a simpleton. What we give him is a world he can understand with simple language and strong pictures. We bring him the news cogently and clearly. We bring him Americanism.")

Others invited to the party gave Vivien Madden more elaborate reasons why they would be unavailable. These were people who were frightened of Adam Scofield; they weren't entirely sure they knew why, but they preferred to stay clear of him, as they preferred to avoid swimming in tranquil blue lakes with sudden, unexpected drops.

But many of the eighty were thrilled by their invitations, those invited for the first time and even those who had gone to Parnassus before. Professionally and socially, they believed they could only benefit by remaining in the larger-than-life tycoon's good graces. And, they conceded, honourable or not, he was an exciting man to be near.

Eugenia, frequently a gracious hostess for Adam, decided at nearly the last moment that she could not go with him if liquor was served. Besides, she said, since her mother's death her sister, Cornelia, was alone except for the servants in New Haven, and not well, and she felt it was her duty to take Harmon there to visit.

"Why," Adam asked with an exasperated sigh, "do you insist on making *every*thing in our life so damned difficult? I built Parnassus for you—"

"Hardly," she interrupted. "That monstrosity, dear Adam, is your monument."

Adam, wearily: "Explain something to me. Why won't you let go? I've asked for a divorce a dozen times and a dozen times you've given Harmon as an excuse. But we might as well be divorced for all the time Harmon's seen you and me together. I've wanted this marriage to be a good one. You can't deny that."

162

"No divorce. Never. The Lord joined our union and only the Lord can dissolve it."

He left that evening for Parnassus, seated in the Rolls-Royce beside his chauffeur, Thomas.

"Are you married, Thomas?" he asked.

"Oh yes, sir. Be twenty-six years."

"Children?"

"Only seven."

They laughed. "What's your wife's first name?"

"Joetta."

" 'Joetta'—what a pleasant name. Is she a good cook? Good mother?"

"Best there is."

"First-rate wife to you, too, I'll bet."

Thomas grinned. "We have our spats now and again. But yes, sir, it's worked out just fine."

Does she warm you, comfort you? Adam asked silently. Does she kiss you, just to kiss you? Tell me all about it. Tell me everything.

"That's wonderful, Thomas," he said, instead. "That's wonderful."

He gazed at his reflection in the window glass and admonished Eugenia, *You've tricked me and trapped me long enough. You've turned my son against me, the one person on this earth I'd walk through fire for. He used to listen to me, ask me questions, love me. Now he runs to you. I'll never forgive you for that. Why could you never meet me half-way? Why couldn't you have been half of what I've wanted, needed, all these years? This loneliness is painful. I'm strangling. . . .*

"How old are you, Thomas?"

"Fifty-four, Mr Scofield."

"You're a spring chicken. I'll be fifty-five tomorrow."

"Go on! I didn't know that. Happy birthday, many happy returns."

"Thank you."

"Then that's what this big weekend shindig's all about, is it?"

"Yes. That's what it's all about."

The Fourth of July weekend at Parnassus began on Thursday afternoon. Nearly a quarter of the guests were there and settled in their rooms in the main house and guest cottage when Adam arrived. Some of them were napping, some swimming, some walking the grounds. Caleb Buckminster, who was soon to become the Company's executive vice-president, was on his annual pilgrimage East, and he stood now near the main house, alone, regarding the deer and zebras that grazed in the wildlife sanctuary.

They welcomed each other, and Caleb shook his head and looked around him. "Can you remember what I told you the first time I was here, when you outlined all you had planned? You asked my advice—not that you ever want it when your mind's made up—and I said that if you'd asked me before you got started on this, I'd've told you you were clean out of your head."

"Do you still think so?"

"Yes. More than ever."

"What do you really think?"

"I'd like to retire and move in."

Adam laughed. "Did you bring Nell with you?"

Caleb nodded. "We got here about three hours ago. She's lying down now, probably with her mouth still wide open. Nell's even a bigger hayseed than I am. She never saw anything like this back in Council Bluffs, and she got overwhelmed. Where's Mrs Scofield?"

"She—couldn't make it, unfortunately. Her sister's been ill."

"That's too bad. Nell was looking forward to seeing her again," said Caleb, who certainly had long known about the state of Adam's marriage.

The July sun was still high, and Adam, proud of his firm, flat-bellied, uncommonly youthful figure, changed into a bathing suit and hastened to the outdoor pool. He smiled and chatted with guests who were there, calling them by their first names, flattering their wives, thanking them all for coming. As he was about to climb the steps to the diving board, he caught sight of an utterly stunning young woman reclining on a lounge chair, a blonde, lovely girl, her marvellously etched face tilted towards the sky. She seemed completely at peace, oblivious to him, to everyone. Grady Honeycutt, Caleb's East Coast counterpart, was near, and Adam quietly inquired, "Who is that?"

"Her name's Venus Montgomery," Honeycutt said. "Arthur Dunbar brought her; she's evidently his little cup-cake from Hollywood. Isn't she a knockout? Everybody's been giving her the twice-over. She's small, but what's big's packed in the right places."

Adam frowned. "Dunbar's married, isn't he?" Arthur Dunbar was a sales representative in the New York offices of Pageant Pictures, the one Hollywood studio that was claiming, in these mid-1920s, that talkies were definitely the wave of the motion picture future. Adam had listened to him from time to time, with canny questions and guarded interest, as the clever salesman had presented him a series of reasons why the Company should invest in Pageant's present and future.

"Yes, he's married," Honeycutt confirmed. "Don't worry, Mr Scofield. I saw to it that she's on one floor of the main house and he's on another."

"Worry? I never worry. Not even when an invited guest confuses Parnassus with a brothel." Adam left him, poised at the edge of the diving board, and viewed the beautiful young woman, disappointed that she was a whore if indeed that was what she was. Those in the water who were under or near the area of the board looked up and scattered. He dove in, cleanly, and surfaced, grey-flecked brown hair plastered over his forehead, at the side of the pool closest to where she lay. She saw him. She smiled, and crossed her ankles, but she appeared not to know who he was, or to care.

Dinner was served sharply at eight o'clock in the vast

165

refectory. There were many tables, a tropicana rose in a vase on each one, and festive menus that offered the guests a wide selection of meats, fowl, and fish. Adam was at the head table, effortlessly carrying on a collection of conversations at once, now jovial, now serious, covertly glancing at Arthur Dunbar's table and at the young woman, dressed and even more stunning than she had been at the pool. Dunbar, fortyish, the kind of high-powered Hollywood type Adam found contemptible, had introduced them briefly before dinner. She had been pleasant, nothing more, almost as if she had been wound up and instructed to be cool, even a trace distant. Adam had bowed, wished them hearty appetite, and removed himself.

Unforgivable, he thought as he ate and addressed himself to Paula Reed Armstrong, who had come alone and who sat directly across from him. *The child can't be more than eighteen. I don't care if she's slept with Dunbar or the whole Marine Corps. She's a child, and she's not Dunbar's wife. The guests will talk. Unforgivable.*

Adam and Paula Reed Armstrong had never met until this day, although she had been by far the chain's best crime reporter for the past year and a half. She was from the West Coast, hired on Caleb Buckminster's strong recommendation as a crackerjack newspaperwoman, and indeed her day-by-day coverage of the Leopold and Loeb case in Chicago had been the most electrifying of the lot. She wrote tough and, Adam had heard, talked tough and drank whiskey, but her typewriter smoked with brilliant copy and he had agreed to an unprecedented five-year exclusive contract, to pay her twenty thousand dollars in each of the first two years, with each succeeding year's salary to be negotiated. He had half expected to meet an ageing lesbian, with short hair and mannish clothes and a bulldog jaw. She was perhaps thirty-five. She was strong-looking and angular, but not masculine. She wore a perfectly respectable, feminine dress and she was presentable.

She also nodded every time the wine steward came by, and once, Adam had noticed with private displeasure, she had summoned a steward who wasn't nearby to refill her glass.

"What I most admire about you, Miss Armstrong," Adam declared, "is that you write like a man. You have an acute eye and ear for detail and nuances that somehow escape our other female writers and reporters. I trust you'll accept that as a compliment."

Smiling, she raised her glass and said blandly, "I prefer to think of myself as a competent reporter, period, Mr Scofield."

"Indeed. Certainly."

On the way to the theatre auditorium after dinner, he asked the child named Venus Montgomery if he might have a word with Mr Dunbar alone before the films began. She nodded, said in a surprisingly untutored voice that she'd go inside and find a place, and both men watched her walk away. Enthusiastically, Dunbar asked, "Well? What's your opinion?"

"Of your bringing a woman other than your wife to Parnassus? My opinion, Mr Dunbar, is that Parnassus isn't a Hollywood fleshpot. My opinion is that you exhibited a moron's lack of respect and common sense and I want you out of here first thing in the morning. No, I'll change that," he snapped, and beckoned to a servant and directed, "This gentleman is leaving on the next train. See that one of the chauffeurs gets him safely to the station." Then, to the awed Dunbar: "Get your belongings together as quickly as possible. No need to fetch the young lady; just go."

"What did I *do*?"

"What you planned to do was to commit adultery under my roof, and that I won't tolerate, now or ever. It isn't important whether that girl is your mistress or not. What is important is that I respect womanhood, obviously more than you do, and I'm not about to hand her back over to you. I'll arrange for her to get where she's going, on her own. If she decides that you're where she's going, without any of your coercion, I'll hear that from her lips. There are stairs and an elevator, there to your left."

He turned to Norton Hilliard, who wanted to be the next

governor of New York, and Mrs Hilliard, and welcomed them with an expansive smile. "What a magnificent home you have, Mr Scofield!" Mrs Hilliard gushed.

"Graced by your presence, my dear. If you and our future governor are ready, the pictures will be starting presently. I'm told there'll be a comic short and a full-length Chaplin feature that hasn't been shown yet to the public. I'm sure you'll enjoy it."

The spacious theatre was still lighted, waiting for the host to appear. Normally Adam sat in one of the davenports in the rear of the auditorium. He saw the blonde child on a davenport halfway up front, went to her, asked, "Is this seat taken?" and then sat, without waiting for a reply. He nodded to the organist, whose fingers flew into an overture.

She looked behind her, for Dunbar. "You friend was called away," said Adam. "He asked that we look out for you."

"Called away?" She was almost flawless, her skin as clear and pale as liquid gold, her huge eyes questioning yet holding a secret brightness, an alert and exquisite young woman.

"Back to the city. He said, and I agree, that there was no reason for you not to stay and help yourself to our hospitality. I have it on A-One authority that the weather this weekend is going to be ideal. And tonight, up there, we can see Charlie Chaplin."

A glint of suspicion moved across those wondrous eyes, but then, abruptly, they were amused and smiled and she smiled with them. "I'm nuts about Charlie Chaplin," she said.

Adam offered, later, to take her on a personally escorted tour of some of the grounds; he would first, he said, bid good night to the guests, most of whom knew that he disapproved of late hours at Parnassus. "Can you find your way to the outside zoo in about thirty minutes?" he asked, and she nodded. "Fine. Be sure to take a wrap. It could get chilly."

He chatted with those who hadn't yet retired, he was

affable, and he was certain he was insane. She was where they had agreed to meet, talking to a deer that licked her hand, and she looked up at Adam with that glorious smile and exclaimed, "He knows me! I always thought deers were scared of their shadow. Or is it deer?"

"It's *deer*, and no one, not even deer, is frightened of anyone at Parnassus. Come, I'll show you part of the gardens. You won't see much, even with that full moon, but you'll enjoy the smells of the flowers. We have over five hundred different varieties of flowers."

"Do they all smell at once?"

"Sometimes it seems so, especially on a clear night like this."

He led her to the first garden path, and talked about the peonies and how they had been imported all the way from China, but he soon recognized that she wasn't any more interested in peonies than he. "What'd you do," she asked, "order Arthur Dunbar to get himself lost?"

"Yes. Exactly."

"Why?"

He told her.

"Translated, that means you wanted the field all to yourself, right?" she said cheerfully.

"You're a very perceptive young lady for—How old are you?"

"How old are *you*?"

Adam nodded. "No inquisitions, then, on either side."

"And this 'nobody's scared of anybody here.' . . . Dunbar sure must be scared of you, to take off like a bat out of Hell. Are you really as powerful like they say?"

"Like who says? *As* who says?"

"That's good. I like being corrected on my English; some people can't stand it, but I always appreciate it as long as whoever's doing the correcting isn't treating me like I'm some dope, which in some ways I am."

He laughed. "Just one small inquisition, because I'm curious: what do you know about me?"

"Ummm. I know you run *The New York Outlook*. I know

169

that because I live in New York now and I read it. I was born and raised in coal-mine country in West Virginia. We used to take *The Wheeling Item-Ledger*. That was your paper."

They walked. "It still is, last time I heard."

"Well, what *I* heard is that you're not supposed to be a very nice fella. That you'll print a lie just as easy as the truth if it'll sell papers. You don't seem like that to me. I don't know how far I'd trust you, but you don't seem so hard-boiled."

"I'm actually a rather honourable man, my new friend. I can be trusted." And, lying, added, "I didn't invite you on this walk to take advantage of you."

Impishly she asked, "Why did you, then? Not that you'd get anywhere, but thanks, anyway. Listen, are you really fifty-five? That's what Dunbar said. My father would be around fifty-five now if he's alive—I left home a couple years ago and we're not much for writing letters—and you look a good ten years younger than him. Or it's 'than *he*,' I guess."

"It's *he*, and we don't seem able to stay on one subject for long, Miss—Montgomery, isn't it?"

"Janusz. Anita Janusz. Polack. You ever hear of the Hawley Theatre on Twelfth Street?" He shook his head. "No reason you should. It's a vaudeville house, pretty third-rate vaudeville. I'm in the pony line there, and once in a while I do a tap solo. This fella Biff Striker—he has an act there he calls Biff Striker and His Daffy Hoops—he made up that name for me, Venus Montgomery. I'm still not used to it."

"I'd like very much to see you perform sometime."

"Oh, I stink! I don't fall down much anymore, but that's the best I can say. It's not too bad a show. Oliver Wendell Holmes came to see it once. He's a judge. Could we sit down on that bench awhile?"

The bench was under a line of lighted Japanese lanterns. As they sat, Adam's hand accidentally, not altogether accidentally, grazed her breast. He apologized and waited for a reaction. There was none. "Now that we're friends,"

170

he said, aware of the danger of what he was about to say, "tell me why you didn't insist on leaving when you knew Dunbar had gone."

"Because I'm nuts about Charlie Chaplin. I told you."

"Is that all of it?"

She sighed. "You want my life story, I'll give you my life story. This Dunbar fella came around to the stage door about a month ago, and asked me out. I don't do that sort of thing—not because I'm a goody-goody, but because this other pony, the first week I started at the Hawley, she went out with a stage-door Johnny she didn't know and she got half her throat slit. Anyhow, he kept showing up, and pestering me in a nice way, and finally I figured, What's the harm? I'll get a meal out of it. So we had supper and he made a couple of passes . . . that's all right, I can always handle that. I didn't believe him when he said he was with the movies—turns out he *is*, isn't he? But he was nice enough, kind of refined. I went out with him again. He didn't make any time with me, mostly because he was like an octopus and I don't go for that. Lonesome. What you could say is that I was lonesome to be with some guy besides Biff Striker and his daffy hoops."

I want you, Adam thought. I want you.

"So he said he had this invite to here, and I should take off work for the weekend and come," she continued, suddenly lurching forward to slap a mosquito between her palms. "Got it! He said where you were this big shot—well, I knew *that*—and there'd be all these other big shots here, I could wind up a headliner if the right people met me. So I said okay. I figured, if nothing else, I'd get to see this place. I've been reading about it and seeing pictures."

"And you stayed because you might end up going home with an even bigger big shot than Dunbar. One who could make you a headliner."

Incredibly, she glared at Adam. "You hold on a minute, Mr Moneybags," she snapped. "That makes me out to be a whore. You can believe this or not, whichever way you like, but I don't mess around unless I want to! I may not

171

have the greatest bucket in the world, or the greatest soul, but who I am is yours truly *me*! I stayed here because I liked it here, I didn't have anywhere else special to go. I stayed because somebody would maybe sign me up to be a real big star, but I'm not as dumb as I look, I know I got nothing but a face and no talent, I know that signing-up business is fairy-tale stuff. All I—"

She shot to her feet, and wheeled on him, and cried, "*You* know something? *I* better go back to the city. It's late, but I guess taxis run all night to the train station."

Adam rose, too, not at all certain if this was the shrewdest act in theatrical history or a cry of genuine hurt, certain only that he desired her, almost desperately.

"One," he declared, "there are cars but certainly no trains at this time of night. You'd have to huddle outside that station and fend off derelicts and bandits. Two, I see nothing wrong with wanting success, but if I offended you I'll cut off both my arms, here and now, with delight."

"And three? What's three? You wouldn't mind getting jazzed before you turn in for the night."

"Now, really, Miss Montgomery, you—"

"Sure, why not? A piece of meat is a piece of meat, why not, I'm the available kid on the block, I hang around and that means easy pickin's, I'm—" she was saying gaily until, quite without warning, the blithe, impudent-brave tone suddenly broke and then she was crying, softly, sadly. Adam, appalled, tried to enfold her. She retreated swiftly, perhaps as appalled as he, and said, "Uh-uh. Sorry about the water-works, Pop. Sorry I couldn't accommodate you on cue. You're right: it's crazy to sit around outside a train station when I have a nice room here with silk sheets. Just do me one favour, just one: I know how to get back to that house. What I want to do is go there by myself. I walk pretty fast, so you won't have to stall around here long, but I don't want you going along with me, and most of all I don't want you to say a word. Not till after I go in the morning, and after that you can sing opera for all I care."

She fled.

Angry and mortified, Adam presently returned to the main house, to Parnassus, to the barony he had conceived and built and nurtured, to what was and probably had always been a hollow chase, halls and corridors rattling with empty drum sounds.

Only the sounds of busy crickets could be heard in the otherwise still night as Adam made his way to the main house. The ground floor was lighted, as he instructed it always be at night, and quiet. The door to the central library was ajar. He looked in. Paula Reed Armstrong was in his overstuffed leather chair, a book before her, a drink beside her, lighting one cigarette with the stub of another.

"What are you reading?" he asked.

She glanced up and then blinked at the book's title. "*Critique of Pure Reason*," she said.

"Since when has reason been pure?"

"Since forever, according to this edition."

"Would you like to come with me and see my private library? We might find an updated edition there."

"Shall I bring my drink?"

"Leave it. We'll probably find you an updated drink, too."

She wasn't entirely steady on her feet as they walked to the elevator. Adam, tired, still angry and mortified, supposed it didn't matter. "Do you turn the clock around, like most reporters?" he inquired. "Work at night and sleep during the day?"

"The last time I slept, if memory serves, was in 1919. It sounded like a good year."

He showed her his third-floor study where, by day, Teletypes constantly chattered, phones never stopped ringing, telegraph equipment clicked on without end, where Scofield staffs collected and transmitted his instructions. Now the study, like the night, was still. "What were you drinking?" said Adam, who distrusted men who drank seriously and was baffled by women who drank at all.

"Rum ought to be fine."

He lifted a receiver. "A bottle of your best Jamaican rum,"

173

he said. "One glass and a pail of ice."

"The caliph abstains?"

"Drinking's never interested me much."

"The caliph has no vices?"

Why this baiting? he wondered. "My single virtue is that I keep whatever vices I have well hidden."

"How virtuous."

"Tell me your virtues."

"Virtues. I always remember to put the cap back on the toothpaste. Otherwise, not a one."

"Vices, then."

"Vices. I accept the caliph's command to come to Parnassus. That's a hundred and eleven vices, right there."

"Were you forced to come?"

"No one gave me a chloroformed handerchief, no."

"Were you concerned you might lose your job?"

She grinned and winked. "Things like that don't concern me. I know I'm the best at what I do."

"Then why?"

She shrugged. "To needle the caliph, maybe. I like your money, caliph, but I'm not sure I like you. Would you be tremendously eager to learn why I think I don't like you?"

Tightly: "Yes."

"I think, for studied vulgarity, you and this place were made for each other. I think something was left out of the caliph. Like this place: it has everything that's buyable, everything except naked dancing Nubians in the chapel—although I haven't had enough time to check; they could be there—everything except soul and heart. But, then, what was I really expecting to find, Nirvana among the gold spoons and the Etruscan clocks? Is there a bathroom around here? Simple one, that doesn't flush champagne?"

"That door," Adam pointed, and purposely averted his eyes as she left. He sat, experiencing rushes of nothing. The rum and the pail came. He dismissed the servant.

She returned, her angular face glistening, smiling rather prettily now. "Where was I?" she asked. "I was saying something shocking, probably. I tend to do that when I've

174

had a drop too much of the barnacle. It doesn't mean anything."

The cheap sparring had begun to weary Adam. "You were saying your reason for coming to Parnassus was to observe an ogre."

"Not completely." Only a trace more controlled in her walk, she poured some rum, drank resolutely but with grace, and came to him, pleasantly now. "I was hoping you'd show me where you sleep."

His eyes widened. "Why?"

"I've never had a genuine caliph inside me before."

He watched her as she contorted beneath him, heard her gasp, "Good for you? Is it good for you?"

He watched her drain her glass, watched her cumbrously gather her undergarments together, watched her begin to dress and pause to pour more rum, and dress some more, and drink some more.

"Will you be able to stay the whole weekend?" he asked.

"Yes," she said, still smiling, nodding a bit too extravagantly. "Then I head back to Chicago."

"You're doing a superb job there."

"We-all tries ouah best, bozz."

"Will you be all right—getting to your quarters, I mean?"

She straightened, worked her knuckles as a brush through her fuzzy, unruly hair, smiled mischievously, and crisply saluted. "Onward, upward, to-the-quarters-ward. I read that in Bartlett's Familiar—uh—"

"Quotations."

"Read it in Bartlett's Familiar Pears, matter'f fact. Better go, right?" She sat, tentatively, at the side of the bed and her hand moved along the line of his thigh. Too close to him, she asked, "No hard feelings?" And chortled and hurriedly said, "It wasn't supposed to come out that way: 'Hard.' . . . I meant, ah—"

"All's well. You get a very good rest."

"I'll do that. Yuh." She lingered for a moment. "Did you like me? What we did?"

175

"Yes."

She rose and once more straightened, suddenly majestic and dignified.

"*Bonne nuit*," she whispered, and even touched her finger to her lips and pointed the finger to him.

He watched her go out, stagger out. She closed the door after her, ever so carefully. He called Grady Honeycutt, waking him, and said, "Paula Armstrong. She'll be in Chicago, early next week. She's to be fired. Pay her off."

In the morning, Venus Montgomery was on her veranda, wearing white shorts, feeding pigeons.

"Am I still Count Dracula?" he asked.

Her smile was both sly and cherubic. "Yeah!" she answered happily. "Want to suck some blood?"

ELEVEN

GREENWOOD.

I left Mary's town house before seven on that Friday morning, not long after Martin Hargill and Leonard Slater saw themselves out. I was in my apartment by half-past seven. No messages. I told my houseman, Luis, to wake me at ten, or at any time if there was a call, any call, and proceeded to squirrel as much shuteye as possible into a couple of hours. The day ahead was sure to be a buster.

By nine I was out of bed, having dozed and wakened, dozed and wakened. I lumbered around the bedroom, coughing half my head off, and listened to the top of the nine o'clock radio news. Nothing. Not that I was expecting anything.

I read my AP wire. Floods, famines, fires, weddings, wakes, catastrophes, and comedies. Frances Holmes, attorney for McCabe and Hendrix and Skinner, reiterated on a taped interview that the verdict was a purely political verdict that would, if there was a scintilla of justice left in the land, be resoundingly overturned on appeal.

> REPORTER: On what will the appeal be based?
> HOLMES: The judge's innumerable errors and his over-all belligerent conduct during the course of the trial will do for starters, followed by his loaded charge to the jury, which was a masterpiece of bias. Plus the hang-them-all climate the media created, especially the New York newspapers; their daily lurid allegations made an impartial jury obviously impossible.

Otherwise, nothing. I phoned my office. My secretary, Arlene, wasn't in yet, but there were no Carole-type messages for me. "Connect me with Berney Kristall," I said, and the *Outlook*'s managing editor came on the line. He gave me a rundown of the day's playable news stories. I asked him if the crank calls were still coming in. Some, but they were tapering off. "It's playing itself out," he added. "Those slobby youngsters who were picketing and yelling in front of the building aren't there now. I'm looking down at the sidewalk from my window, and it's empty."

"That's heartening as hell."

Kristall laughed. "Joe the nail-biter. Relax. It's a beautiful morning."

"It was a beautiful morning at Pearl Harbor," I said. "I'm getting dressed now. I'll be there in an hour." I cut my chin shaving.

The first boom was lowered during my twenty-minute taxi ride to the Scofield Building. I was in my office at ten o'clock and so was Berney Kristall a moment later, with the just-in wire story that an All Points Bulletin was out for Carole Enright, multimillionaire Mary Scofield's teen-age daughter, missing for more than twenty-four hours. The generally imperturbable Kristall was good and perturbed now, with questions about how long I'd known and whether Mary knew. I reread the skimpy story. I wasn't perturbed, I was ready to kick butter-wouldn't-melt-in-his-mouth Leonard Slater's chest in—the APB had been directed from his office. "The calls are pouring in from the other papers," Kristall said. "What do we tell them? How do *we* run this?"

"For the time being we run nothing," I said. "There's no story yet. We have every reason to believe the girl will turn up safely before the end of the day."

"That's it? Just that?"

"Just that. For now. We have us a tightrope here, Berney. Publicity can hustle her home, and publicity can give her some bumpy detours, too."

"But the cat's out."

I nodded. "The cat's out, and I'm no dummy: if the kid isn't accounted for fast, we can't expect the competition to lay off playing it big. In the meantime we sit tight and hope it doesn't have to become a story. If it's a kidnap, we'll hear from somebody, won't we? That's when it's a story; not till then."

"So what now?"

"So what now is that you politely ask any and all of our gentle competitors who come around or phone to please keep a temporary lid on. It won't work for long—some rag in Squeedunk's going to run it—but try, anyway."

Alone, I buzzed Arlene to get me Leonard Slater, and stared at my desk and the day's work on it. Arlene buzzed me back. "Slater's secretary says he's occupied but he'll return the call as soon as he can."

"Get that secretary back on the line," I said. The secretary repeated that the commissioner was occupied. "Unoccupy him," I said. "Now."

Presto: Leonard Slater. He wasn't responsible for the All Points Bulletin, naturally. He'd alerted his first deputy to the disappearance so that a quiet investigation could be begun. The deputy, or *some*one down the line, had got ten wires crossed and, meaning well, had jumped the gun. Sure, and now spilled milk. The FBI was ready to step in the moment they were requested, said Slater. I told him to make the request official, and hung up. And hoped we all knew what we were doing.

The eleven o'clock radio news sandwiched the Carole story, or non-story, briefly between two other items. I went down to the room where the daytime round of cops were monitoring and recording the incoming calls. The calls were stepping up again slightly, a cop named Thardik told me. One anonymous patriot was phoning from time to time, warning imminent vengeance on the Jew-Commie *Outlook* for having consistently covered the McCabes' trial as though they were martyrs rather than killers; the patriot had it on impeccable authority that the Scofields were working a secret deal to buy the McCabes' freedom once the front-page smoke cleared away; the *Outlook* had encouraged the McCabes' murderous acts by questioning capital punishment and promoting gun control; the Scofields were a clear and present menace to every right-thinking American, and this patriot and his thousand associates would see that every Scofield would soon be blown off the face of the map.

Another periodic caller, Thardik went on, was a soft-spoken nut who recited retribution passages from Scriptures. Most of the callers now, though, were spouting basically the same canned speech in praise of the people as represented by the People's Resistance Army and in we'll-get-you-for-hanging-the-brave-PRA-defendant condemnation of the Nazi Scofields. How they were going to get us was still unspecified.

I listened in for a while, listened to young, overheated voices repeat adolescent, underbaked litanies about oppressors and the oppressed, once heard someone giggle in the background, and presently had to agree with last night's monitoring cop and today's Thardik that all it added up to was that every cretin with a dime to make a vicious, big-shot phone call was making it.

A nuisance, yes. To be watched, absolutely. But my mind just couldn't seriously connect any of this passive psychopathy with Mary's daughter. Not yet, at any rate.

I was ready to go back upstairs when Thardik, a receiver to his ear, beckoned to me and said, with his hand over the mouthpiece, "This is the Christer I was talking about."

I listened. I heard, " '—for I the Lord thy God am a jealous God, visiting the iniquity of the fathers upon the children unto the third and fourth generation of them that hate me.' "

He rattled off more quotations, in a vaguely familiar, Woody Woodpecker voice, outlining the punishments God had in store for the disobedient. *Transcano? Carole's gas-pump swain?* I listened harder, stiffened. Maybe. Maybe it was Leo Trascano. I couldn't be sure.

"What's your point, boy?" I asked. "Speak it out so we can understand."

He stopped suddenly. Maybe he recognized me. Maybe he was merely knocked off balance to realize he had a live audience. Maybe he *was* Trascano. Maybe not.

He hung up. "You know where to get me," I said to

Thardik and took the elevator to my office. I told Arlene to find me the Manhattan address of Sister Florence Cody, the God's Love lady. She brought it to me. I phoned Ernie Collinge, who was in charge of Pearlin's in New York, read him the address, and said, "Find out if she's in her house today, and get right back to me."

This has to be a prime goose-chaser, I thought. But you have to start somewhere. You can't just sit around.

Mary phoned me shortly before noon. She'd just wakened, hadn't heard the radio. I had to tell her that, in Berney Kristall's soaring phrase, the cat was out. She was silent—I could see the brain cells clicking together—and then she said, "Kill the Vienna series, starting as of the next run if you can catch it in time."

"Wait a minute," I objected. "Muscling Hargill and Slater in your living room was one thing, but actually going the capitulation route is another. It's still early. We don't know anything yet, and—"

"That's just it, we don't know anything. And until we do, nothing's more important than Carole's safety. I don't mean kill the series dead; I mean put it in the drawer. Print something like this, in the front-page box: 'The remaining articles will appear in due course, but we're temporarily suspending them owing to the uncovering of new facts about the Vienna operations and the need to pursue these facts.' Whatever. You know how to word it. Vienna should get the idea that we can go either way with this—we can ease off in the rest of the series or we're prepared to take him apart, bone by bone. It's a combined threat and bribe, and it could smoke him out."

I reminded her of the no-name calls from the friends and lovers of the People's Resistance Army, reminded her that the calls hadn't stopped. "They're the vocal ones," I said.

"And the Viennas are the unvocal ones." Almost coldly: "Let's assume I've given this some thought, *Yussele.*"

"Are you coming to the office?"

181

"No, probably not. I want to keep moving; it's pointless to look at the telephone and wait for it to ring. I'll keep checking with you. If there's anything to tell me and I'm not here, Stefan can find me in a minute." She hung up. I rang Berney Kristall, vamped a till-further-notice paragraph about the interruption of the Vienna series, and directed that it start running in the very first edition from which today's article could be pulled. Then I buzzed Arlene for coffee and Bufferin. The Gelusil I had in my shirt pocket.

By early afternoon the news of Carole's disappearance, and of the FBI having been called in, was on every broadcast, coming out of every electronic device but electric toothbrushes. The ground-floor monitors were doing a land-office business. So were my phones. I divided my time between my office and the monitor room, shuttling back and forth. I accepted only two personal calls—one from Mary, who was checking in. I couldn't tell her anything new except that there was heavy flak from the stations and wire services and newspapers, including our own, for a Scofield statement. Her order was to say nothing and run nothing. The other call I took was from Pearlin's Ernie Collinge: "Your Sister Florence is at home today, Joe. As of a few minutes ago, anyway. One of our men delivered a registered letter that she had to sign for."

"What was in the letter?"

"Just a mash note, signed 'A friend.'"

"Not bad imagination for a gumshoe," I said. "Good work, Ernie."

I called for Harry, my sometime driver, to have my car brought around and to be available to drive. A cab might have been simpler, but the car had a phone. Then I went again, for the fourth or fifth time in a matter of hours, back to the monitor room, still hoping, still debating the sense of a crosstown *shlep* to the God's Love headquarters, not seriously suspecting the Sister Florence people but needing, maybe like Mary, to keep on the move. The no-name phone calls were now turning really hairy. I knew, of course, that the Company had enemies, some legitimate. I also knew there was never a short supply of crazies, or of malicious cruds. What I wasn't altogether prepared for was the onslaught of white-heat hate: human beings, with normal voices, timid voices, voices hard as cleft rocks, hysterical voices, but voices that belonged to human beings, not savages, were hoping the girl was dead, were glad she was dead, had seen her mutilated body in a ditch, prayed the villainous Scofield family would be punished—on and on and on, calls and clicks, no pattern but generous helpings of psychosis. I tried to keep some of them, any of them, on the line. No sale. I stomached as much as I could and then I rang up Slater and insisted that people be sent over who'd had more than a day's experience in tapping telephones. Not that a fresh platoon was going to do any good, I supposed—I knew very well the tangle of complications involved in collaring phone cranks—but I insisted, anyway. And went to the basement garage, where Harry was waiting for me. I got into the back seat and read him Sister Florence Cody's West Side address.

Halfway to Twenty-third Street, as I was imagining a raft of calamities, the car phone rang. Arlene said that Howard Bradway was on the line.

"Okay, I'll take it."

The senator's brother had just heard that Mary's daughter was in some kind of danger, and was calling to commiserate.

"Nobody's verified yet that she's in danger," I said. "Do you know something I don't?"

"What's that supposed to mean?"

"Let's stop the riddles, Howard," I said, obviously too testy. "If you're calling to say you're sad, thanks. If something else is on your mind, spill it."

"I'm sorry you're taking that attitude. I've just this minute spoken with Bill. He's at home today, in Georgetown, and he heard the news on the radio and he feels terrible about it."

"That's nice."

"Tsk. We were all so close not too long ago, Joe—Mary and Bill, you and I, the four of us. . . What I regret is that this coldness has set in, on your part and Mary's part. Now I guess you and she are beginning to see what it feels like to have family threatened."

"You're losing me, Howard, or it's the other way around. The only threat I hear seems to be coming from you. Either that or satisfaction that someone besides the Bradways is hurting."

"That's a filthy thing to say!"

"It probably is. What I regret, Howard, is that you're evidently still looking to chop off the head of the messenger who brings the bad news. We reported what Bill did; we didn't invent it. As for jeopardy, there's one hell of a world of difference this minute between his and what might be Carole's. So let's go to the mat one more time: if you have something to tell me that bears on the girl, other than those phony tears, talk. If you're calling just to rap my knuckles, leave it lay."

"I won't forget this sort of treatment, Joe. Bill might—trusting people's always been his biggest weakness—but I won't. When you—"

I hung up.

Hung up, and stared through the car window, and idly re-examined my Charlie Chan theory, that the killer invariably turns out to be the least likely suspect. In its own cockeyed way, it did make a fleck of nightmarish sense: the Bradway brothers believe our sole purpose in running our exposé on Bill is punish him, and so they punish in return. They snatch the kid.

Oh, for Christ's sake, I thought. Enough Loony Tunes, already.

And yet. And yet.

Crossing from the East Side, moving and then inching, Harry got caught in a garment-centre traffic tie-up that featured stalled trucks, rolling dress racks, and yelps and rages. I couldn't get Bradway out of my head. I sat back, and thought back . . .

Indirectly, I was responsible for bringing Mary and Bradway together, just as, indirectly, I was later responsible for bringing her and that wild-man actor, Rick Tovar, together. Leave it to me. Greenwood the matchmaker.

Bradway materialized a little over three years ago. In those days, when I was still roaring along like every kid who knows he'll never die, I made periodic, unannounced trips to our various out-of-town newspaper offices. That June—right around the time Mary finally unloaded Owen Enright by divorce—I made a sneak attack on our Rhode Island paper, *The Providence Times-Banner*, and had a long day's session with its managing editor, Phil Diamant, and asked him, among other things, what the chances were of Walter Osborne's not getting re-elected to the Senate that fall.

"Pretty zilch," Phil said, not surprisingly. Osborne, nearing eighty, had been United States senator from Rhode Island since the state was one of the thirteen original colonies, or so it sometimes seemed; his punch as an effective legislator was nothing but memory, but he was one of those entrenched fossils that keep staying on, courtesy of past glories and smooth flacks good at reselling the same old package every six years, the "Vote for Experience" kind of package—"experience" meaning seniority and the attendant perks. Mary had asked me to ask about Osborne—and about a young congressman named William Bradway, Jr., who was beginning to make a little noise of his own in the state and who was anxious to take Osborne on.

Phil shrugged when I mentioned Bradway's name. "No money, and only some ragtag organization at this point. We're planning to boost him for the nomination to run against old Walt, but whether we can swing any help his way . . . well, it's just too early to tell. Frankly, I think he's a loser."

"Osborne has it that sewed up?"

"That's partly it. By 'loser' I mean he's seen *Mr Smith*

185

Goes to Washington too many times. He's a very young thirty-two, all shining idealism."

"That's bad?"

"That's suicide. When were *you* born, Joe? This Bradway calls 'em as he sees 'em. He publicly raps powerhouses in his own party, guys like Matt Tierney who cut enough ice to bury him. Not playing ball is the quickest way to get out of politics."

"Get me all you have on him for me to take back home."

For a youngster in Congress less than one full term, the file on William Gathings Bradway, Jr., was impressive. Freshman congressmen are expected to sit still and mind their manners. Loudly but clearly, this boy was on record as having entered a succession of combat zones, from blasting the Pentagon for its military cost overruns to promoting a national health insurance. His speeches on and off the floor called for line-toeing integrity in industry, in business, and for damned sure in every cranny of government. Phil Diamant sneered at the shining idealism. I didn't. I'm certainly not Captain Romantic—I'd been around long enough to know that excessive boat-rocking isn't recommended in politics—but the more I read, the more I warmed to the young fellow's innocence and sharp mind, and the more I began to feel that, handled right, he just might have a future.

He was good-looking, too, which could only help. He was, as my mother would have burbled, so handsome he belonged in the movies, lanky and boyish, with all-American clean-cut features. Extra added attractions were the vivacious Betty Coed wife who'd licked the campaign envelopes, the sunny son and daughter, the obligatory beagle and hamsters, the steady church attendance. He'd worked part of his way through college and law school playing trumpet at weddings and Bar Mitzvahs, laying pipe, waiting on tables. Pop Bradway was a motorman, retired early when an accident cost him a leg. Mom Bradway had helped to buy shoes and milk for young Billy and his four sisters and brothers by working as a maid. "No, don't call her a hired housekeeper," went one William Bradway, Jr., quote. "Mother was a maid. A dollar fifty an hour when she could get it, and sometimes carfare, to scrub other ladies' floors. We kids never once heard her complain. If it's corny to call my mother the wisest and most dignified human I've ever met, then let it be corny."

Perfection. I sent the *Times-Banner* clips by night despatch mail to Mary, who that week was at a publishers' conference in the Midwest.

One of her handwritten memos to me, two days later, was about Bradway: "Hunch fears he's a jot too perfect. Check out fully. If as good as seems, bombard & elect. M.S."

Bombard meant see that everyone in Rhode Island knows there's a William Bradway, no expense to be spared. *Elect* meant—well, just that. Mary was getting ballsier and ballsier in her publisher's chair, becoming more and more convinced, in her soft-sell, unarrogant way, that her press and her money could, seven times out of ten, part the Red Sea.

I put our Pearlin's cops on the job. Bradway was a hound's tooth. Mary met him for one long talk and said to me, "Let's go." We spent a lot of money, and the Company's papers and *Scofield's* played him up and, at Mary's specific directions, praised Walter Osborne's Year One accomplishments while concluding regrettably that the ancient dragon was now a bit of living history rather than a functioning senator. Our Rhode Island radio and television stations gave Bradway as much exposure as, and often more than, the law allowed. He wasn't a polished performer on camera, but neither was he a used-car salesman; he avoided prepared speeches, he answered rough-house questions without ducking, he had an unforced sense of humour, he talked gut issues with such energy and obvious intelligence that you started to believe for real that Rhode Island was goosing the apocalypse if it let Osborne have another go-around.

187

What Bradway also had was a party that didn't want him. "What we do first," Mary said to me, "is to make the voters want him. The rest ought to fall into place." She watched his videotapes and dictated a series of observations and recommendations to his older brother and decent-but-klutzy campaign manager, Howard, directives always couched in Velvet Claw "you-might-disagree" gentleness, but directives nonetheless:

> *Poking that index finger to emphasize points was patented by JFK. A little less churchgoing schmaltz, however sincere; it too often comes across as playing to the peasants. It might be time to phase out the loyal wife and children and mortgaged-house references; the Checkers stuff made Nixon, but that was ages ago. Stress and restress Osborne's lack of interest in his constituency, his taking it for granted, but avoid referring to his age. The venerable elder statesman is what he has going for him; we can and will press that he's long over the hill; WB mustn't. Ease up on crowding too many facts and figures into a single sentence; statisticians rarely win nominations.*

The day before the nominating convention, Mary jubiliated, "We're going to win it, *Yussele*, we're going to win it!"

It was won. Mary honoured her quiet promise to contribute a hefty cash gift to the debt-ridden party. The contribution must have been very quiet because Bill Bradway, Mr Integrity in Government, would surely have made yowling sounds, maybe even in public, if he learned he'd been bought. I heard of nary a peep.

And it must have been very quiet because Osborne's party would certainly have squeezed that goody hard, and they didn't; they knew Mary was in Bradway's corner, but obviously didn't know, or couldn't prove, that he was in her purse. At the outset of the campaign they didn't do much of anything except parade Osborne's yellowed but indisputable record and pointedly ignore Bradway, the way Roosevelt had ignored Dewey and Dewey had ignored Truman. When Bradway began to make some minor inroads, they attacked not him but what they called the "Scofield media empire" for giving a questionable amount of publicity to a young, radical, inexperienced, naïve upstart. On television and in public halls, with Mary's covert string-pulling, Bradway debated Osborne's empty chair. The Osbornes countered by plastering a line across the state—*"Who'll look out for YOU—the senator from Rhode Island or the senator from Scofield?"* It was a lulu of effectiveness, and a week before the election all the polls, including ours, showed Osborne perched squarely in the catbird seat, having uttered not a word. Mary's money wasn't cutting much mustard, nor, evidently, was the so-called Scofield media empire.

Then, three days before the election, Walter Osborne made his single mistake, and it happened to be a beaut. The Company's television station in Providence was releasing a prime-time hour on election eve, with both contenders invited to participate. Mary ordered the *Times-Banner*'s front page to feature a large photograph of an empty chair— a rocking chair, the kind seen on the porches of nursing homes. To our surprise, Osborne bit. He magnanimously agreed to appear—"not to enumerate my qualifications, which this state and this country know full well, but to shake hands with this charming young lad who just might benefit from a short course in civics." The weathered pol was deigning at last to squash the toy mouse.

A beaut. Mary spent the entire day prior to that telecast with Bradway in her suite at the Continental Hotel, coaching him. She didn't go to the studio. I did. Osborne sauntered in, a few minutes before air time, a jolly, self-assured, beneficent Santa, his step too springy to be close to eighty, vigorous, A Presence. He was grandly cordial to Bradway, who was suddenly taken with the shakes. I did a silent groan. It was Dempsey about to get into the ring with Donald Meek.

Osborne had remembered to bring his familiar countenance and patronizing good humour. What he forgot to bring was answers. Bradway tore in early on, with an avalanche of specific, clear, faultlessly homeworked questions that all added up to *What have you done for us lately?* The kid kept pressing hard on current problems, kept asking what the senator had to offer in the way of current solutions, kept carrying the ball with his own current solutions. Osborne wasn't evasive so much as he was fuzzy and general, the in-charge smile never leaving his face. Near the end of the hour, the fact seemed apparent to everyone but him that the toy mouse was sandbagging him.

The next night, Mary and I sat in her Providence suite and watched and listened while Walter Osborne wearily read his concession speech. She was exultant. She kissed me and asked, "How long has this kingmaking business been going on? I think I'd like to make it a career, if it pays a living wage."

"Lay off the power drunk, Jim Farley," I said. "Your little hobby set you back a bundle in a pea-size state like Rhode Island. The next time you could get clobbered."

"You're the financial wizard, *Yussele*. Give or take a few dollars, how much do you estimate it would cost to send someone to the White House?"

I played along. "That depends on the candidate. If you're thinking of running yourself, I can tell you this right now: I'd never vote for a broad with brown eyes."

"I'm thinking of Bill Bradway."

It was said a little too reflectively to be a gag. "Sure, why not? But shouldn't we let him be a senator for a few minutes first?"

"Just noodling, *Yus*. You know I'm never serious. Anyway, he's only thirty-two, isn't he? The minimum age to be President is thirty-five."

Bradway walked into the Senate, that exclusive club for ageing power brokers, and made few mistakes. He made the right connections, too, got the right appointments, and turned up as co-sponsor of some solid legislation. And he was liked.

As a Mary-watcher from way back, I would have been willing to bet a substantial amount of my Company stock that her interest in him was purely as a kingmaker. I would have lost. I still don't know when their affair began (although I'll bet *all* my Company stock that it wasn't until after he was elected, well after) or how long it lasted, but they did have an affair, all right. No, I didn't festoon blessings, for a number of valid reasons. But it was her choice and her business.

Within a scant year, Bill Bradway was on the way to becoming a national figure, thanks to his own unquestionable talents as a shrewd and constructive politician and to our papers' and *Scofield's* continual support. Everything good was going for him. And, in time, he might really have had a serious shot at the White House.

If he had stayed Senator Spotless, that is. Or even if he'd pocketed a little harmless graft along the trail, or quietly belted a few too many bottles, or discreetly balled the chorus line at Caesar's Palace. Everyone's human, right? Voters will forgive a hero or applicant hero his Argentine Firecrackers or even his Chappaquiddicks, right?

Maybe, but Bill Bradway, devoted husband and father, evidently had classier commandments to break in his leisure time. Ten days before Mary flew to London for the Publishers and Journalists award, cops rapped at the door of a late-night, noisy party in a Washington suburban apartment, on a neighbour's complaint. They warned the merrymaker who opened the door to cool it and were about to leave, but then one of the cops thought he caught a whiff of marijuana. They broke into the house, and they found something juicier than grass: among the half-dozen revellers were a sprinkling of Lolitas, one of them partially dressed, one starko. The flat's tenant and host was a musician in his early twenties. The oldest guest, booze-bombed and wearing blue undershorts, was Senator William Bradway, Jr.

They were all hustled to the station house, Bradway sobering up fast. As Van Avery, our Washington man, was able to piece together the rest of it from a jigsaw of tips, Bradway wasn't even booked. Either because some dollars were slipped under a desk, or because the station house's top cop was experienced in the art of soft-gloving big-star senators, or conceivably a bit of both, he was hustled in one door and out the other.

The story stayed buttoned for all of twenty-four hours, till Avery unbuttoned it. He brought it to me with the obvious question: "What do we do with it?" My answer was just as obvious: "It's a matter of time before the others get it." I took it to Mary. I had to.

Her immediate impulse, though their affair was long since over, was to fly to him, to hear his side of it—there *had* to be some sane explanation, she said, and repeated—to help him however she could. Almost as immediately, she changed her mind and phoned him, instead. She came to me later, looking glummer than I'd ever seen her, and ordered more digging.

We dug. And what we dug up proved that the Washington suburb party wasn't Bill Bradway's only knuckling under to the pressure cooker, wasn't his only adventure in kiddie land. There had been other parties, starring Bill and the underagers, in particular a lissome chick just a shade shy of sixteen. Even in these days of sexual revolt, that was, no contest, a trace too revolting.

She was a looker, by the way; I had to give Bradway that. In a few more years she might have looked a little like Mary.

That had to hurt. I'm sure it did.

Harry, my driver, parked the Coupe de Ville around the corner from Sister Florence Cody's house on West Twenty-third. I told him to take messages, and walked to the front.

If only to keep Internal Revenue off her aged tail, not to mention her public disavowals of worldly goods, I expected Sister Florence's dwelling to be small and spare. I was right:

192

from the outside, at least, it was a drab, sagging brownstone. I pressed the bell, half anticipating the chimes to ring out "Bringing in the Sheaves." Two long rings later, the door was opened, ever so cautiously, by a wizened man who had surely played all the Fritz the Hunchback roles in the early talkies. I gave him my name and said I wanted to see the Sister. And added fast, because the Sister knew who I was and certainly wasn't about to welcome me in without coaxing, "Tell her if she doesn't see me now, *right* now, I'll be back with a warrant on the basis of information that she's harbouring underage runaways."

Fritz shut the door, bolted it. I stood, just stood, wondering if the closed door meant for me to wait or to go away, they don't want any. And I felt like a sap; this wasn't how Mike Hammer would have handled it, or even Nick Charles. A minute passed, maybe more than a minute. The door came unbolted and open again and Fritz nodded and ushered me in.

I followed him up a wide flight of stairs. So I was in, which meant—what? Enter Gung-Ho Greenwood who sprang from the diving board before noticing that the pool had been drained. What the hell did I expect I was going to find, Cody bouncing the kid on her knee?

Fritz preceded me into a parlour, motioned for me to help myself to a chair, and split. Did I say parlour? It was dark and it was brooding, and it could have contained a polo match. There were candles and religious ornaments everywhere. There were scores of photographs of Sister Florence, some in meditating repose and others in action, baptizing and blessing believers. The furnishings weren't Georg Jensen, but they weren't thrift shop castoffs, either; the smell of incense didn't quite cover up the smell of money. The pictures of Jesus were here, probably autographed, and so was a fully stocked bar. Soft music was being piped into this half-holy, half-zonky stadium from somewhere. "People Will Say We're in Love," yet, and for a dreamy moment I found myself waiting not only for Sister Florence but for someone in striped pants and a white carnation to appear behind me and inquire, in cathedral tones, if my pleasure was to view a loved one's remains or get laid. In that same dreamy moment, I was dazzled to realize in a burst of insight that the first three letters of *funeral* are *f-u-n*.

Sister Florence Cody swept in at last, not smiling, though not shooting rays of hostility, either, a formidable-looking woman who ate heathens for lunch, her jewellery clanking so loudly as she walked that it sounded like she was being screwed by the Good Humour man. "Mr Greenwood," she greeted.

"Yes."

She wore heavy rings on eight of her fingers, so heavy that I wondered how or if she could lift her hands. The perfume she brought in with her reeked of a combination Mayfair musk and football practice socks. She didn't lift either hand. What she did do was to ask me what this underage runaway nonsense was about.

I told her the Scofield girl was missing. She said she was sorry; she even seemed surprised. I filled her in on my trip to the Willows in Florida. I filled her in on the phone calls to the *Outlook*, the repent-or-ye-shall-perish cutesies.

Sister Florence, tough cookie that she was, didn't bat an eye. "So the little girl's not at her fancy school where's she's supposed to be. Youngsters disappear all the time."

"Right. They chase off to a God's Love station house, and they're brought back, and they disappear again, and all of a sudden in comes a bunch of hellfire and brimstone calls. Happens every day."

She shook her head. "Honey, I took you to be a whole lot sharper than that. Maybe that little girl's sharper than all of you. Maybe God was what was lacking in her and she decided to up and leave what was cold for what's warm. But for you to crowd *me*, that's plain—"

"It's plain sensible, Flo. You're a grifter since Genesis. You have a cushy racket going for you, and the Scofields helped to get you leaned on a little, so you have plenty of reasons to hit back." I heard myself as I talked and of course it came out senseless, senseless because there was nothing specific to pin on her. "I'm here with a deal. The law, or someone, is going to find her. If you and your crew are connected in any way, you're done for. If you co-operate with me now, get her back and safely, we can't get you out from under the tax people, but we'll lay off formal charges."

She stayed tough, even unruffled. "Appears to me like you need a different kind of help, honey. What's two and two add up to where you come from? Just what would *I* gain out of messing with a kidnap? What'm I, courting more toothaches than I got now? You sic Uncle Sam on me, he's watching me when I go to the toilet, and I get even by rolling a felony? You're kidding. You got to be kidding."

"No, I think you'd better take me seriously. You know what farms and ranches and houses your sweet kiddies are settled in as well as the FBI does. You can find out fast if she's in any of them."

"You're crowding again, honey. I don't like it. There's thousands of parishioners to God's Love. I can't account for what one of them might be doing or thinking at any one time, any more than I'd figure you can in your line, with all your people. But if I hear anything, I'll let you know."

"You do that."

"And you quit crowding. I hate your wicked guts, all you Scofield bloodsuckers, and I hope and pray you get what you deserve."

There wasn't much point in continuing the petting session. "Here's a quick recap for you, Flo," I said. "If she shows up anywhere in your network of funny farms, or you hear *any*thing, and I don't hear about it in thirty seconds flat, all that Scofield wickedness is going to come down on your business, and you, like three million tons of bricks."

Tex Greenwood then mounted Old Paint and rode back to the corral.

Some cowboy.

By eight o'clock that Friday night, waiting in my office

195

for Mary to phone, I was set to pack it in. What I wasn't ready for was Rick Tovar.

That's right. The actor.

There was still not hide nor hair of Carole Enright. Hargill's and Slater's offices were keeping in touch with me but nothing was breaking yet, I would tell Mary, and I would emphasize the *yet*. I knew better than to con her with silver-lining language, but I certainly wasn't going to repeat what a suddenly civil-tongued Martin Hargill had confided to me an hour before: "If it's a kidnapping, there should have been a definite ransom message of some sort by now. My own feeling—and that's all it is, for the time being—is that money isn't at the heart of this. If we don't get some tangible signal by morning, I'm afraid we may have to assume she's not alive."

Roughly eight o'clock was when Tovar barged in, pursued by the night receptionist who was protesting that he had to be announced first yet who at the same time was obviously in a state of bliss to be so close to Nirvana. I nodded to her that it was okay, and waved her out, and asked Tovar, "Where did you drop from?"

"An Air Force jet. I hitched a ride as soon as I heard the news," he said, and added that he'd tried to reach Mary from Ireland and then from the Jersey field where he'd landed. He kept his white raincoat on. He seemed to be in a finger-snapping hurry. "Has the kid shown up yet?"

"No. Sit down."

"I don't want to sit down. I want to know what gives."

So he didn't sit. I'd never liked this overrated clown much —I had him sized up as a slick, crafty opportunist, light on talent and heavy on nerve, the kind that manipulates people like Mary into handing him the Kingdom of Heaven by down-playing his ambitions while looking out for numero uno every minute. But I had to admit to myself, as I answered his questions about the girl and what was being done, that there was maybe something solid to him after all, that he was really concerned, that his impulse to help Mary was a decent one, not look-at-my-muscles stuff. I told him

196

that Mary had checked in with me at intervals through the day and that I was expecting to hear from her. I told him about the APB.

He threw me a mean squint. "So what're you doing, man? Sitting on your executive butt and waiting for the junior G-men to find the kid with their two-way wrist radios? Why don't you send out for a ouija board? You'll find her a whole lot faster that way."

That kind of talk was my domain, and I didn't appreciate it. "All right, let's hear you be smarter."

"Ramon Vienna's boys," he said. "They know how to make things move."

"Vi— I hope that's not the extent of your wit and wisdom."

"It's a damn better beginning than anything you've laid on me so far. I'm talking about cracking this thing quick."

"*Oi,*" I groaned, slowly shaking my old, old head. "*Oi* means you either have a terminal case of jet lag, sonny, or you think you're shooting one of your picture epics. We've been exposing the hell out of the Viennas, which happens to put them up there near the tiptop of possible sus—"

"In the meantime, I know Pete Vienna, the big man's brother. He lives here in Manhattan. I have his address."

"Is that a fact? I know Joyce Brothers' kid sister. I have her address, even her picture. Watch your step there, cowboy. Two can play at this name-dropping game."

Tovar got sore, but he didn't quit. "Pete Vienna buddied up to me in Vegas a few months back. I let him buy me a beer and that made him King Kong to his girl friend. He sent me a case of booze and a promise that I'm his pal for life, that I name anything I want and it's mine."

"Did he also tell you that hoods say that to every clown who shakes hands with them?"

"Terrific. So point me in a better direction."

I wanted to point him out the door, but then I thought: What was to lose? Maybe he *could* get to the Viennas, and come up with information, any kind of information, that I didn't have. "All right, Clark Kent, you want my permission to leap tall buildings? The window's over there. Go be a hero."

"Cute," he said. "I come to help, and Mary's friends sit around and crack wise. Cute," he said, and turned to leave.

"Okay, wait," I said. He stopped. "If you're going after the Vienna crowd, I guess the least I can do is give you a driver and car, so you don't have to stop for autographs on the way. But you don't know if Vienna's brother's at home now, do you?"

"No, but I can find out by showing up."

I nodded and called Harry to bring the car around. I wrote the number where I could be reached, handed it to Tovar, and said, "The driver will be waiting for you downstairs in the lobby. Just stay out of draughts, movie star. The weather could turn cold out there."

He didn't answer. He left. I watched him go, and hoped we both knew what we were doing.

I washed my face, and studied my bloodshot eye in the mirror, and started to cough again. I surveyed that damned telephone. It and my ear had been going steady since the moment I'd come back from Sister Florence's, and I wondered how old Adam Scofield, my first important boss and the founder of this candy store known as the Scofield Company, had amassed all his candy without enslaving himself to phones. One of the Adam legends is that he used them when he had to, but distrusted them, that he preferred when it was at all possible to play Adam Hurd Scofield on a strictly face-to-face basis.

Dandy for you, Adam. Not so dandy for me. I'd begun this latter half of the day by accepting only scrupulously screened calls, and graduated into a Ma Bell addict, lifting the receiver to deal with the press and the rest of the media with a frammis technique that grew more eloquent as I grew more irascible and exhausted. It became like the need to drive cross-country in a day and a half, hoping to make all the lights, the compulsion outweighing the sanity. I'd listened to Christers and right-wings and left-wings, and to

198

one birdlike lady whose never-failing extrasensory perception had assured her Carole was safe as could be and rapturously happy, but that was all her extrasensory perception wished to convey at the moment. I'd taken a call from Anna Halversen, the Hartford sanitarium psychiatrist, who'd asked once more about Harmon and implied that the Scofields were criminals for making no attempt to find him.

At a little before nine, I took one more call. From Mary.

She was at home after a long day of moving about—she chose to be hazy about where she'd been or what she'd been up to—and I gave her the edited version of what Hargill, the FBI man, had said to me. I decided against mentioning Rick Tovar's visit. A mistake, maybe. Maybe not.

"Here's Doc Greenwood's orders," I said to her. "You're to take the fastest-working sleeping pill you have in the joint and get under the covers. Starting now."

"How much rest have *you* had?"

"More than enough," said the most accomplished liar on the Eastern Seaboard. "I'll ring you the instant there's anything to ring you for."

"You're very dear to me, *Yussele*."

"And you have terrific taste. Sleep like a top, kiddo."

Within minutes she called back. "Joe . . ."

"Yeah."

"A request. Above and beyond. Would you come here, and get under the covers with me?"

Talk about inappropriate. More, talk about strange. We'd been living under separate covers for over twenty years. Did I tense and quicken, though, exhaustion and all? Yes indeed.

"Joe?"

Warily: "Yeah."

"Will you? For just a little while?"

Talk about inappropriate. Talk about strange. Talk about urbanity. My sophisticated rejoinder was, "Yeah."

I phoned for a taxi. I stuffed my shirt-tail in, combed my hair by scissoring my fingers through it, dressed in a streak and sped to the elevator, Methuselah at—excuse the expression—sword's point.

The elevator was my private elevator and, if you please, I had to wait a good three minutes for it. I kept punching the button. Adam Scofield, Mary's grandfather, Carole's great-grandfather, wouldn't have had to punch the button. The elevator would have been there at the ready, its door open.

How would old Adam have handled Carole Enright's disappearance? I banged the elevator button with my fist, and considered . . .

TWELVE

A MONTH after their first meeting at Parnassus, Adam Scofield moved Venus Montgomery into an airy, furnished apartment in a select part of Manhattan, roughly halfway between his New York office and his town house.

He knew what Caleb Buckminster would have cautioned, if Caleb's advice had been sought:

> The joke, if it's a joke, is all our editorials about the sanctity of the home and family. I'm not talking about hypocrisy; if most men want to fool around, more power to them. But you're mighty vulnerable, and you know it, or you ought to. Just let the rumours start and you risk an awful lot of egg on your face—a fifty-five-year-old face, by the way. How would we run the headline if it was about somebody else? Let's see: "Ageing Married Tycoon in Secret Love Nest with Blonde Dancer Forty Years Younger."

Adam knew, and knew as well that he could handle it.

His single qualm, a minor and fleeting one, was that Venus was barely eighteen, not quite forty years younger but still a child. And yet (he would have argued with Caleb) she was a child only in the sense that she couldn't be corrupted, even if he were a corrupter. She was thoroughly honest, to begin with, and honesty was not the trade of calculating gold diggers. On that weekend at Parnassus, she could easily have taken quick advantage of his invitations, some implied, some explicit, to help her in what he called the theatrical business. She hadn't. She could easily have let him seduce her, or at least led him on. She hadn't—not with any conscious design, certainly. She'd had every reason to suspect, and perhaps did, that if she rebuffed him, however engagingly, that first visit could well have been the last.

During the long Fourth of July weekend, devoting hours at a time to her, perhaps too often and too rudely ignoring his other guests, walking with her over the acres upon acres of grounds, sitting with her, being amused by her, treating her now as a child in need of fatherly guidance and now as a bright young woman wiser than her years, convinced she was both, he had grown capitvated by her.

And mystified, for she wished absolutely nothing from him.

"Sure, I guess I wouldn't mind seeing my name up in lights someday," she had admitted at the end of his birthday party, shortly before one of the limousines drove her to the city. "But I'd have to pay you back, and I don't think 'Thank you, kind sir' is what you have in mind. You sort of have to try and understand me. I suppose I belong in the booby hatch. I've been on my own for a good couple of years now. I'm no prude, and I don't tell anybody else how to live, but I have to know a fella and like him a whole lot before I get hooked up with him."

"You're jumping at too many conclusions. I'm not a devious man. If I had improper intentions, I can assure you I'd be a great deal more direct."

She had laughed, impudently. "Somebody's kidding somebody, maybe without meaning to. I guess I sound conceited and in love with myself, figuring you're after me." Touching his arm, looking up at him, with affection: "But listen, nice Mr Scofield: if you want to use your pull without ever even seeing me on a stage—I could have three left feet—or not knowing anything about me, then what that has to mean is you got something up your sleeve. Or somewhere. I like you. And I don't want anything from you. See, I told you I should be in the booby hatch, but that's the way I am. This was one terrific weekend, and thanks for the free ride back to town."

The following Tuesday evening, Adam went to the Hawley Theatre on Twelfth Street. She had been right: it was third-rate vaudeville, and she wasn't a very good dancer, yet there was a buoyancy, a winning spirit, a special innocent quality

202

about her that made her stand out far more than any other girl in the line. Moments before the finale, he left the theatre through a side door to wait in the Rolls, lest someone in the audience recognize him. His chauffeur, Thomas, came to him ten minutes later with the message: "She said to say thank you for the flowers, Mr Scofield, but she has some other engagement tonight."

"Is that all she said?"

"Well, no. . . She was very nice to me, personal, but she said if she goes out with a man, the man's got to ask her, not the man's driver."

The Company's private detective agency found where she lived. Adam ordered a gold brooch at Cartier and sent it to her, accompanied by a note that insisted he was neither tyrant nor lecher and, since she apparently had no telephone, asked her to phone him at the number he furnished. He signed it, "Yours faithfully, AHS." As he waited, the detective agency brought him all they had learned. She lived with a female roommate and she had no known bad habits. She had dates but was not promiscuous. She earned fourteen dollars a week at the Hawley and had no other known income. Her current beau—though "beau" was scarcely a correct description—was Biff Striker, who did a hoop act at the theatre. The relationship appeared to be platonic. They occasionally ate together, always Dutch treat. If there was anything even remotely grasping about her, the agency failed to uncover a single evidence of it.

She phoned Adam. "That was a classy letter and this is sure some classy piece of jewellery," she acknowledged. "But you put me in a pickle: I'd be afraid to stick it in the mail. I know where the Scofield Building is, but if I return it in person I wouldn't know who to give it to so's I'd be sure you get it."

"It doesn't carry a curse. It's for you to have."

"Oh, yeah, I figured that out all by myself. The problem is, I tried it on in front of the mirror and somehow it doesn't go so good with my dress from Macy's basement." Hurriedly, cheerfully, she added, "And you can forget about what you're maybe going to say next: that you can fix that up, too. I wish you'd listen to me when I say I don't want anything from you. I love getting presents—who doesn't?—but not *these* kind. It makes me feel funny, and I don't like feeling funny. I told you I liked you and that was the truth; I lie once in a while, but most of the time I tell the truth. But it—well, it just wouldn't work out. For one thing, you're married, aren't you?"

"I seem to recall that that Dunbar fellow who brought you to Parnassus was married, too."

"Yeah, but I wasn't planning anything fishy with him. With you . . . no, I don't want to get fishy with you, either. Look, for the sixty millionth time: you're a nice man. You're about the same age as my father—I forget; did I tell you that?—but that doesn't bother me; you must've been all over the world and I could learn a whole lot from you. I— boy, I'm not making too much sense, am I? It's just that— all I'm trying to say . . ."

There was a very long pause. Adam asked, "Yes? What are you trying to say?"

Her pause continued, and then she answered, "If you want to see me again, I guess it's all right. On one condition, though: you take this jewellery back. You know what you could buy me? Popcorn, with butter on it. And big red apples that squirt when you bite into them!"

That's history's most proficient con artist, *Caleb Buckminster would have sneered*. On a fourteen-dollar salary, and no prospects of Flo Ziegfeld or Prince Charming in the wings, she's wounded that you'd even think of buying her favours. She's wise as can be. And you're the saddest platitude there is: the old fool who thinks a young chicken bats her come-hither eyes because she's interested in you and not a silo full of Cartier brooches.

Caleb, Adam thought jubilantly, you're dead wrong. Caleb would indeed have been dead wrong. Venus Montgomery, button-bright and full of life, clearly enjoyed

Adam and the hours he could steal from the *Outlook* to be with her, was clearly unfazed by the cavernous difference in their stations and ages, enjoyed their secret picnics, enjoyed making him laugh, was neither intimidated by him nor intimidating. She would let him know when her room-mate, Diane Margerum, was expected to be away from her Jane Street flat—a drab cell Adam considered suitable only for retired chambermaids and copy boys—and there she would cook spaghetti for him and listen to him talk about the world and his place in it, spontaneously interrupting him to have him explain what she didn't, or couldn't, fully follow.

She came to ask fewer and fewer questions about his marriage, gradually replacing them with earnest questions such as, "Why do you keep coming around and sending me all these presents?" But she was accepting the presents now, the extravagant ones as well as the buttered popcorn, receiving them with nearly the same joy he experienced in giving them to her. "Why? I'm still not paying you back, *that* way, and I'm not going to," she argued.

"You give me pleasure. I'm happy with you."

"Then I'm a whadda they call it, a court jester."

"No, you're a Galatea. There are depths to you that haven't begun to be tapped. That's my real ulterior motive. I'm going to see to it that you become every good thing you've ever dreamed of."

"What's a Galatea?" she asked, pouring his coffee.

Adam threw his head back and laughed.

"What'd I say *now* that's so funny?"

"I don't know—it's just your way, just your manner. I love it."

"Listen, I've been thinking: what if we start kissing a little bit? If I don't like it—not that I won't like it, but if it starts to, well, get out of hand—then we'll just quit, okay?"

Adam took her to the airy, furnished apartment, the one he had leased under the name of Montgomery. "Boy," she said, barely aloud. "This is bigger than my whole home

205

town. Is this where they store elephants in the winter time?"

"It's yours, on the complete understanding that I'll never come here without telephoning first and being invited. And you'll stop that ridiculous job at the Hawley."

"Stop, just like that? What'm I supposed to do with myself after I file my nails and make crazy faces in the mirror?"

"You'll work," he replied, and detailed his ambitious plans for her. "I'm arranging for a few people to help me help you to help yourself: a tutor to nudge your education along, an expert to counsel you in style and grooming. I want you to be the very best person you can be. You want that, too."

"I—guess," Venus said haltingly. "I'll do anything you want me to do."

"No, no, no, not just because *I* want it. You have the potential for exciting things. Believe that. Believe there's nothing you can't achieve, and there *will* be nothing you can't achieve."

Adam personally interviewed and hired a carefully investigated woman named Bertha Atworthy to go to the apartment for an hour every afternoon to start Venus on grammar and vocabulary, to guide her to the right books to read, to stimulate her towards the desire to learn. He personally interviewed and hired a carefully investigated woman named Alice Kerr to meet with Venus three times a week, to teach her how to sit, how to rise, how to wear her hair and use cosmetics, how to dine at proper dinner tables, how to select the right clothes at good shops.

And he kept his promise to Venus, who had not asked for it, and never arrived without calling first and requesting permission to come—kept the promise so that she would not feel she was his mistress, which she was, or his wife, which she was not. There were times when he called her and came to her in the middle of the night, sometimes only for minutes, sometimes to stay till dawn; sleepy, occasionally moody, she was nonetheless always there, to make a sandwich or serve coffee, to be his companion in conversation and in bed. In those initial months, as his newspapers boomed, he revelled in sending and bringing her gifts, revelled in her little-girl open joy in receiving gifts and receiving him, revelled in being the young man he had not been as a young man, in playing Pygmalion, in asking her questions about what she was learning, in applauding her for her newfound poise. If this is a cartoon of the ageing duffer and the saucy minx, he thought, then so be it; this is what bliss is all about.

In those initial months, Adam left New York only when some Company crisis outside the city demanded his personal attention. He first realized the extent of Venus' importance to him on the September day his private railway coach carried him and his private secretary, Isaac Duncan, to Harrisburg. He telephoned her late that night and said, carefully keeping the sound of a plea from his voice, "Please hurry here. Harrisburg is the home of hot buttered popcorn." Venus growled something about Lincoln having freed the slaves. In his hotel suite the following day, she trembled in his arms, and tugged to free his suspenders, and murmured, "The things I do for some old men . . ." The Company's board meeting, across the street, waited. Venus was here.

Adam could and did expect his employees to keep their mouths shut when necessary, but he could not control raised eyebrows. After a while it didn't matter. He took Venus with him when he travelled, always discreet enough to have her situated in a separate suite yet practical enough to ensure that the suites adjoined. They travelled together on Adam's business trips, and they travelled together on short holidays, Adam delighting in showing city sights to the West Virginia coal miner's daughter. They spent the days and weekends he could spare at Parnassus, quietly served there by the year-round staff, some of whom had met Eugenia Scofield, most of whom had at least seen her. They dined in public restaurants. They did not go out of their way to be observed, but neither did they hide. At Delmonico's one night, Venus asked bluntly, "Tell the truth: would you be as out in the open like this if your wife and boy wasn't out West somewhere?"

"'Weren't, not 'wasn't'. Rubberneckers have never bothered me. Do they bother you?"

She shrugged. "Nothing bothers *me*." Then suddenly, smiling mischievously: "Well, one thing does. I'd like to finish up this steak and go find me some old man to give me a really good loving."

He returned the smile, his large body tautening. "Let's pay the bill and get out of here."

Late in October, as general circulation figures took an unaccountable drop, Adam placed an impulsive long-distance call to Caleb Buckminster. "I want us to look into motion pictures, Caleb," he said. "I understand Pageant Pictures is hurting for some fresh money. Nose around—nothing direct yet—and see what kind of deal we can get for Pageant to rent us its facilities here in the East and distribute Scofield Films."

"Sco—"

"Now don't but-but me, Caleb. I want to get rolling as of yesterday. I have a star all set to go."

"Something tells me I know the star's name. Would it be Venus Montgomery?"

"That's a fantastic crystal ball you own out there, Caleb. What else does it tell you?"

"It tells me I should thank you for calling me instead of the other way around. Maybe we ought to've been talking before today. Your private business is your private business. But if the gossip about you and that young girl is as noisy as it is 'way out here, I hate to imagine how loud it is back East. Part of the gossip—and I sit here with the ledgers and I can verify that it's not just idle chatter—is that the Company's boss isn't at the grindstone as much as he might be."

"I'm in a hurry, Caleb. Ring me back with facts and figures and projections as soon as you get the lay of the land."

"Speaking of lay of the land—"

From their first meeting and on through hundreds of personal meetings, phone conversations, letters and wires and memos, Adam had taken particular care never to speak sharply to Caleb Buckminster. Now he said, sharply, "Another word, one more word along those lines, and I'll accept your resignation from the Company, effective immediately."

". . . Heard and noted."

"Excellent."

Adam stood that day in his Scofield Building office, forcing himself to push Caleb's absurd grumblings from his mind, and glanced at the desk calendar and saw that today was Eugenia's birthday. He thought about phoning her. Eugenia, who had come to dislike New York and had never liked Parnassus, was at the Arizona estate with Harmon, had been since July, preferring it as a base, if not a permanent address. The pace was more tranquil there, she had explained, and the climate kinder to her sister, Cornelia, and to Harmon, who was fragile and continually subject to colds. Adam telephoned Scottsdale often, not so much to keep in touch with Eugenia as to relieve the guilt he felt at not being closer to his son. The conversations with Harmon were, when Eugenia wasn't within earshot, always rewarding to Adam, certifications that the boy loved and missed and respected him. He wanted the boy with him, here, wanted Harmon and Eugenia, the affectionate and loving Eugenia he had married, here with him, a family. The fact that they were so far away gave him more freedom to see and be with Venus, yet he wished to welcome inhibition, for he wanted his family.

He decided against calling, for now; Eugenia might natter, and he was in no mood for it, especially after Caleb's jabs at his eye. Instead, he went to Venus, stopping on the way for Thomas to go into a florist shop and buy a single yellow rose. Inside the tissue that wrapped the rose, he placed the diamond pin he had ordered that morning.

He had forgotten to phone first. Venus was in her living

room, drinking beer with a tacky-looking young man who wore a rummage-sale suit and who seemed completely at home. Venus didn't appear disturbed, and certainly not guilty. "Chet," she began, "I'd like you to meet—" The young man's long legs came off the hassock and he shot up, his hand outstretched.

Adam stood frozen. Ignoring the hand, he said, "You'll leave now." The man blinked. Venus started to protest. "Now," Adam repeated stiffly. "At once, and without a word."

"You have some frigging hell of a gall!" she cried when they were alone. "Chet Bourne's a *friend* of mine, from the Hawley! What'm I, not supposed to have *friends*? You don't *own* me, you know!"

Sighing, still holding the box with the flower and pin, Adam instructed, "Lower your voice."

"I don't lower *any*thing, mister! I didn't do anything wrong and you're not gonna treat me or my friends like some piece of garbage! You hear? You *hear*?"

He threw the box on the floor and slapped her, hard, across the face.

She fell back, and gasped. Quietly, Adam said, "You'll be still and you'll listen. You can gather your belongings and go off with that riffraff, or you can stay here and abide by one condition, only one: you'll let *me* choose your friends, if you need friends. This isn't a flophouse or a soup kitchen or a brothel. I'll have no misunderstandings about that."

"What're you so *mad* about? I'm staying because you mean a whole lot to me, that's why. I cross my heart: I'm not two-timing you or anything like that. I'm trying to do the right things so you'll be happy. Why're you so *mad*?"

Adam left her and went to his town house and lifted the telephone receiver to call his family. He replaced the receiver and summoned Enoch, his valet, to pack a suitcase, and then he phoned Roger Fellows, his pilot, to have the private plane ready for takeoff within the hour. They flew through the black night to Arizona. Eugenia, tanned and healthier, lovelier than ever, was obviously pleased to see him. "To what do we owe this honour, Adam?" she asked with only mild sarcasm.

"I want you and my son home," he said. "This isn't good the way it is, it can't be good for Harmon to be without a father, it's so very hard for me to be alone."

"How can I keep up with you? When we do talk, or when you write, it almost always centres around your desire for a divorce."

"Because we haven't worked at the marriage. I'm willing to take ninety percent of the blame; I've been selfish, pre-occupied, I haven't tried enough to really see you, hear you. Let's all go home where we belong, Eugenia. I want to be a husband and father. We have wonderful years ahead for the three of us."

Eugenia agreed, with stipulations. He would have to accept Christ, as she had. He would have to make a series of fundamental changes, commencing with his vow to turn his newspapers and magazines from their course of high-lighting and in effect fostering scandal and moral degrad-ation to one of instruments for uplight that would please Jesus.

"I see," he said. "Is that all? With that pipeline you have to Him, maybe you can arrange for Him to become chair-man of the board and guarantee that we're all fed."

Her hands went to her ears, and Adam tasted the sinking feeling, the realization that he had come for nothing, that it was all gone. "You've always disapproved of me, haven't you?" he charged. "You've always seen me as something of a lowlife, a guttersnipe. Very well, I want to put a question to you: Where's *your* morality, madam? You reject how I earn money, but you stop short of rejecting the money, don't you? You're living and eating under a roof that the grubby Scofield press pays for. Why don't you prove how truly moral you are? Why don't you hand me back every-thing my dirty press has bought for you and go move into some holy mud hut and feast on grass with all the other Christers?"

"I won't hear any more!"

"No, I didn't think so," he said in sadness and revulsion. "While I'm here, would I have your permission to see my son, if I promise not to get too close to him with my dirty hands?"

"He's in bed, with a cold. He's very frail."

"Because he's babied," Adam said, and found Harmon asleep, under mounds of blankets. Adam bent down and kissed his son's moist forehead, sat lightly at the bed's edge and regarded his son, eleven years old, his son who wrote him amazingly mature letters about the books he was reading, about his plans to become either a doctor or a navigator, letters that were too often formal but nonetheless the letters of a loving son. The boy came awake, stared for an instant as if he wasn't sure of what he was seeing, and his thin, pale, beautiful face lit up and his skinny arms instinctively raised to embrace his father. That, thought Adam, deeply touched, enfolding him, was worth the whole trip.

"I had this dream the other night, Father," Harmon said, "that you were here. I'm glad. I'm sorry I have this cold."

"So am I. Let's catch up on old times. Tell me what's keeping you busy." The bedroom door opened. Adam turned his head from the boy and glared at Eugenia, signalling her to leave them alone. She obeyed. "The last time we were on the telephone, you were reading *The Last of the Mohicans*."

"Oh, I finished that long ago. Here's what I'm reading now," Harmon said and showed him *The Count of Monte Cristo*. "Did you ever read it?"

"I'm afraid you're the scholar in the family, lad. No, I was never very much for stories when I was your age, I regret to confess. Tell me about it. Tell me everything under the sun."

Harmon talked, indeed about nearly everything under the sun, like a caged animal suddenly allowed to run. He talked, and they talked together, and he laughed at Adam's jokes, and Adam laughed at his, and presently Adam asked him, "Are you having much fun, lad? All this reading is great, and I'm proud of the grades you're making in school —I wouldn't know how to be anything but proud of you, ever—but you know what they say about all work and no play. Do you have many friends?"

"Well, a few, from the church. Not many."

"This church stuff—are you really all wild about it, or do you go because you have to?"

The boy seemed worried. "Relax," Adam said. "This is strictly between you and me."

"No, I don't like it too much. Once in a while it's all right, but it's sort of all the time, prayer meetings when there're other things I want to do . . . But it's all right, I guess. It keeps Mother happy."

"Harmon, you think about this for a while before you answer. Would you like to be back East, to live with me? To go to school there, with friends that enjoy having fun?"

"What would be best would be if we were all together."

Adam nodded. "That's right, that would be the best. But you're old enough and grown-up enough to know that that probably just isn't going to happen. I revere your mother, no finer woman ever walked this earth, and I believe she cares for me, too, but we don't get on as both of us wish we could; I'm very sorry, but that's the way it is and I don't see it changing. I'm asking you something important, son: Would you like to come stay with me?"

The boy's pause answered before he did. "No, Father. You always told me to be truthful."

Adam nodded again. "So I did." He opened his billfold and extracted two fifty-dollar bills. "I want you to put these in your secret drawer; every young man has a secret drawer, or ought to. Your mother's not to know; certain secrets ought to be kept from mothers, too. Spend it on fun. If your mother catches you spending it, you can always pin the blame on me, but try not to let her catch you. Buy treats for your friends. You'll be surprised how many more friends you'll have before long. And give your old pappy a thought now and again. Okey dokey, scout?"

On the lawn outside the house, Eugenia was calmer,

gentler, softer, almost as though she were prepared to start over. "It seems a pity for you to go all the way back to New York so soon," she said. "How many hours did it take you to come here?"

"About twenty-four."

"And that many back, without proper rest. You're not a youngster anymore, Adam."

"Fit as a fiddle. Do one favour for me, Eugenia: give Harmon some elbow room, let him have his childhood."

"What do you mean?"

"He's a marvellous boy, and he's going to be a cracker-jack man. But you mustn't stunt him or smother him."

"What you're saying is that he talked against me."

"I'm saying the opposite. He loves you, as he should. He wants to stay here with you, he—Lord, Eugenia, why are you and I like cats and dogs the minute we get together?"

"I have a better question. Why do you speak the Lord's name when you don't believe in him?"

"Good-bye."

Minutes after landing in New York, he telephoned Venus.

"Could anyone there be interested in some buttered popcorn?"

"Only if it's hot."

He raced to the apartment. "Where were you?" she asked.

"Out looking for myself."

"Did you find you?"

"I found you, and that's better."

"Then where's the hot popcorn?"

"Here."

She helped Adam undress, and drew the shades, and slipped into his arms that were quaking with exhaustion, fifty-five-year-old exhaustion. "You want something to eat?" Venus asked. "Or drink? You want to go right to sleep?"

"No."

"You want me to do all the work? I'd like to."

"Why would you like to?"

"Oh, can all that, all right? I don't do anything I don't feel like doing. I feel like doing all the work. All I was asking was, Is it okay with you? Sometimes you don't go for it that way."

"Yes. Right now, yes."

"You're lying, seven ways to Sunday," she said when his erection collapsed. "What you want is to go to sleep."

"Stay with me."

"Try kicking me out."

Venus held him, and whispered, "Sleep, baby. Sleep, baby. Sleep, baby." And soon, at peace, Adam slept.

THIRTEEN

IN THE EARLY afternoon of that Friday in May, one hour after Joe had reported to her that an APB had been sent throughout the country and she had directed him to have the series on the Ramon Vienna empire temporarily stopped, Mary was in Carole's dorm room, at Pearce School in Westchester, alone with Carole's roommate. The girl's name was Phyllis Meacham. She was plumper than Carole, not as pretty, and, though she seemed uneasy, she also seemed to have an innate confidence that Carole lacked. Her side of the airy room was a chaos of scattered clothes and books, whereas Carole's side was immaculate, dresses hung neatly, the desk and bureau tops in faultless order.

"I need all the help you can give me, Phyllis," Mary said.

"I told Miss Deane all I knew, Mrs Enright. Carole wasn't—isn't somebody who usually talks very much. I mean, we room together, and I guess we're friends, but we're not *close* friends."

"But you're the one she confided in before she flew to Florida."

The girl nodded.

"When she came back here on Wednesday night—that's what I have to know about," Mary pressed. "Any clue, anything she might have said that you didn't think was important enough to repeat to Miss Deane . . . She must have said *some*thing to you. Please try to remember, Phyllis."

"Well, she did talk. But . . ." Phyllis Meacham stopped and regarded Mary.

"But what?"

"This is sort of putting me in a corner, Mrs Enright. I guess I'd never forgive myself if anything happened to Carole because I left something out—I've been thinking and worrying about that since yesterday—but there's . . . well, there were some things she said that I'd rather not repeat. We had this agreement that the private things we said to each other would stay private. And, well"—squirming slightly in her chair—"if I repeated it, it might, ah, hurt some feelings . . ."

"Let's hurt some feelings, and see if that can help me find my daughter. You have my word, my firm promise, that whatever you tell me will be between you and me."

"Well, she was awfully upset that night, that's for sure. She knew she was in for the whole detention and demerit business from Miss Deane, and she'd never had anything like that before. She kept saying she couldn't understand why she went off with that Leo creep. I'd tried to talk her out of it ahead of time, and she kept saying I was right, that she should've listened to me, that she should've listened to herself. She called it a dumb stunt and she was sure she'd let everybody down, that no one would trust her anymore. You, especially."

". . . Me?"

"She never really talked about you before, Mrs Enright, but she did that night. Some, anyway. She talked more than I ever heard her talk. She kind of rambled all over the place. That's not like her . . ."

CAROLE: "Did you ever meet my mother, Phyl? No, that's right, you wouldn't've; she's never been here."

PHYLLIS: "I've seen her pictures, and I think once I saw her on television. She's beautiful."

CAROLE (nodding): "And smart. And glamorous."

PHYLLIS: "But you were talking a second ago about taking off with Leo. What's that go to do with your mother?"

CAROLE: "Nothing. I don't know. Everything."

PHYLLIS (tapping her temple): "You're making brilliant sense."

CAROLE: "I ran away once before. Three years ago. I had a terrific crush on a man my mother was . . . I suppose she was sleeping with him. Oh, of course she was, only I didn't know that then, I didn't think about it. All I knew was he was the most wonderful person in the world. We'd talk together. Once we took a long walk—it must've been for an hour at least—and that was the most perfect hour of my whole life. I felt so free that day, so—warm. I talked my head off. I don't remember what about—it must've been stupid, all of it—but he listened to me. He didn't make fun of me or give me any of that you're-a-little-kid stuff. He treated me like a grown-up. And a few weeks later I got on a bus to go to him. Just to be with him. I knew it was crazy, as crazy as this dumb thing with Leo. I was so scared on that bus. I was just as scared yesterday, going with Leo, and all day today until the man who works for my mother came to get me. Yes, my mother's very beautiful. And sometimes I wish she was dead. Or I was dead, so I wouldn't have to be scared of her anymore. Isn't that a terrible thing to say? I've said it to Dr Marco. It's terrible, and sometimes I can't help it.

"You're so lucky, Phyl. You have family that cares about you. I see it when they come here to see you. I see the way they look at you . . . pride, love. They care what happens to you. Oh, my mother would care if I died or something bad happened to me, but it's not—She never looked at me the way your family looks at you. I hardly even remember my father. He's alive somewhere, but I never hear from him. But they'd be there for only a minute, like they were doing me this big favour and they were restless, and then they'd disappear. Evaporate.

"I don't mean it, what I said about my mother. She's really a good person. I sound like the world's biggest crybaby, don't I? What I did, running away without telling anybody—that was terrible. Inexcusable. You'd never do anything like that. I don't know anybody else who would. Well, I've learned my lesson, Phyl: you don't start to grow up till you stop expecting everybody to take care of you. From now on, ol' Enright starts to buckle down. I'll make my mother proud yet.

218

"My lousy, selfish mother."

Suddenly, tearfully: "Why did I do it? Why do I do everything wrong? My mother's going to hate my guts when she finds out!"

"Excuse me, Mrs Enright," Phyllis Meacham said. "But you asked me."

"Yes," Mary said. "Thank you."

Carefully, maintaining control, deftly feigning composure, Mary had brief, individual meetings with two of Carole's teachers and her guidance counsellor. They were in agreement in their concern and in their praise of Carole as refined and well-behaved and always ladylike, a painstaking student, shy and at times perhaps a bit unsure of herself and less outgoing than many of her classmates, but a sweet and certainly fastidious girl. They bubbled with clichés. They meant well. They were of no help at all. They had never truly touched Carole, nor been touched by her.

And then Mary sat in the spotless, cheerless office of Pearce's headmistress, Hazel Deane, a meticulously groomed woman of seventy, dainty except for the contradiction of unusually large hands, the hands of a man. "I'm afraid I have something rather distasteful to report to you, Mary," Miss Deane asserted after they had exchanged pointless small talk for several minutes. The first-name familiarity was suitable; Deane had taught her sophomore biology.

Mary waited.

"This may not be the proper time to bring this up—our main consideration is that Carole is safe and well, of course —but I think you ought to be prepared for a decision the board made here this morning. We're praying for her, naturally, but when she's found or returns on her own, we've unanimously decided it would be better for everyone concerned if you look into some school other than Pearce for her."

Mary waited.

"As I say, this mightn't be the appropriate moment to be

somewhat—blunt, shall we say?"

"Go on."

"It's the feeling of the board, Mary, that it simply can't afford the notoriety, the bad publicity, that this incident is almost certain to bring. Pearce is bound to suffer as it is. We've guarded our reputation for unblemished respectability for ninety years, and—" She smiled benignly. "But you're aware of that as anyone. You're one of our most successful products."

Mary still waited, watching without expression, beginning to experience a slow welling of impatience, of resentment.

"Obviously, I hesitated to mention it, but it's said, isn't it, and I think you'll concede we have very little choice. It goes without saying that I'll be glad to recommend some other good schools, and I'll write only the most glowing letters about Carole." A pause. A questioning, inquisitive smile. "You understand *our* responsibilities, Mary. I'm sure."

"What I don't understand," Mary said quietly, "is your institutionalized insensitivity. I don't know if my daughter is alive, and you're nattering to me about reputations. Repu*ta*tions?"

"I'm sorry if you heard it that way," Deane said calmly, folding her Gene Tunney hands. "No one has any desire to be insensitive, as you put it, but the rather harsh fact is that Carole did leave here, without permission, to chase off somewhere with some common riffraff from town. That's defiance. We can't be sure it won't be repeated, that it isn't being repeated at this moment. Unfortunately, Pearce isn't equipped to handle behavioural problems."

Eyes narrowing, Mary said, "I didn't send you a behavioural problem. I sent you a child, to be taught and moulded. If she became a problem—to this school for robots, but more importantly to herself—she learned it here."

"May I say something about insensitivity?"

"No. I've heard quite enough."

"I'll say it anyway. In all the time Carole's lived and studied at Pearce, you haven't come to visit her once. If I'm

220

wrong, then I stand corrected, but I believe I'm not wrong. She gave a piano recital this past February. I happen to know as a fact that she was terrified about performing in public, and her friends and instructors were able to prop her up, as it were, only so much. I know she was looking forward to your being here. The parents, at least one parent of all the girls who were in the recital that day, found the time to come."

"I won't be lectured," said Mary, who hadn't known about the recital.

And who abruptly recalled that she *had* known, had been invited, had vowed to appear, had been called away the day before, had made up for her absence with a long, loving telephone call to Carole, and bouquets of flowers to be delivered just before the recital.

"Very well, no lectures. You seem anxious to leave."

"There isn't anything more to discuss," Mary said hoarsely, rising.

"I regret your antagonistic attitude, Mary. I regret that it's come to this, that we couldn't have talked sooner."

"About what? Your self-righteous explanations of why you couldn't be expected to perform the job you were paid to perform? I entrusted my daughter to you and you failed in your job. Now your hands are washed clean because she's a 'problem'. Thank you. Thank you for nothing. Thank you for letting me down."

Stefan drove her the mile's distance from the school to Dr Marco's office. She had phoned him at noon, had asked to see him either before or after her visit to Pearce. "My hours are booked until later this evening," he'd said. "I'm sorry; I'm sure there's a great deal of stress. I could fit you in at, let's see, nine tonight."

"What time does Carole see you on Fridays? I'll take that hour."

"Her Friday sessions begin at seven-thirty in the morning, before school."

"This is becoming almost ludicrous, Doctor. I don't care

to be 'fitted in'. You won't lose a session's fee, if that's crossed your mind. I'll triple whatever you're normally paid. My daughter has disap*peared*."

He seemed at last to hear her. "I'll rearrange the afternoon's schedule somehow. Let's put you down for two-fifteen. There'll be no fee, of course."

Now, at ten minutes past two, Mary moved restlessly about in his empty waiting room, unused to waiting, felt Carole's presence in it, vacantly leafed through a month-old issue of *Scofield's*, vacantly gazed at the festive Breughel on the wall, still unclear about why she was here, certain only of a controlled panic rising in her.

"Control, control," Gramp had taught. "*Don't let the bastards catch you without it, or you're sure to be stomped on.*"

She looked at his closed door, heard nothing from behind it. She had spoken with this Marco exactly once, two years before, when the fourth physician to examine Carole had agreed with the first three: the child's formidable array of symptoms—the extended dreamy and withdrawn moods, the loss of appetite, the stammering, the extreme nervousness—were emotional, not physical. Alan Marco had been recommended as the best psychoanalyst within reasonable proximity to Pearce School. After several interviews with Carole, he had suggested that Mary come to see him. "Yes, Carole can certainly benefit from treatment, and I'll take her on," he'd said in that phone conversation. "But it'll be useful to all of us, Miss Scofield—to you, to her, and to me—if you and I can talk together."

"I agree. I'll phone you for an appointment the moment I'm free," Mary had promised in full sincerity, submerged that week in the very real crisis of a paralysing printers' strike. The strike was settled. It was replaced immediately by fresh crises. The meeting never materialized.

Two-twelve. What will he say to me now, two wink-of-an-eye years later? she thought. Will he be openly accusing, condemning? Solicitous, supportive, comforting, evasive? Will he do a Hazel Deane reprise: *Your child's in trouble because the people most meaningful to her—you, Mary Scofield—left her on the train and forgot to claim her.* Will he come on as the High Lama? A bogus-profound cliché factory? Will he scold me? Will it be justified?

Waiting, weighing the urge to knock at that closed door that was becoming a nose-thumb of rejection, of indifference, she thought of the analysts and therapists and psychiatrists she had met over the years, socially and as the working Mary, never as a prospective patient. She remembered herself at Carole's age, perhaps a little older, longing to be helped by someone trained and uncensuring but always afraid to broach the subject to Gramp, who would have been appalled at the request, who would have viewed it as unconscionable weakness.

> " *You'll never be hurt if you protect yourself from being vulnerable,*" he'd preached. "*Defend yourself against relationships that might get too close. In the long run, you're the only one in your life you can rely on. And that's good, that's the way it has to be.*"

"Head doctors," he'd once snorted. "A pack of charlatans, the lot of 'em!" *And why does Gramp keep popping up in my mind now—Gramp, who was a love and who was so woefully wrong so often about so much. Gramp who needed a family so badly that he crippled his child, and his grandchild, and, by a tricky bit of sleight-of-hand, his great-grandchild...*

Charlatans. Of course there were charlatans. And competent professionals who were nonetheless not sufficiently wizardlike to help the heads of the devoutly hopeless like her father, Harmon, Gramp's child. Or perhaps Carole, her own child . . . She thought of Marco, on the other side of that forbidding door, wondered which he was, charlatan or prof—

Ah, you fraud, she cursed herself in disgust, in agony.

Ah, you two-faced, hollow, superficial, blame-shifting

223

phony. Two years after you remember you left your baby on the train, you suddenly wonder if the conductor was nice, if he soothed her with lollipops, if he was a responsible surrogate parent.

"Carole," she said softly, aloud. "Carole," she repeated, touching the table and windowsill and chairs that Carole had surely touched.

She saw Carole wilfully, spitefully punishing her, heard Carole's toneless voice: "*I want you to suffer. I want to hurt you for leaving me on that train. I want you frozen with guilt for the rest of your life.*"

She caught a glimpse of herself in the waiting room's wall oval mirror, and instantly turned away. You charlatan, she thought, you fraud, you phony.

You were never really cold and removed. That's only how it must have seemed.

What you really were was—cold and removed.

In one way or another, he'll tell you that. He'll drown you in it.

Two-fourteen. What the hell was he doing behind that closed, fearsome door—practising for this meeting by brushing up on his tea leaves, gathering his defences together?

Tension built. Hostility built. She imagined him, half William Powell with the lapel carnation, half Erich Von Stroheim with the riding crop, opening the door, motioning her into his office, fixing all seventy-seven eyes on her.

MARCO (from Olympus): "What do you want me to do for you?"

MARY: "Reassure me. Tell me I'm blameless."

MARCO: "You're not. Carole hates you, and rightly. You're worse than a stranger to her, you're a play-acting mother. You've always been insincere and selfish, you've always held out tantalizing promises to her you never had any intentions of keeping, and now you're getting the punishment you deserve. Look at you: you not only don't know what your feelings are, you don't even know

224

what they ought to be."

MARY: "I paid you to help her, not to teach her to hate me and run away!"

MARCO: "Yes, she's running. She's a Scofield. All Scofields run. It's easier than facing responsibilities, fulfilling obligations. She's a lonely child, an unloved child; she's looking for warmth, for safety."

MARY: "*I'm* a lonely child! *I'm* unloved! *I'm* looking for warmth and safety! Let me start over. Let me be a child again. I'll do it right this time."

MARCO: "Too late, much too late. Everything in life is a re-enactment of the past. You're locked into your legacy. All Scofields are doomed to the past. Repetition compulsion, repetition compulsion, re—"

MARY: "I *paid* you! I *paid* you! I *paid*—"

Two-seventeen. The doorknob turned and Mary instinctively straightened, determined that he recognize at once by her pretence of authority that, for this hour at least, he would be working for her. He charged out, neither William Powell nor Erich Von Stroheim but an open-faced young man, pleasantly homely, necktie askew, and he said, his manner hurried yet not rejecting, "Two more minutes at the very most, okay?" And then he was gone again, the door shut after him.

She sat, trying to be angry at his abruptness, and instead her mind was flooded again with images she had successfully suppressed all day. She saw Carole being harmed by sick, hateful people. She saw her baby helpless, terrorized, pleading for help, calling out to her mother who had ignored her, her grandfather who could not even help himself, her great-grandfather who would surely have come to her if he had been alive.

She stood, alone, fighting to suppress the horrible images. Abruptly, then, she fled.

FOURTEEN

ADAM TOLD VENUS that she would become a motion picture actress.

"Wouldn't that be the limit!" she scoffed, both flustered and flattered. "Me in the movies? I'd be horse-laughed out of town."

"Possibly. But how do we know that unless we investigate it? How do we know anything unless we investigate it?"

The subject wasn't discussed again until a week later, when he telephoned Venus and said, "I would like to come to dinner tomorrow evening and bring a guest. Does the name Harvey Coles mean anything to you?"

"No."

"It will. Coles is a novelist, a hack but a quite competent one. He's interested in writing photoplays, and I think he could write a clever one for you."

The following evening, he brought Harvey Coles, a small, tense man with a small, tense moustache. Eulalie, the housekeeper Adam had hired for Venus, served a splendid lamb. During dinner, as Coles squinted and twitched and surveyed the glorious-looking Venus, Adam outlined a notion he had devised for a film story, a lighthearted family picture about a girl who innocently gets mixed up with a gang of spies. At the end of the meal, Coles nervously played with the knot of his necktie and remarked, "I'll study the possibilities, Mr Scofield."

"You'll find them most workable, Mr Coles," Adam said softly. "And most profitable, too."

After the writer had bowed and scraped his way out of the apartment, Venus surprised Adam by asking if he was really serious about putting her in the movies.

His eyes widened. "When am I not serious?"

Weeks before the scenario was completed, he ordered

that an item be carried in all his papers: The Company had formed Scofield Films, and the Hollywood studio Pageant Pictures would be Scofield Films' distributor. He arranged for Venus to pose for more than a hundred photographs, published his favourites, and began a saturation campaign to inform America that Venus Montgomery, "gamine and goddess," would be Scofield Films' star player.

He observed, when he had the time, that Venus went through the paces of preparation somewhat like a fevered sleepwalker, unsure of whether she wanted to be a star or a spectator, bewildered, frightened by the prospects, thrilled by the prospects. By the time Harvey Coles submitted his scenario, the campaign was roaring along in high gear. The West Virginia coal miner's daughter named Anita Janusz read about a fresh, scintillating beauty named Venus Montgomery, a young, vibrant personality and a sensitive artist from the New York theatre who was destined to out-Pickford Pickford, and marvelled, "The New York theatre? The Hawley on Twelfth Street is the New York theatre?"

Grinning at his creation, Adam said, "Before we're through, my dear, we'll have you born of royalty." She read the photoplay, half comedy, half melodrama, all Adam, calling for her to be a professional actress, and protested that she couldn't go through with it. He soothed her, declaring that he hadn't the slightest doubt in the world she was going to be a fine artist.

"Why do I do everything you tell me to?" she moaned.

"Because enough of you is satisfied that I'm right about you. Come here, stop fluttering. It would be nice to kiss you."

"No! Damn you, quit grabbing my tits like I'm some toy, like I'm not even human! I'm *human*, you know! I *breathe*, you know!"

"And you love me."

"Hell I do! Hell I do!"

The picture was to be entitled *Susie and the Spies*, Adam instructed, and filmed at Parnassus. He took personal charge, summoned the best technicians and artists recommended to him to make the picture memorable. He told Venus' acting coach, "I don't expect you to transform Miss Montgomery into Bernhardt or Duse, but I do want you to concentrate on bringing out her natural vivacity so that it comes through on the screen. There's also a special comic quality about her, a talent for laughing at life's setbacks and pitfalls. I want the audience to be able to warm their hands near her." Within a week, the coach confided to Adam that he would do all he could to work miracles but that Miss Montgomery, in his opinion, had many limitations. Adam fired him and hired a coach who praised her.

Through rehearsals and in the opening days of filming, Venus wailed that she was hopeless, and that everyone else knew it, too, everyone but Adam, who stubbornly insisted the public would adore her. She begged him to free her, to save her and him and the good people connected with the picture from sure embarrassment. His certainty of triumph grew, and she went through with it. By the day of the world premiere in New York, most readers of the forty-three Scofield newspapers knew there was a new, shining star in the film firmament named Venus Montgomery, a classic beauty and gifted actress. Adam bought her a lavishly beaded gown and escorted her to the packed theatre. In the lobby he introduced her to Company executives and congressmen and businessmen and their wives he had personally invited as "my protégée, who'll have some outstanding experienced players looking to their laurels after tonight." Applause began and swelled as they walked down the lighted aisle. "I'm gonna sink straight through the floor," Venus mourned.

"Smile," Adam commanded, smiling.

Susie and the Spies had cost him two hundred thousand dollars, and looked it. He had seen the picture at a private screening, had watched Venus as Susie, prominent in almost every scene, frozen-faced and moving clumsily, had kept the nibbling doubts to himself, had assured himself that he was too critical because he was too close, that a live audience would be patient and love her.

Now, as Venus fidgeted beside him, groaning quietly and whispering that her eyes were shut tight, he was conscious of an indignant silence in the theatre. Then he began to hear sounds, people coughing and making seats squeak with their restlessness, heard no laughter when the picture was a comedy, heard laughter when the picture was a melodrama. Anger rose in him. He heard spiteful hisses, and his anger shifted to cold fury.

"Sit tight and sit tall," he ordered, squeezing her wrist. "They're scum and you're a lady."

"Can we go?"

He squeezed all the harder. "You are a lady," he repeated.

Then the picture was finally done and there were scatterings of polite applause mixed with the hisses. The lights went up and the organ played, but he refused to release his grip. Looking nowhere except straight ahead, at nothing, he prompted, "You're to put on a big smile and keep it. We will get up and walk up this aisle when we're ready, not an instant before. If anyone congratulates you, be gracious. If any hoodlum is insulting, even if he glances at you in an insulting way, ignore him but walk straight and keep that smile on your face."

In the lobby, some people pumped his hand and congratulated Venus on a dynamic performance. She thanked each of them, and Adam was proud of her courage and her charm. She didn't burst into a flood of tears until they were in the Rolls and the rear seat's window shades were closed.

"I hope those are tears of excitement," he said, holding her. "Hoodlums aren't worth tears."

"I was so rotten," she sobbed. "You're the only one who doesn't know that. Or you do, and you're not saying because you're so stubborn."

"I know no such thing. You were marvellous—sensitive and funny and breathtaking. Now, not another word. Hooligans are people to fight, not bow down to and be bullied by. You haven't learned that yet. I'll teach you."

They went to Adam's catered party in honour of Venus Montgomery and *Susie and the Spies* at the New York Scofield Hotel. The huge room was crowded with guests, some who had been at the theatre, some who had not. An orchestra played and glasses clinked and Adam drank some wine and let Venus have some, too, and introduced her to everyone who came to them. She danced with Adam and with men whom Adam, subtly nodding his permission, let her dance with. In her apartment that night, after his arms cradled her, she asked, "Why are so many people so scared of you?"

"Scared? Are *you* scared of me?"

"Well, no, I don't think so, but everybody at that party was. You don't raise your voice and you're cool as a cucumber in public, but I see how people are when they're around you. They're real respectful and friendly, and they act like you're just about ready to shoot them smack between the eyes."

He laughed. "If that's true, is it bad?"

"Sure it is, if they don't have a reason to be scared of you. I wouldn't want anybody scared of me for all the money in the world."

"That's a great amount of money you're prepared to forfeit, love. Don't give it up so easily. Don't give anything up easily." Brusquely he said, "Yes, I have a certain degree of influence, and that's because I have a very large degree of self-confidence; I'm confident that there are many things I can do better than anyone else. If some people are scared of me, as you put it, it's because they're afraid of themselves. Simple. If they had a lick of the confidence I have, they'd be spending less time being afraid of me and they'd use that precious time to be their own men. Do you see how clear it is?"

"Oh, yeah, clear as mud."

He laughed again. "Very well, clear as mud. Stop being such a worry wart; you're much too young, with too much promise for that. Be happy, Venus; it bothers me when

230

you're unhappy for even a second. You know that, don't you?"

The Scofield newspapers called *Susie and the Spies* a wonderful treat and the luminous Venus Montgomery's portrayal electrifying and brilliant. Other newspapers called *Susie and the Spies* a horror and the leaden Venus Montgomery's performance a disaster. The reviews had nothing to do with her, Adam worked to reassure her; his competitors were continually seeking ways to hit at him with their jealous venom. "Don't concern yourself with what those nickel-and-dime animals write," he said. "You're still going to out-Pickford Pickford."

Well before the final financial report arrived that *Susie and the Spies* would earn none of its investment back, Adam ordered his papers to announce that Venus' second photoplay would be *Guinevere and the Knights of the Round Table*, a fantasy melodrama. She called him at his Scofield Building office, something they had agreed she would never do. She had just read the item in the *Outlook* and she swore at him, spitting gutter profanity, for having let the announcement get out without consulting her, without even mentioning a second picture to her. She would never be in any more of his crappy movies, she raged, and he could go straight to hell for treating her like some rag doll without a brain.

His voice controlled and frigid, Adam said, "It is now one o'clock in the afternoon. I will be there shortly after eight. In the meanwhile, I suggest you teach yourself some telephone manners and do something at once about your fishwife tone. Do you understand me?"

"I—All right."

She was docile and apologetic when he appeared. "I will not tolerate filthy language, particularly on the telephone," he stormed, his eyes burning. "Ever. Is that abundantly clear?"

"I'm sorry . . ."

231

"And I'm disappointed in you. I'm always disappointed in ladies who don't behave as ladies."

"I'm sor—" she began, and then her face suddenly darkened, and she said, "Wait a minute. What've I got to be sorry about? *You* quiet down a minute."

He blinked.

Venus was still for a time, as though assembling her thoughts. Then she spoke softly. "Some things you do, I don't like. Butter wouldn't melt in your mouth and still some times you can be a real shit of a bully. You're good to me and I may be a dumb Polack from the sticks, but I don't like you making me be something I'm not and don't want to be. I just don't like it. I never said anything before because I've always trusted you and I'm crazy about you, I guess, but I don't like it."

She put her hand out, to stop him from interrupting. "I have feelings, too. I don't understand them all the time, but I got them. I'm not some floozie. Maybe that's what some people would call me and maybe I can't blame them—you pay my rent and you buy me nice things and maybe that's what a floozie is—but I have feelings like everybody else and I don't want to be somebody's trained horse, not even yours."

Adam watched her pace, and softly asked her what was really upsetting her.

Venus stopped, and turned, and looked at him.

"I don't like being your girl friend," she said weakly. "I want to be your wife."

Her fingers covered her lips, as if to erase what she had said.

No, Adam thought. No, I want your life to stay the way it is.

"Yes," he said, "I want that, too." He had asked Eugenia for a divorce, he explained. Eugenia had refused. He would press it. It wouldn't happen the next day, he said, nor would it be pleasant, but it would happen.

Adam promptly cast the subject from his mind. He had become reliant, almost as a shield, on Eugenia's adamant refusal to free him. His affection for Venus was deep, often abiding. She could anticipate his moods and needs, and catered to them. She knew how to amuse him, soothe him. She was frequently a matchless companion. The idea of losing her was unthinkable. The idea of marriage was unthinkable. She was empty-headed, a leaf, a child, a whore.

Venus made *Guinevere and the Knights of the Round Table*. It was a flop, too, in spite of all the hard work, the new acting coach and the new director who magically coaxed a performance from her that approached a level of tolerable inadequacy—not so violent a flop as *Susie*, but a flop nonetheless.

This time out, however, there was an important difference: even the critics whom Adam did not own wrote fondly of Venus Montgomery. None of them referred to her as an actress, yet they wrote about her with approving words like "fresh" and "charming" and "impish" and "lovelier than her single wooden expression in *Susie and the Spies* would have led us to suspect." When the customers still stayed away, Adam simply, and quietly, leased theatres in six key cities in the United States and ordered that the film continue to be shown, whether the theatres were packed or empty, until he directed otherwise. It ran continually for more than half a year, during which time Venus began and finished her third movie, *Spoonin'*, and during which time Adam exulted in watching her grow, expanding her interests while still maintaining a touching, almost total dependence on his decisions. He agreed with Caleb Buckminster that his determination to make a major motion picture star of her was costing enough to ransom a dozen kings. He agreed, and it didn't matter, for the Company's earnings had never been higher, the country was financially sound, and he was, singlehandedly, transforming a West Virginia coal miner's daughter into a queen. "Soon," he would answer when she pressed him about marriage. "All in good time. I'm working on it. Believe me." She seemed to. In his own good time, when the moment was precisely right, he

233

would carefully explain why a divorce and remarriage were and would forever be out of the question. Later. Presently. Timing was everything.

In the autumn of 1929, a month before *Little Lady*, Venus' fifth movie and first talkie, was to open, Adam received a telephone call from Eugenia's sister, Cornelia. Harmon had been rushed to the hospital in Scottsdale with a burst appendix. Eugenia was of course with him. Adam telephoned his own physician, George Hunt, and they both were airborne within the hour.

The past weeks had not been kind to Adam. Lon Starkey, an Alabama circuit preacher with a vigorous sense of showmanship and a genius for publicity, was storming revival meetings and radio stations with brimstone sermons against the hypocrisy of all forty-seven Scofield newspapers for fraudulently advocating the Seventh Commandment. "What do we have here in the rich and powerful Adam Hurd Scofield and this painted actress that calls herself Venus Montgomery?" Starkey had bleated until one week before, loudly enough to be heard cross-country. "What do we have when a self-proclaimed professor of morality, a self-appointed spokesman for the straight and narrow path, exclaims, 'Do as I say, not as I do,' and takes unto himself a harlot? A mockery, my friends, a cynical nose-thumbing at the Divine Word. 'Adam' is fact, Jehovah's first man. 'Venus' is myth, the goddess of beauty. Ironical, heathen mockery, good friends! I'm here to give you all some ripe food for thought: before you buy your next Scofield newspaper or any of its unholy publications, pause a bit and decide for yourself where your hard-earned pennies are going, for the answer is right here in Psalms 50: 18, 'When thou sawest a thief, then thou consentedst with him, and hast been partaker with adulterers.' And before you go to a movie picture show where the yellow-hair harlot flounces and bounces her iniquity at you, stop and read here what Isaiah 57: 3 has to tell you: 'But draw near hither, ye sons of the sorceress, the seed of the adulterer and the whore.'

It's all right here in the Book, dear Christian friends, we who have . . ."

In his office that day, Adam had summoned Karl Keyes, a magician at getting unpleasant jobs done swiftly and cleanly, had shown him the transcript, and asked, "How soon can this matter be attended to?"

"In three or four days, to do it right."

"Do it right in two," Adam had said quietly, annoyed that he hadn't been told about the preacher sooner, fearful that the Starkey poison had already taken hold in crucial pockets of the country, poison that could hurt *Little Lady* and, particularly in the Bible Belt, the Company.

When the news came over the Teletype two nights later that the Reverend Lon Starkey, on his way to a meeting hall in Savannah, was found unconscious on a dirt road, a quarter mile from his automobile, his wallet gone, his throat cut, Adam had ordered editorials decrying the violence. Now, four days after the bungling, as Adam's plane flew him to his son, Starkey was still alive—his vocal cords slit, and no one seriously associating the incident with the Company, but alive. Fantastic, Adam thought, still appalled; a professional is hired to perform, and he botches it. Fantastic. . .

Eugenia was in the hospital's second-floor solarium when Adam and George Hunt arrived. Adam was terrified when she rushed into his arms and wept. "What?" he demanded. "What?"

"We— Adam, we almost lost him."

"He's living?"

"Yes, thank God, thank God, thank God," Eugenia murmured. "But it was so close."

Adam took charge. He insisted that the surgeon, a Dr Markland, see him at once, introduced himself and Hunt, stayed as Markland explained the situation to Hunt, listened as Hunt asked questions, asked his own questions, punctuating them with repeated commands to be assured that everything possible had been done for the boy and that the boy would be all right, his voice rising and his impatience

235

evident when the answers weren't concise enough. "What I keep hearing you say is that the operation was extremely delicate and the child almost died," he exploded. "*What* brought him to the brink of death? Would it've been less delicate if there had been a surgeon who knew exactly what he was doing?"

Hunt flushed. Markland, polite at first, said, "To begin with, Mr Scofield, this is a hospital and you're going to lower your voice at once."

"I'm well aware it's a hos—"

"One moment, please. I'll assume this behaviour of yours has to do with strain and anxiety, but you're not to bark at me as if we're hired hands around here. I'll be happy to discuss the case with Dr Hunt and let him make his own examination. If you wish, I can have a release paper brought for you to sign, and the moment *I* decide the lad's health won't be jeopardized by being moved, you're free to take him anywhere you choose."

Adam, silent, nodded.

He was allowed to look in on Harmon. He bent down and kissed the sleeping boy's head and whispered, "I love you. I'm glad you're safe." A tight ball suddenly formed in his throat and he hurried to the lavatory, where he turned on both sink faucets at full force to mask the noises of inexplicable, ungovernable sobs. Then he found Eugenia, put his arm around her, and together they went home.

"I've come to a decision, Adam," Eugenia said. "If a divorce is sincerely what you want, you may have it."

They sat on the patio. Eugenia looked tired, older, lovelier, softer.

"That isn't all what I want," he said.

"We share Harmon, really nothing else. No, no, don't worry, I'm all out of resentment and bitterness, so there'll be no lectures. I just don't see what I thought I was holding on to all these years. We're a million miles apart; I look back and we were always a million miles apart. I have a contented life, of sorts. You have your work, and that wonderful energy, and you have that—actress."

"I'll make you a pledge. Come home—to stay—and you have my solemn pledge that I'll never see her again."

She shook her head. "It isn't that easy, Adam. There was a time when each of us could have at least tried to make important compromises. What I didn't bring myself to realize until the past month or so is that I just don't love you."

Adam was alarmed. "You know that isn't true. You mustn't say it. If I thought—" He was mute for a moment. "If I thought you meant that, then I'd have nothing, absolutely nothing."

"The actress—"

"The hell with the actress! She's meaningless, it's all meaningless! Christ Almighty, Eugenia, don't ever say there's no feeling for me! I know my faults, I think I know most of them. I know there's always been the seesaw inside of me, the honourable man and the guttersnipe, I know backwards and forwards what I'm made up of. I need to have order in my life, respectability—"

"I can't give that to you." Again she shook her head, more firmly this time. "As for my offer of a divorce, it's offered genuinely, Adam. I assure you it's not a ploy. What it all comes down to is that there's much about you I admire, and I'll never stop praying for you, but otherwise I simply don't care about you anymore."

Little Lady premiered in New York on October 28, 1929. On the afternoon of that day, Venus telephoned Adam and asked him to come to her apartment immediately. He heard anguish and asked what was wrong. "Just come, okay?" she entreated.

She opened the door for him, her face drawn. She had been to see her doctor. "I'm about two weeks' gone," she told him.

Adam frowned. "No mistake?"

"No mistake."

"How in hell did that happen?"

She smiled. "The usual way, I guess," she said. Adam

stormed across the length of the parlour to the telephone and called Grady Honeycutt, the *Outlook*'s executive editor. "That woman in Washington Heights," he declared. "Have her arrange to be free tomorrow morning." He replaced the receiver.

"Weren't you listening to me?" Venus asked. "I tell you I'm knocked up, and you go making business calls."

"We go to the theatre at eight o'clock tonight. In the morning, you have a date with a woman who'll rid you of your small problem."

"Whaa-at?"

"The sooner the better. You don't need to have the slightest worry about this woman. I'm told she's the best there is."

"You want to back up there a little and explain what you're talkin' about? What 'woman'? What 'best'?"

"An abortion is what I'm talking about, you idiot!" he thundered. "You begin the next picture in ten days. You'll be shipshape by then."

Her eyes widened, as though in something approximating disbelief. "You just hold your horses, general. This is *me*, remember? My baby. Our baby. I'm not going to go cartin' off to some butcher. I have some say."

Irate, beset, Adam snapped, "you have no say! You're not going to saddle me—us—with a *baby*, of all insane things!" He glanced at his watch. "It's almost five and you're not anywhere nearly ready for tonight. What time is the hairdresser supposed to be here?"

She sat.

"I asked you a question."

Quietly she said, "Get out of here."

"Fine, exactly what I need: a bout with a prima donna. Don't you give *me* instructions, you insolent, ungrateful Polack! What did you expect me to do, throw you up in the air and tell the papers to print hooray, hooray, I'm going to be a daddy?"

She stared at him.

"I asked you when the hairdresser is to be here, and I

want an answer!" She continued to stare. "Very well, now I've seen your imitation of a stone wall." He applauded, knowing how childish it was. "Congratulations, it was an outstanding performance. Is *this* how you figured you could become Mrs Scofield, by letting yourself get pregnant? Did you honestly image that would do it? *Our* baby? How do I know it's mine?"

He glowered. At last she stood—with the flawless poise he had paid for—and she spoke. She spoke evenly, softly, without emotion.

"Okay. You get what you want. I'll get rid of the small problem. Only I don't go to the show tonight. I'm staying here. You want to go, you go by yourself."

"That's infantile. The theatre will be packed. I have the whole block set up for the rubberneckers to watch you step out of the car."

"No." Wearily: "No." She walked to her bedroom. Adam heard the lock click.

He returned to his office, where he stayed and worked, pausing only to direct the word to be spread that Miss Montgomery had come down with a touch of ptomaine and regretted her inability to attend the premiere. Soon before eleven o'clock, he accepted a call from Emily Wallington, the *Outlook*'s film critic. "What you missed!" she gushed. "Tonight was a triumph. The second the picture was over, everybody clapped their hands! I mean everybody!" Adam paid attention to what surely weren't the sounds of ass-kissing. "I saw the other reviewers on the way out. Some of them winked at me; that never happened before with Venus' other movies. It's her best yet and she was divine in it. She's really and truly a star now. There won't be any holding her back after tonight."

He placed a call to Venus, to personally report the exciting news, to hear her squeal that delicious little-girl squeal of glee.

There was no answer. He had thought repeatedly through the lonely, agonizingly long evening about going to the apartment, about caressing her, about making everything

239

right. Now he decided against it. She would have to learn better manners first.

In the morning, Adam summoned Grady Honeycutt to escort her to Washington Heights, wait, deliver her back to the apartment, and phone when it was done. She knew and liked Grady. Adam had ten dozen roses, carnations, and orchids sent to the apartment. He absorbed himself in work. Honeycutt didn't phone, but appeared. "It went like a charm," he said. "She wasn't even weak in the pins when I took her home. She didn't have much to say, except that she wants to rest up and be by herself."

"You know more about this procedure than I do. Will she be all right?"

"Oh, sure. The maid's there, so she won't be alone. She's strong as an ox."

"I want to go there."

"My suggestion would be to wait till tonight. Give her a chance to sleep it off."

"Many thanks, Grady. It's good to know I can count on you."

"Any time."

At eight o'clock that evening, Adam collected the brace of newspaper notices that praised Venus Montgomery and *Little Lady*, patted the diamond necklace in his pocket, and entered his limousine. He sat up front, beside Thomas, his chauffeur, because the rear seat was stacked high and full with bags and boxes of buttered popcorn. "Look like Sanny Claus comin', Mr Scofield," Thomas guffawed.

"Our young friend likes popcorn, Thomas."

"Gits in the teeth, you ask me."

Thomas and the apartment building's doorman needed two elevator trips to carry out Adam's instructions, which were to line the corridor outside Apartment 7G with the popcorn, ring 7G's bell, and vanish. He rode the elevator to the seventh floor when they were finished, emerged, and saw Eulalie, Venus' maid, standing in the doorway, staring dumbly at the bags and boxes. She saw him. He smiled and said, "You seem perplexed, Eulalie. Why don't you go back in and tell Miss Montgomery she has a visitor with several presents?"

"Miz Montgomery? Oh, she gone."

Venus had slept through much of the day, the maid explained. At about six she had wakened, packed her smallest suitcase, wrapped herself inside a light coat, said, "See you later, sweetie pie," and disappeared.

"Six o'clock? Why wasn't I notified?" he demanded.

"Miz Montgomery, she always tole me you was never to be contacted, nohow."

He searched through every room in the flat, almost as if he might find her. He found nothing missing, except Venus and the small suitcase he had bought her.

He went home, concerned about her well-being, maddened by her adolescent pique and wrathful independence. He would give her twenty-four hours to stew in some corner, as she surely was doing. If she hadn't returned by then, he would have her located and would impress on her that he was done with her, once and for all, unless she swore that she would never upset him this way again.

The stock market convulsed the following day. She had still not returned. He hired private tracers to locate here and resolutely kept close to his desk and telephones and Teletypes that day and the next, satisfying everyone that Wall Street would come around and right itself in due course, striving to satisfy himself that Venus was not only perfectly all right but wouldn't be so foolish as to cause him and the Company any embarrassment.

It took his agents nearly two weeks to track her down. She was staying with friends, a retired vaudeville couple, in a Chicago suburb. He was asked for further instructions. There were none, he said. He directed Scofield Films' publicity chief to send out releases that Venus Montgomery had temporarily removed herself from movies and the lime-light owing to overwork but would be back, bigger and better than ever, in the reasonably near future. He studied the receipts of *Little Lady*. The picture was instantaneously successful, everywhere it opened, despite the country's bewilderment about the economy.

She continued to stay away. Everything of value Adam had bought for her remained in the apartment, which he stubbornly continued to rent. There were no letters, no calls, no signals that she wanted to be invited back. He gave up the apartment on the day in January he learned that she had dyed her hair black, had taken another name, was living quietly in Michigan with a sick and jobless actor named Chet Bourne. He learned that she, like Bourne, had become a heavy drinker. Discreetly yet firmly he had the message delivered to Hollywood that she was never to be employed in motion pictures again. Someone would eventually hope to defy him and offer her a role, he knew. He would handle that when he needed to.

He buried himself into his work harder, more intensely, than he ever had in his life. It showed, for he was rewarded by Caleb Buckminster. On his birthday, in July of 1930, he received a glowing financial report from Caleb, who scribbled in pencil, *Welcome home, drowsy giant*.

The Depression adversely affected some of the Scofield magazine sales, but few of its forty-eight newspapers. In 1931, the year Harmon was fifteen, Adam introduced *Scofield's*, his eleventh magazine and the first to commit him personally, a weekly magazine to report and comment strongly on the world's current news, vogues, and mores. "One line is never to appear in *Scofield's*," he ruled, "and that line is, 'As everyone knows.' " He was advised that the timing was altogether wrong ("*Who's going to pay twenty-five cents to read there's a breadline?*") and he was advised, ever so circumspectly, that the success of the press arm of the Company was predicated upon its gift to titillate and entertain rather than provoke thought. ("*Don't interfere with a winning streak, especially in these times.*")

Adam assumed full control of *Scofield's*, from inception to delivery, frequently working uninterrupted stretches of seventy-two hours.

The magazine was an immediate hit. He continued to

make the magazine, and the Company, grow, pouring in money against the counsel of hired experts who vigorously advocated that the corporate belt be tightened. He pressed on, listening to the experts, nodding to them, ignoring them.

And the Company grew. He drove himself deeper into the business of its success.

Harmon wrote to him occasionally, respectful and implicitly affectionate letters, beautifully worded letters about books he was reading and the future in engineering or architecture he was planning, letters that always ended with oblique requests for money. Adam sent him money, usually a hundred dollars at a time, folded inside letters of his own that praised the boy and proffered sound advice about the joys and responsibilities of becoming a man, always ending his letters with declarations of love and pride in his very dear son. He addressed these letters to Harmon in care of the Scottsdale Post Office, where Harmon had his own box.

"My life now centres wholly around the receipt of your letters," Adam wrote one night in his town house study. "I realize and appreciate how busy you keep yourself, and appreciate as well that writing to one's father as a duty can be a toilsome chore.

"I ask you, however, to write to me just as frequently as you can. Your letters thrill me, give me nothing but pleasure and vast pride. I cannot stress enough their impor—"

He tore the letter into four neat sections. A whining letter, an unmanly letter. He walked from room to room and then impulsively, though it was past midnight, dressed and drove himself, choosing not to disturb the chauffeur at this late hour, the thirty miles to Parnassus. The caretaker let him in. He swam from one end of the indoor pool to the other. He was suddenly ravenously hungry, but he decided it wouldn't do to ask for a meal in the middle of the night. In the kitchen off the refectory, he scrambled six eggs, fried six strips of bacon, poured milk into a large glass, and carried his meal to the refectory. There he ate, at the head of the table where seventy guests had more than once sat at a single dinner. A fork dropped to the floor. It clattered, and the sound reverberated throughout the entire room.

Late that summer, Adam received a telephone call from Eugenia, her voice aristocratic as always, though uncommonly shy. She had decided to move back to New York and enrol Harmon at Stormbridge, a private school for boys in Southern Connecticut that emphasized scholarship, sobriety, and the rigid building of character; she had found no comparable school in or near Scottsdale. "I see no reason why we can't share the town house," she said. "It's certainly large enough for my sister and me to have our privacy, and for you to—do whatever it is you do there. Naturally, it's your decision. I don't want to foist us on you if there will be the least inconvenience."

"This is your home," said Adam.

"I ask you only one thing: that you never bring that woman to the house as long as our son and my sister and I are there."

"She's long gone, Eugenia. When will you come? I'll send the plane."

"Thank you, Adam, but I've never been in an airplane and I don't intend to start at my age. And Harmon won't admit it, but he has a dreadful fear of heights. The train is a much more civilized way to travel, anyway. I should think in about a week or ten days."

On the day his family was to arrive, Adam went to the railroad station to meet them and collect them. His heart swelled as they emerged from the train. Harmon, still skin and bones, had grown like a weed. Adam's sister-in-law, Cornelia, was still half-ramrod, half-prune, complaining that the trip had been endless and insufferably dirty. Eugenia, Adam's exquisite Eugenia, greeted him with genuine warmth; she didn't kiss him, and her head turned so that he could kiss only her cheek, but her smile was a true smile, a smile that said she was where she belonged and wished to be.

Hatcher drove them all home; Thomas, Adam's easy-going chauffeur for so many years and almost exactly Adam's age, had died suddenly one week before of a massive stroke. "What're you now, seven feet tall or eight?" Adam roared lovingly at Harmon.

"Not quite, sir," Harmon answered, grinning, blushing. "A shade under six."

"What's this 'sir' business? I don't see any Army officers around here." To his wife and his magnificent son, Adam exclaimed, "All I see is my family, the Scofield family together, and I couldn't be more tickled."

"You're looking well, Adam," Eugenia said.

Once home, Eugenia and the servant staff exchanged greetings. Mrs Gans, the head housekeeper, asked who was to be put up where. Adam heard his wife select the north bedroom for herself, not his bedroom.

In the town house's library that evening after dinner, after Harmon had said good night, after Cornelia had retired with the announcement that she was positive she was incubating influenza, Adam said to his wife, "Believe what I'm about to tell you, Eugenia. I'm sincerely happy you're here. Sincerely."

She examined the hem of her skirt. "I've never really stopped caring for you, Adam. I have a sharp tongue and I say things I shouldn't say—I phrase them so badly—and I kick myself afterwards. I hate it. I make a New Year's resolution every night in the year to reform." She looked at him with a curious, almost apologetic smile. "Are we leopards too old to change our spots, Adam?"

"Old? We're newlyweds. Talk to me, Eugenia. I'll change every spot on this carcass if you'll tell me how. I *want* to. I want these next years to be nothing but good ones. Starting tonight. Starting with one bedroom."

He saw her face flush, saw the smile remain, saw her sit forward. "*This* newlywed, the one with the greying hair, is going straight to sleep. In her own bed. I'm terribly tired

245

after that long train ride." She paused, and rose. She walked to him, stood near him though beyond his reach, and said unsteadily, "Let's be patient with each other, dear Adam. Both of us have spent these past years nursing resentments. I want every last one of mine to evaporate, and I'm going to try—I mean that—but I need to move carefully. We both do, but the—bedroom isn't the place to begin. Not yet." She raised his hand, fondly kissed it. "I lied to you in Scottsdale. I said I have no love for you. It was an absurd lie. Do be patient, and I'll prove to you how absurd it was."

Adam sat alone for many minutes in the dimly lighted library, savouring the sweetness of her, feeling the stirrings of a newlywed, reminding himself that he was sixty, conscious of lust, conscious of Eugenia's gentle admonition, understanding her wishes, prepared to indeed move slowly, cursing the wasted years, happy at last, happy with himself, happy that order had been restored to his life. He yawned, scratched his chest contentedly, and mounted the stairs. He saw a light under her door. He lingered there for a moment, and then knocked. She was sitting up in bed, with a book that looked suspiciously like a Bible.

"Let me come in with you," he said hoarsely.

Sharply: "No. I was as clear as I could be downstairs. I'm not—"

He switched off the light. She struggled and whimpered that he was an animal, that her sister was in the next room and was a light sleeper. Her fist punched at him, fiercely at first, and then gradually her fists opened, and her lips parted and her thighs parted. "Ah yes, I do love you, my darling, ah yes, yes . . ." she breathed, and he made love to Eugenia, to Eugenia Scofield, to his only beloved. They clung to each other and Adam repeated her name, the sound of it heightening his passion, repeated *Eugenia, Eugenia, Eugenia*, his wife, his anchor as the whores could never begin to be. They lay in the dark afterwards, still clinging, and she asked if he remembered the Woodmont.

"Our wedding night hotel?"

"Mm. I remember it as if it were yesterday."

246

"It was yesterday. It's now."

"Do you know what I remember? It's so vivid to me. I adored you, I worshipped you. And I was petrified because my mother talked to me before the wedding about the—'bridal experience,' she called it, and she said, 'If you hold your breath and think about something else, the pain won't be as excruciating.' She wouldn't say that word, 'sex.' I remember she spelled it: s-e-x. She said that men—even good men; she liked you, Adam, even though she mightn't have shown it—could be the wisest, most sensitive, most considerate people on earth, but they all turned into jungle beasts when it came to s-e-x. I was so positive you were going to be a jungle beast."

"Wasn't I?"

"Not at all. Ever. You saw how frightened I was that night at the Woodmont, how nervous and unsure, and you said that if I preferred, would could postpone the—ah—"

"S-e-x?"

Eugenia giggled like a child. "That's what I hold on to, Adam, your goodness that night. Every time I've felt bitter thoughts towards you, I've stopped later and remembered how kind you were that night."

She kissed him, full on the mouth, something she never had done. "Thank you, my precious husband," she whispered. "For being my precious husband."

Not quite a month after Harmon entered Stormbridge, Adam and Eugenia received a letter from the school's headmaster, Walker C. Oates. "Personal letters to the parents of our students, so soon after the beginning of a first term, are the exception rather than the rule at Stormbridge," it read. "Your son has shown himself to be so exceptional, however, and so quickly, that I take great personal pleasure in directing this note to you both. Every one of Harmon's instructors has informed me that he is a diligent and challenging student with superior intelligence, that he has made a rapid adjustment to his curriculum and classmates, and that, while working within the frame of our requirements, he is a joy to teach. He demonstrates individual initiative and a sincere desire to learn. We at Stormbridge wish to thank you for having provided our school with an outstanding young man who is certain to make his mark in any field of endeavour he selects."

"I wouldn't take ten billion dollars for this letter!" Adam jubilated, and dictated a letter of gratitude to Oates, and enclosed a cheque made out to Stormbridge in the amount of five thousand dollars, and concluded the letter with, "Please know, sir, that your taking the time in your surely busy schedule to write such a kind and thoughtful message about our son has made Mrs Scofield and me profoundly happy. If I may be of any additional material benefit to your excellent school, do not hesitate to advise."

He received three more letters from Walker C. Oates. The first arrived within days, acknowledging his philanthropic support that would go into the school's scholarship fund, requesting permission to call it the Adam Hurd Scofield Scholarship Fund, repeating praise for Harmon, and extending assurances that further contributions would certainly not be rejected. Adam signed another cheque for two thousand dollars.

Winter struck New York with whipping vengeance in November, a week before Harmon was due home for Thanksgiving. "Cornelia is convinced she won't be able to stand the winter cold," Eugenia said. "She wants to go back to Scottsdale, or to Florida."

"May I help her pack?"

"She doesn't want to go alone."

Warily: "Which means . . . ?"

"I'm the only one she has, Adam. She needs me. She's getting on in years."

"No. I know what can of peas you're opening. No."

"You're being unreasonable, aren't you? It would be only through the winter."

"*I'm* unreasonable? We have a partnership here. We have a son—"

"—who's doing beautifully at school."

248

"*We're* doing beautifully, you and I. I don't want to hear any more about it. If your sister has to have a companion, I'll gladly buy her a gross of them, but you and I have just started to learn how to be married to each other, and I won't tolerate this only-through-the-winter claptrap."

Oates' next letter arrived on the day Harmon arrived home. It was couched in cordiality but contained a deadly serious charge: a boy's briefcase had been missing for a period of days, had been reported stolen, and was found under Harmon's bed. No disciplinary action was taken because Harmon, confronted by a student court, had sworn total innocence and proof of guilt could not be produced. Adam was being apprised of the incident, Oates's insulting letter went on, purely to maintain Stormbridge's consistent policy of keeping parents informed of important episodes in their son's school lives. The inference was clear, nonetheless: Harmon Scofield, the exceptional son of a generous contributor to Stormbridge, was being called a common thief.

"It's good that I got to this piece of filth before your mother did," Adam said. "Who planted that briefcase beneath your bed?"

"All I have is a suspicion, Father. I can't prove it, but I'd bet anything Chang did it himself, planted his own crummy briefcase in my room out of spite. A couple of weeks ago I took a math test he was going to take the next day. He wanted to pay me to give him the questions and answers in advance, and I said no."

"Chang? What's that, a Chinaman?" Harmon nodded. Incredulous, Adam asked, "They raked *you* over the coals because of a *Chi*naman? I'll straighten this out. I'll get that Oates' ass down here today and see that you get a personal apology."

"No, that would just make it worse. I'm the one who has to go back there."

"This is a matter of honour."

"Please, let's just forget the whole thing. If the story got out that I had my father fighting my battles for me—well, you know what it's like with a bunch of guys."

"Are you sure this is what you want?"

"I'm sure. Yes, sir."

Weighing doubts, Adam said, "Very well, then, it's dropped for the time being. But your word against a Chink's! Amazing!" Then: "Your mother ought to be home from that hallelujah church meeting of hers any minute now. Mum's the word, scout. Your mother would worry. Your aunt—my God, your aunt would have a litter of kittens and ducks!"

They laughed together, mock-punched each other, and raced each other down the stairs.

At the beginning of December, Adam watched Hatcher and the butler carry Eugenia's luggage out of the town house to the car. Deeply hurt, determined she would not have the satisfaction of seeing and hearing him blow up, he said, "I'd appreciate the answer to a single question, if your sister out there allows you and me to have half a second alone. If your sister and I somehow happened to both get sick on the same day, which one of us would you run to to take care of?"

"Don't put me through that again, Adam. The train leaves in exactly one hour. You and Harmon will come to Hallandale for Christmas and we'll all—"

"All right, go. The world would stop if you missed your goddamn train. Don't let your sweet sister out of your sight for an instant or she'll turn to dust. Well, what are you standing there for, what are you waiting for? Your sister hasn't had you at her beck and call for a whole minute. You'd better hurry, you mustn't upset the poor finger-snapping bitch."

"Adam, the servants can hear . . ."

"Then clear the hell out of *my* sight! This is the last time you trick me, this is the last time *any*one tricks me!" he shouted.

Walker C. Oates' final letter, received shortly before the

250

beginning of the Christmas vacation, notified Adam that Harmon, who had exhibited such a promising start at Stormbridge, had been caught stealing money from the locker of another student, had offered to bribe that student into not pressing charges, and was herewith expelled. Expelled with the school administration's regret, in view of the boy's undeniable potentialities and in view of Adam Scofield's generosities to the school, but expelled. To reinstate him, Oates's moralistic tract lumbered on, would be to condone inexcusable conduct.

"They got it all cockeyed because they have it in for me," Harmon explained to Adam. "All I was doing was fooling around. The 'money' was exactly one dollar. One measly dollar. Why would I have to steal *any*thing, let alone one measly dollar?"

"Would you like to go back to that place?"

"No *sir*. Never. Leaving that jail is just about the best thing that's ever happened to me."

"Why?"

"Because that's what it is: a jail. You've been paying to keep me in jail. They don't care about me, all they care about is my toeing the line— 'Do this at nine, do that at nine-oh-one.' They give you demerits if your socks are crooked."

Adam, who himself had never mastered the knack of riding conveyor belts, searched his son's face and finally nodded. "Then you're well out of that cookie cutter nonsense. We'll look into something else, something more suitable. In the meantime, we'll come up with something better-sounding than 'expelled' to your mother. Right?"

The boy—the young man—smiled. "Right, sir."

"Speaking of your mother, Christmas is around the corner. Are you dying to spend the holidays with her and your gorgeous aunt, or would you settle for, say Parnassus? Or our digs in Bermuda, or maybe Mech-hee-ho? The two of us?"

"Guess."

Adam winked. "The two musketeers. Partners. Let's play

251

a joke on your mother. Let's let her wonder where we are. How does Mexico City sound to you? I read in some newspaper—not one of ours, naturally—that you have to beat the pretty young *chiquitas* off with clubs there."

A Company limousine met the private plane in Mexico City and delivered them to the Reforma in midafternoon of Christmas Eve. They swam before dinner and Adam saw his handsome son covertly ogling the young, rounded *chiquitas*, nudged him, and teased, "Are you interested in learning Spanish?"

"*Sí, sí, señor!*" Harmon kidded back and scissored away into the water.

In the bathhouse, alone, Adam picked up the telephone receiver, asked for the Company's local man, and ordered that an English-speaking woman tap at the suite's door at precisely eight o'clock. "Roughly thirty years old," he directed. "Old enough to be sensitive but young enough to be attractive. She's to be clean as gold or you'll wake up tomorrow morning without ears."

At a quarter of an hour before eight that evening, as they finished their meal in the central dining room, Adam said to Harmon, "I have an appointment. I'll be away for a few hours. You hop upstairs and wait for eight o'clock."

"Why eight o'clock?"

"That's when someone will bring you your old man's Christmas present."

Adam strolled the evening streets of Mexico City, and drank awful coffee in its side street cafés, vividly reliving his own father's frightening birthday gift to him when he was roughly Harmon's age, a trip to a wondrously overpowering woman named Celeste. At ten o'clock, he unlocked the suite's front door. Harmon was in bed, though awake. "How was your present?" Adam asked.

The boy was embarrassed.

"Bad?" Adam pressed. "No good?"

"She was nice."

"Was 'it' nice? What happened?" Adam asked eagerly. "Tell me. Did she talk much? Did she tell you her name?

What did she say, what did she do? Tell me!"

After Stormbridge, Harmon was expelled from Bowden Academy in Pennsylvania and then from Harkins in New Jersey. The letters to Adam were remarkably similar: that Harmon had started like a skyrocket, an alert student with an outgoing, winning personality, but he seemed unable or unwilling to accept that fundamental rules were meant for him as well as for the other boys; that his irresponsible attitudes were proving a disruptive, even destructive, influence on some of his classmates. An insolent paragraph in the Harkins letter suggested that Harmon had mental problems—the phrase was "certain indications of emotional instability"—and recommended that professional help be sought.

"The *money*!" Adam seethed. "I feed them a fortune and they have the gall to write insulting trash like this!"

Harmon, seventeen and splendid to look at, grinned. "When do I get put in a padded cell, Father?"

"*I'll* be a candidate for a padded cell unless we can figure in a hurry what to tell your mother. We're running out of good stories." Then Adam grinned, too. "Oh, well, we'll pull something out of the hat. We always do." He lightly punched his son's arm and sternly said, "But you know you're going to have to buckle down one of these days soon, Commodore, even if it means playing along with these overstuffed chairs that call themselves schoolmasters."

"I know. I'm not worried, Father, and you shouldn't be."

"Where'd you get the idea I'm worried, big shot? Worried about you?" Impulsively he said, "Come on, what do you say we take a trip somewhere? I'll knock off work for a couple of weeks, a month, whatever—I think the boss'll give me the time off—and we'll just hobo around and enjoy ourselves. How does that sound, Commodore?"

"If I have to," Harmon teased, obviously thrilled.

In Quebec, nine perfect days after they had begun their hobo vacation in Adam's plane, a tobacconist shop's clerk screamed for police, claimed she had seen Harmon stuff a

253

cigarette lighter into his pocket, and demanded he be arrested. Adam rushed to the police station the instant he received the message, impatiently listened to the female clerk's preposterous accusation, impatiently listened to the understandably upset Harmon deny the charge, and thundered at the desk sergeant, "That young man is to be released at once, with apologies from you and this insane woman, or I'll bring a false-arrest charge you can be sure no one here is ever going to forget!"

The demented woman clerk kept gibbering in French, as passionately as if she had witnessed an attempted robbery of the Hope Diamond. It was finally settled, after a grotesquely comic-opera half hour of translating French into English and English into French, when Adam, aware of how pleased the whole absurd incident would make the Company's competition, soothed the woman's sense of moral outrage by slipping her a twenty-dollar bill. Both he and Harmon were silent on the way back to the hotel. There, Adam said, "The truth."

"I was going to pay for it, Father."

Adam winced from the pain. Quietly he asked, "Why? Why does my son have to steal?"

The answer, spoken as quietly, was incredible. "I don't know."

"Jesus," Adam breathed. A horrible silence, and then: "Talk to me. Tell me what that means."

"I—can't."

"You'd goddamn well better try. What is this you-don't-know, you-can't? I'm your father. We've always talked straight from the shoulder with each other. All I want out of life is to make a good and strong man of you, a man of character. Real men don't say, 'I don't know, I can't.'"

The boy nodded.

Adam, thoroughly uncomfortable in this new, foreign role, asked, "What was the price of that cigarette lighter?"

"I don't kn— I'm not sure. About fifty cents. I know I shouldn't've done it."

"Suppose we put an agreement smack on the barrelhead, here and now. The next time you're in the market for anything that can be bought, suppose you remember that dandy time you spent with those cops gawking at you. Because the next time your old man just might be out to lunch."

The boy nodded.

Relieved, Adam nodded in return. "All right, case closed. The air's cleared, and maybe it was all for the best. If we have to make mistakes, we ought to get them to teach us something." His arm wrapped around his son, his son who *surely* felt wretched. "Let's go put on the feedbag. There's a waitress in the restaurant downstairs who has frogs' legs and pigs' knuckles—"

Harmon said, imitating Adam, " '—And boy oh boy, is she ever a mess!' "

"Did I tell you that joke before?"

"Exactly sixty-seven times."

"Well, you have to admit it's still a belly-buster."

In the summer months preceding Harmon's eighteenth birthday, the good schools willing to accept him as a student in September became fewer and fewer. "Your exceedingly generous endowment offer is noted and most tempting," Catlett Academy wrote Adam. "We would naturally welcome it, but we must, reluctantly, reject Harmon's application to enter Catlett. [Signed] R. J. Rolfe, Dean of Admissions."

Adam telephoned R. J. Rolfe and demanded, "What the hell is this about?"

"To the point, Mr Scofield, we don't believe your son is Catlett material. His dismissal from three schools in under four years is something less than an impressive track record. Catlett's scholastic and character requirements are quite high and—"

"I know about Catlett's requirements. I also know it's crying for money."

"Indeed it is, as are most private schools in the country."

"Then you'll excuse me, Mr Ralph—"

"Rolfe."

"—but you're a goddamn fool. I'm offering to save your business from going down the drain, with the guarantee of the kind of annual donation I'm sure you don't receive many days in the week. *Track* record? What've you heard, that my boy cuts up a bit now and again? That *track* record talk is childish! Harmon Scofield is going to be a giant!"

"Perhaps we have different interpretations of 'cutting up,' sir. I have reports on him from the other schools here in front of me: 'Repeatedly offered sums of money to others to take his final examinations under his name.' 'Attempted to bribe an instructor into giving him an A in a course he was failing.' 'Stoke money.' 'Attempted a homosexual act with—' "

"No! Stop that! I won't sit here and listen to any more of those lists of lies! What did you say—'homosexual'? Your head's sick, Mr Ralph, the whole lot of you belong in an insane asylum. You can take your hifalutin school and stuff it in your hat. You haven't heard the last of this, Ralph, Rolfe, whatever your name is! I recommend you spend less time blackening the name and trying to block the future of a prince—a *prince*!—and more time reading the Scofield press. Before we're done with you, your cow's-ass school will bankrupt itself out of existence!"

Adam slammed the receiver down on its cradle, and breathed heavily for a very long while.

Lies.

The boy had admitted snatching a couple of dollars out of that school cafeteria's cash register. A prank. With more money than any youngster would begin to know what to do with, he had grabbed a dollar or two as a prank, a—

Attempted a homosexual act . . .

No.

No. No no no no no no.

Not Harmon. Not my son.

You vicious, mother-milking sons of bitches, I'll ruin you, all of you. This is my whole world you're trying to destroy

256

with those vicious, filthy rumours, those obscene lies. I won't let you get away with it, any of you.

At Adam's diplomatic urging, Harmon went to California that summer, promising to gather himself together, find himself, decide exactly where he was headed, and come back with his sleeves rolled up. In August, Adam learned that the boy had got drunk with some floozie there and crashed his car. Harmon did come back, with the floozie, a pregnant floozie, with the adamant declaration that he was going to marry her. Adam struck him and cried, "Get out of our sight and our life, you foundling-home garbage collector, and take your scabby whore with you! This is the day you'll regret till the minute you die, and I hope that's soon!"

Adam Scofield, sixty-three years old, stared through his office window.

Is this all there is? he asked. *Is this all I have? After everything, is this all I have?*

FIFTEEN

MARY FLED from Dr Marco's office to her car and told Stefan to start driving, anywhere. She huddled in the back seat, struggling with the images of Carole in a dozen perils, and at last she suppressed them and sat up straight, in control.

She phoned Joe for developments.

"No, nothing yet," Joe said, and offhandedly mentioned, within his catalogue of non-developments, a call from Howard Bradway. He gave Mary the essence of the call, criticizing it as patently self-serving, and she interrupted him to ask if anything more had been said about Bill. "He's at home today, according to Howard, and sorry to hear about Carole," Joe acknowledged. "Why?"

"I'm not sure. Let's you and I keep in touch," Mary said, and hung up.

"Where now, Miss Scofield?" the chauffeur asked.

"Find out, unless you know yourself, where the nearest private airport is."

Stefan picked up his own telephone and soon had the answer. "It's called Ackerman's. It's six, eight miles north of here. I wrote down the number. Do you want me to call?"

"No, just drive there. I'll call."

The breezy voice of a man who identified himself as Hap Ackerman declared, "Yes, ma'am, we can fly you to Washington, but not till tomorrow morning."

"Why is that?"

"I'm short of help."

"Are you a licensed pilot?"

A booming, irritating guffaw. "I hope to tell you, ma'am."

"Then I'll appreciate your taking me to Washington, and waiting for me for a matter of hours, and then flying me back."

"Who *is* this?"

"The name is Scofield. I should be there within fifteen minutes. Kindly be ready to go."

"That's not a whole lot of notice, is it? It's only right to advise you, ma'am, that this'll run you into some fairly sizeable money—I'd have to close up—and my policy is to collect in advance."

"Fifteen minutes," she repeated. "Oh, one moment: what's the name of the airport where we'll land?"

"It'd be Gowan. How many'll there be of you?"

"Myself." She replaced the receiver and directed Stefan to contact someone at the Company in Washington to arrange for a car and driver to meet her at Gowan.

Hap Ackerman, a blocky giant with vermilion cheeks, greeted her with palsy-walsy effusiveness as she came out of the limousine. "Hey, sure, I reca'nize you, honey. I know the Scofield folks," he said loudly. "Talk about small worlds! My father, he's gone now thirty-one years, he used to fly Adam Scofield, back in—wait a minute, I have a snapshot somewheres of the two of them togeth—"

"Mr Ackerman," Mary said coldly, "is the plane quite ready?"

"Yes, ma'am."

She produced a cheque she had signed in the car. "Tell me the amount, and we can get going."

"Well, now, let's figure this out. I want to be more than fair and square with you, because I hope we can do a heap of business in the future. Right?"

She took a pen from his shirt pocket, wrote the sum of one thousand dollars on the cheque, handed it to him, and said, "You'll do three things for this money, Mr Ackerman. You'll deliver me to Gowan, you'll return me, and under no circumstances, unless it's absolutely necessary, will there be any conversation between us."

The plane was an eight-passenger Cessna, and Hap Ackerman lifted it into the air with tranquil grace. She had never been to Bill's home in Georgetown, but she knew the address. This impulse could be the fool's errand of the age, she thought. Bill might be out, and that stainless-steel wife

259

of his mightn't know where he is, might know and refuse to tell her.

What do I really expect to find there?

Carole?

Cavorting?

The image hit her like a stab of migraine. *Silly*, she thought, banishing it; *silly beyond words. Whatever stupid thing or things Bill might have done, however angry he might be, he wouldn't hurt Carole. Nor me, not that way.*

And yet who *was* Bill? The fine, good man she had loved, who had loved her? The man with inner conflicts so sick that he almost sent up smoke signals for police to arrest him, for the world to find him out?

Could anyone change so much, so drastically, so hurtfully?

Hadn't they *loved* each other . . .?

I knew of the whispers: that my motives for pressing Bill Bradway's nomination and election to the Senate had bedroom overtones.

The whispers, certainly at the outset, were absurd, if for no other reason than that I was then recently divorced from Owen Enright, still smarting, numb to the prospect of another close involvement with a man, any man.

I guess I had expected that the final separation, after several years of preparing for it in a series of subconscious small claims courts, would reward me with a sense of well-being. It did bring a feeling of relief to have the ankle chains off, to at last be free of someone so lavish with his weaknesses as Owen. It also brought a feeling of failure, my own failure. The first two marriage strikeouts—the teen-age rebound elopement with Tommy Moran, the abrasive pleasure-packing mismatch with Gil Stafford—could be blamed on being still very young and easily receptive to the movies' guarantee that love solves everything from insecurity to sunburn. But the third marriage ended when I was nearly thirty-seven years old, scarcely an age to take Valentine card poetry as gospel. And it ended because

Owen's inadequacies had become an unendurable drag.

Towards the finale, the language in our mostly dispassionate-sounding arguments belonged at a social workers' conference.

HE: You've castrated me."

I: "No man is castrated unless he wants to be."

It got funny. It got tiresome. It got obscene. Then it was done, and he was gone for good. I felt no love for him, no hate, yet no twinges of satisfaction or sadness, either. Nothing but the weight of being weightless. Nothing but the resolve to work at something I *was* good at—the Company —and to stay clear of anything hinting at entangling alliances.

Bill Bradway caught my attention because everything I was able to learn about him indicated he was the kind of person who belonged in elective government, particularly at a time when the country was becoming increasingly suspicious of government; young enough to regard honour as honour and corruption as corruption, wise but not a wise guy, insights keen, proposed programmes ambitious yet enactable with pointed leadership—a politician who took the trouble to find out what was troubling "the plain people" as he called them without once appearing patronizing.

Yes, okay, my investment in helping him get elected was sparked partially by vanity, too: I enjoyed the fantasy, and then the partial reality, of playing puppeteer.

But that was all. We were together perhaps a dozen times, from those preliminary meetings till the night of the victory, before I asked if I might call him by his first name. I liked him, but I let him know by my reserve that the only strings attached to our relationship were that he knock 'em dead on Capitol Hill. He called me Miss Scofield, when he addressed me at all. The fact that he was attractive wasn't lost on me. Nor, on the few occasions when I saw him and his pretty and vapid wife smiling at each other, could I

261

avoid the strong hunch that theirs wasn't entirely the story-book union the public was starting to eat up.

He wasn't interested in me as a woman. I wasn't interested in him as a lover. When we spoke, I was as seductive as a pair of orthopaedic shoes. Which was precisely how I felt, and wished to feel.

Until that December, Christmas Eve . . .

I was in Washington that weekend, alone, using the John Adams Suite of the Washington Scofield as a base, to be on *Meet the Press* the next day, a Sunday, and then to share Christmas dinner with Angie and Neal Pryor in Arlington. Earlier in the month, on Carole's twelfth birthday, I'd promised her we would spend her Christmas vacation from school together, just the two of us, anywhere she chose, at Sandys Parish or on a loafers' cruise or at the New York town house, or maybe at Parnassus, where we could sleep till noon, all telephones turned off, and get up and bake pancakes and make faces at the zoo monkeys and, if there was lots and lots of old-fashioned snow, have an old-fashioned snowball fight. When she was little, Owen and I had taken her to Parnassus often. She'd loved the monkeys, and the ponies, and tea parties in the playhouse that Gramp had built for me when *I* was little. Now she was twelve, maybe too old for that.

"Being anywhere with you will be best of all," Carole had said with hushed but contagious excitement. I was in Toronto on December 21 when I suddenly remembered the promise. I phoned Carole and apologized for not having called earlier, but if she would forgive me for being so busy we could still get together for a little while. She said she understood how terribly busy I was, and then she dissolved into confusion: when she hadn't heard from me, she said, she had assumed the plan was off, so she had accepted an invitation to go skiing at Stowe with Gloria Vail and Gloria's parents. On the other hand, though, she was sure she could still call the Vails and beg off if I really wanted . . .

I broke into the babble to assure her that it was okay,

that she should go on to Stowe. I tried to keep the disappointment out of my voice, a disappointment that was my own creation. We would have other times together, I said.

She wouldn't quite let go. "But I really would rath—"

"It's all right, Carole. Don't think a thing about it. Have fun skiing. I probably should go to Washington then, anyway."

"I—Well, you have a good Christmas, Mother." Her voice sounded flat. "I understand. Maybe I'll see you in March, when I have mid-term holidays."

"Yes, fine," I said, hearing the coolness and hating it. I had never been able to have the kind of easy, relaxed, loving relationship with Carole that the ladies' magazines picture for mothers and daughters. I hated that, too.

I got to the Washington suite at midafternoon on the twenty-fourth. I instructed the front desk that I was to be disturbed only for emergencies, and set to work on a sea of postponed correspondence that simply couldn't be neglected any longer. My secretary, Nancy Morrill, had been ill for nearly a month. The interim secretary was proving hopeless. I hadn't yet met, much less hired, Liz Hale.

The idea of holing up with a Dictaphone had seemed absolutely right. It went badly. I was interrupted continually by kaleidoscopes of Carole, of guilt, of emptiness, of gaping emptiness. By eight o'clock, the labyrinthine suite was suffocating me. The urge became consuming to leave, to fly to Vermont and surprise Carole. Highly impractical; the Pryors would understand my begging off, but *Meet the Press* wouldn't. Surprising Carole . . . what did I expect her to do, alter her holiday and minister to me because I'd come down with a critical case of the guilts and the lonelies? I could ring Angie and Neal Pryor. If they were at home, they'd welcome me to come over. I didn't want to see them, or anyone else in or near Washington. I tried to rivet myself back to work. I tried to read. Three in-room movies were available; none interested me. I opened the Company's Washington paper, the *Clarion*, to the theatre page; nothing there was appealing, either. I glanced at the television listings. Again, nothing.

Until I spotted Senator-elect William Bradway's name. He was on *Names in News* on WETA television at eight o'clock, debating Erik Waldrop, who represented the National Rifle Association. The topic: *Do Guns or People Kill People?* The live broadcast was half over when I switched it on. I sat and watched, sorry to have missed so much. Waldrop, slick and urbane, was explaining why the Bradway proposal to restrict the inherent American right to purchase and own guns would serve only the enemies of the United States. Bradway, grim and passionate, was in effect calling Waldrop a paid lackey—"not so much a hired hand as a hired gun"—for the profits-swollen NRA, who would discover a way to extol the benefits of botulism if it could be packaged and turn a dollar.

I found WETA's number in the directory, phoned there, and asked that a message be got to Senator Bradway, once he was off the air, to please ring me here, at his convenience. Then I phoned the hotel's switchboard and said I would accept one call, from Senator Bradway. The broadcast finished at 8:59, and I began to regret my call. He would return it, *if* he did, with the resentment of a plantation hand commanded to shuffle. His wife, a garland of pompoms with mildly buck teeth, would very likely be at his elbow. The call was senseless.

My phone rang at ten minutes past nine. He was pleasant.

"You've persuaded me not to pack a rod, Senator," I said.

"Every little bit helps, Miss Scofield."

I invited him and Mrs Bradway to come by for a drink. "That would be nice," he said, "but Virginia and the children are in Akron right now with her parents."

"Do you have other plans for the evening?"

"Yes. A satchel full of work."

"Where are you staying?"

"At the Mayflower, till our apartment is ready."

"The Mayflower? Who's paying for that?"

264

"Not the federal government."

"But there are *grosses* of accommodations here at the Scofield, free of charge. And you're paying for your quarters? Who's responsible for that oversight?"

"I am. The man who never relished being called the senator from Scofield. The Mayflower suits me, and my take-home pay, just fine."

"Have you eaten?"

"More or less. A hamburger. Why?"

"How about a simple steak and salad? Here. And then you can run on."

"I might just do that."

I wore a lavender dressing gown, neither maiden-auntish nor flimsy-clinging, and he looked tired about the eyes, his good shoulders slumped, his grin genuine but weary, and I indicated the sitting room's bar and asked, "Would you like to pour yourself a drink while I phone down for the steak?"

"I'll tell you what I'd like more than anything. A shower. I've been on the run since daybreak and I'm gritty from the mines. Is that an overly freaky request?"

"Not at all. We get requests like it here all the time. I'll have a drink ready for you. What's your p'ison?"

"Anything. Scotch. One ice cube, no water."

"How do you like your steak done?"

"Overburnt. To a crisp."

"Vegetables? Potato?"

"Just a green salad, with a gallon of oil and vinegar."

"You're barbaric."

"And you're a cheeky waitress."

I heard the shower taps as I called room service. I fixed a scotch-rocks for him, the same for myself. I fantasized his coming back, wrapped in a towel or nothing. The fantasies were getting a bit lurid when he did come back, fully dressed. Straighter, younger than ten minutes before, an extremely attractive man, smiling, probably no more comfortable with me than I was with him. "That shower hit the spot," he said. "Right this minute, there's not a cleaner politician in the whole of the District of Columbia." He thanked me for the scotch—how tall he was!—sipped it, and said as he flopped in the leather chair, "You not only don't pack a rod, you pour a powerful drink."

"My talents are limitless." I sat on the zebra couch and raised my own glass in a toast. "To an obviously exhausted public servant." He laughed. "Was that Erik Waldrop as loathsome in person as he came across here?" I asked.

"As a matter of fact, we had a brief conversation after the show and he was a very likable fella. It's funny, but I've found that when you catch the bad guys off guard—and I do consider Waldrop to be a bad guy—they tend to be a lot more likable than the good guys." He mentioned three senators. "They have colossal credentials, they're completely incorruptible, they're public servants in the best sense of the term—and on a personal level, they're petty, spiteful, back-stabbing little kids. That was my first rude awakening when I came to town—to learn that genuine heroes can have pockmarks."

"What was your second?"

"My second was that I've suddenly realized I broke the speed limit emptying this glass."

I took the glass to refill it at the bar. "My third awakening isn't rude, but it's an awakening," he said. "You as my barmaid. Anyone's barmaid."

"It's legal."

"And surprising."

"What's surprising? That I know how to pour liquid into a glass? I do have a college degree."

And he had a ripe, melodious laugh. "I figured you to be someone who snaps your fingers a lot. Who has your hair brushed for you. Who declares World War III while Butterfly peels you a grape."

"Any other awakenings?" I asked, bringing him the fresh drink.

"Um. One, that I'm going to apologize for. I've decided I don't want to eat, after all. Will they be mad downstairs if we cancel the meal?"

I cancelled the meal.

I was his barmaid, happily his barmaid, over the next hour. He drank rather steadily but only got amiably high, not drunk. The liquor relaxed him, and his growing ease began to relax me as well. We talked casual talk, subdued talk, about the gun lobby and health care and beagles' personalities as opposed to schnauzers' personalities, about Diderot and the giggles of small daughters, about China and —everything. Almost too abruptly, he peered at his watch. "Whup," he grunted. "Rhode Island votes that it waxes late."

The desperation banished from my voice: "How about an omelet for the road?"

"Nope. Thank you kindly, but I have to head back to the Mayflower and save the Republic." At the door, he stood barely inches away from me. He didn't touch me. "In some primitive tribes," he said, "one person was able to say to another person, 'I'm fond of you, I suspect you're fond of me, I would love to express how fond and I think you'd like to express how fond, but the inhibitions are overwhelming to us both.' What was special about those primitive tribes was that they could convey that mouthful in one word."

"What was the one word?"

He shrugged. "I flunked anthropology."

I shocked myself, and surely I shocked him, by asking, "Would you like to sleep here?"

He blinked. "In the guest room?"

". . . Whatever."

A beat. "No."

I nodded.

"No, meaning yes. No, meaning . . ."

"Meaning?"

"Meaning no."

I nodded again, the chin up-smile nod. "Take care, Senator."

"You, too. Thanks for the evening, from the bottom of my liver."

I went to bed and, eventually, to sleep.

My phone rang. "Are you sound asleep?"

"Time zit?"

"Two-ah-seventeen."

"Two seventeen." I came sharply awake. "Did you forget something?"

"Yes. It appears I forgot my satchel. It also appears I forgot to stay there. I've been walking up and down in this room since I got here. I can be there in half an hour."

"Half of that. Half of half an hour."

"Half."

It began.

It was to have ended on Christmas morning, a sweetly uncomplicated incident; to have ended with his going about his business, with my going to NBC and then to the Pryors'. Before he left, on that clear Sunday morning, our conversation was roadshow Noël Coward and Cole Porter. We agreed that no one had been or would be hurt, that it was just one of those things, to be savoured but not hoarded.

I finished *Meet the Press*, and phoned him at the Mayflower. "Can you get out of that dinner?" he asked.

"Yes," I said, and within an hour we were in each other's arms again.

I stayed in Washington for nearly a week, finding excuses to avoid the return to New York, until his family was due back from Ohio. We were careful not to be seen together, yet there was no corridor-skulking; there was delicious talk and delicious closeness, and an understanding between us that there would be a joint New Year's resolution to break clean at the bell. He was married—not blissfully, but married. He was beginning a new phase of his career, with a fishbowl for an address. Scandal, even whispers, could shoot him down early.

Positively. Plenty of sober, realistic nods before and after lovemaking. The first clean break lasted for two weeks, the next for almost that. We devised legitimate occasions to be in the same cities in public—an *Outlook* invitation to interview him in New York, some reason for me to be in Washington, or wherever he happened to be at a given time, to observe this newsmaking new United States senator who spoke out and battled the good battles—so that we could be together later in private. All of it was wonderful. All of it was potentially dangerous, though the danger revolved only around our being caught, not in our seriously falling in love. We both were too much the souls of practicality to do an idiotic thing like that.

Famous last words. By February, scarcely two months after the night in the John Adams Suite, my one vivid fantasy that outdistanced all others was of Bill declaring, "*I've talked with Virginia about a divorce. She promises she won't stand in our way.*"

I kept it to myself, of course. Occasionally from myself, as well. It was absurd. Of course.

In March, quite seriously in love, I used Carole's spring holiday from school as an excuse to arrange a long weekend party at Parnassus; I invited Joe Greenwood and Joe's wife and a dozen other guests along with Bill, a safety-in-numbers ploy. Bill arrived with his cheery dimwit wife and their two small children. I fixed my brightest hostess smile, and greeted his wife as though she were welcome, caught the amusedly helpless glance he threw at me that warned, *No caucusing this weekend. Sorry*, and threw him a glance of my own that notified, *We'll see about that*. I expected him, the first moment we were alone, to apologize or at least explain. He didn't. Instead, he kissed me. He kissed me with a chastity that bordered on insult.

I worked to be a jolly good hostess at the outset of that weekend, nonetheless, keeping the party ball rolling, chit-chatting it up, seeing that the servants stayed on their toes and that the guests were having fun, neither glueing myself to Bill nor ostentatiously avoiding him, watching him move effortlessly and confidently into and out of random conversations, watching him swim in the main house's indoor pool with his kids, who obviously adored him and whom he obviously adored, watching him ignore me, taking care to ensure that no one, including his drippy wife, would guess

I had me a fella, a very special fella.

I watched him, and my nonchalance must have been transparent, at least to Joe Greenwood, whose single eye saw more than Argus ever could. "There's a rumour making the rounds that we're about to reactivate *Bombshell*," Joe teased. *Bombshell* was the Company's scandal magazine, an execrable monthly I'd inherited and closed up early on. "We'll naturally want a cover picture of Wonder Woman and Captain Marvel in tingling embrace, but we ought to have a release. Speaking of release, how *is* the Captain in the hay?"

I said to Joe, surely the only person alive I would allow to be so impertinent, "Go tell *Bombshell*, you filthy old man, that the Captain and I are just good friends."

"You betchum."

Quietly I asked, "Does it show all that much, *Yussele?*"

"Believe it, lady. And while you're at it, believe an ancient Himalayan proverb that begins, 'Them as plays with fire . . . '"

"Okay," I said, and nodded. "You've made your point. The lady herewith cuts bait."

That was my first lie. It tasted divine.

Bill was at ease that weekend, even with Carole—a feat, of sorts, that gave me a fleeting twinge of jealousy

No, not jealousy, really. Envy, a bland case of it. I had tried periodically, from the time when she was very little, to connect with her, to reach her, to have her reach me. She had always been something of a puzzle to me: she was my flesh, yet we were never truly comfortable with each other, almost never spontaneous. When he was still functioning, Owen had been an affectionate, frequently exuberant father; among my compendium of resentments against Owen Enright was that he had only one genuine talent, fatherhood, and he blew even that. I wished Carole well. There were times when I tried to tell her so. She was a tractable child. Passive, really, often so irritatingly passive I had all I could do to hold myself back from screaming, "Can't you have an opinion

270

about *any*thing? When I was your age I had the world by the ears! Can't you be *any*thing like me?"

Bill, though, apparently discerned depths to her that had escaped me. Maybe it was simply because he couldn't turn off the politician valves, but he was terribly nice to Carole, drawing her out, asking her about her interests, asking with evidently genuine curiosity and without condescension. She was painfully timid, but I saw her warm to his attentiveness. On Saturday afternoon they took an hour's walk together over the grounds, just the two of them, leaving me to wonder what on earth he could find to discuss.

"She's sharp as a tack, that one," he said to me later. We were on one of the veiled south terraces, alone. "It's eerie, how perceptive she is for twelve. Did you know she's translating Verlaine?"

I suspected I was being tested. "Why wouldn't I know?"

He shrugged. "I gather you two don't go in much for communicating with each other."

"Oh? And what other criminal acts did she accuse me of?"

He frowned at me, as he should have. "Hey, now, what's with this paranoia stuff?"

Shift the course of this fast, I thought; *don't let him see you without your propah hat.* I smiled and touched him, and said, "You must be Merlin, at the very least. I'm her own mammy, and I'm lucky if I can drag four consecutive words out of her."

"Then *you* ought to invite her on some long walks. You'll learn things. She's shy, and she's got a way to travel before she gets herself together, but that's somebody remarkable you hatched."

"Yes," I said and touched him again. "I want to caution you: if you keep molesting me, I'm going to cry rape."

He grinned and melted, which was exactly what I wanted, needed, to dissolve that moment's awful tension. "I'm innocent, your honour."

"So you are," I granted, and gravely nodded, and cupped his cheeks between my palms.

"Oh, all right. Let's make an out-of-court settlement."

That Saturday night was when I endured a short chat with Bill's wife, an awkward time for me, not because her husband and I were lovers but because she burbled on so about nothing, a time that made me wonder again how Bill had ever got mixed up with such a cute li'l ole bubblehead. (Joe, the consummate sizer-upper, had chatted with her earlier and reported to me, "Whatever you do, don't offer her a rectal thermometer. She's deathly afraid of brain damage.") Virginia Bradway was thirty, friendly, clearly without a gram of suspicion, let alone intelligence, Mrs Senator Bradway to be sure but a woman who came through as far better suited to be Mrs Newark Steamfitter. I was civil to her. And made up my mind, during that chat, that I was going to get my beloved Bill away from her—in time, when the moment was right . . .

And that Saturday night was when I knocked at Carole's bedroom door and entered it. She was in bed with a book. I smiled. So did she. I'd forgotten that she wore eyeglasses. "Hi," I said.

"Hi."

I glanced at the book's author. "Mallarmé. I'm dazzled," I said. *"Ca t'intéresse?"*

"Je fais de mon mieux, mais ce n'est pas facile."

"Sois patiente avec mon français lamentable."

"Tu sais bien que tu parles divinement, maman."

"Ne taquine pas ta pauvre mère." We laughed. I started to sit on the edge of her bed. Perversely, I sat in the little chair near it instead. "You seem to've made a sensational hit with Senator Bradway."

Carole flushed. "What did he say?"

"Well, his general appraisal—"

"No, Mother please! Tell me! What were his exact words?"

"My, you do sound smitten. Let's see: he said he found you pretty, and charming, and very mature for your age." I added some other harmless attributes, and said, "There. Will that hold you for a while?"

272

Her tone was almost cathedral. "I guess he's the finest man I ever met. Thank you, Mother."

" 'Thank you?' For what?"

"For—I don't know, for everything. For coming in to see me."

I stayed for another five minutes, perhaps a bit more. The talk between us was rambling and strained and meaningless; she couldn't give, nor could I. When I rose to go, she asked me, not looking at me, if I would kiss her good night. It was the perfect moment to hug her, to festoon kisses, to say the hell with that world outside this room and to hold her and talk, really talk, to comfort. I kissed the top of her head, and squeezed her wrist, and said, "Don't let the bedbugs bite. Sleep tight, dear."

And two weeks after that Parnassus weekend was when Carole was located on a public bus, bound for Rhode Island.

I didn't worry, for the simple reason that I learned about her mindless prank only after she was returned and safe. I was altogether furious, nearly as much by the inconsiderate act itself as by her fantastic explanation: that Bill had been so gentle, so understanding, at Parnassus, and she'd wanted to see him again, to just visit him. Incredible. I let my temper fly. I'd never ripped into her before, had certainly never shouted. That day I did. She went to pieces before my eyes. I heard myself promising the equivalent of fifty lashes if she were ever, ever, to behave that thoughtlessly again. I also heard the contradiction, of deploring her past submissiveness while raging now about her stab at rebellion. But I kept it up, throughout her hysterics. When it was done, if it was done, I had her driven back to Pearce with her solemn pledge to straighten herself out and cause me no more trouble.

Bill was very upset. Incredibly, he seemed to blame me: "That was a signal for help, Mary. Don't just be angry, don't just stuff her back in the closet. Pay attention."

Yes, I was angry, angry now with him—Bill, who was suddenly, inexplicably, not in my corner. "I'll appreciate it,"

I said, "if you'll stop attacking me. At once."

"At*tack*ing? Because I'm telling you you're handling this all wrong?"

"Yes, you're attacking me. And I won't have it! I'll judge what's best for my daughter. Let's drop it."

"Okay, maybe I'm the one who's been wrong. Let's drop all of it. I'll see you around." Most incredible of all, I needed minutes after we'd finished talking to realize *Let's drop all of it* meant that he saw us as done, through. Merely because I'd snapped at him!

That next week was hellish, interminable. I knew where and how to reach him, but he knew where and how to reach me, too. I couldn't pursue him, couldn't because—I couldn't.

I learned how, though, when the need for him began to run neck and neck with the need to survive. I sent him an Indian peace pipe, a praying stool, a copy of a book titled *Sex After Sixty*, and a note: *The lady wasn't no lady, but she's since graduated from obedience school, with high honours. (Signed) M.E. O'Culpa.* He phoned me in New York from Washington, laughing. I was in Washington within hours.

"Marry me," I said that summer.

We were secluded in my house in Maine, and he spoke one night, with the help of a third scotch, of his wife, till then an unspoken hands-off subject. They'd met at college, where he was a student and she was working in the school cafeteria. He took her out with the express purpose of taking her to bed. He married her because they both thought she was pregnant. He stayed with her for a variety of fuzzy reasons, the fuzziest of them being that she fetched his slippers: "My dread secret's out. I'm the complete chauvinist pig. Virginia's not quite Spinoza in conversation, but she pampers the hell out of me. She thinks I'm Mr Wonderful, and I like that. I like the old-fashioned way she's raising the kids. She'd never hurt me, and I like that. As for sex . . ."

274

He gave me a gauging look. Of course I wanted to know about that. "It happens," he said. "Should I do a cock-and-bull number and tell you I've kept away from her since Christmas Eve? I haven't. Are you shattered?"

"Certainly not," I lied. I even smiled for him.

"You want reasons why a marriage between you and me wouldn't work? I'll give you a bundle of reasons; don't think I haven't thought about it. The most trivial one is that if a recession came along, my only worry would be whether we'd have to unload the eleventh Rolls-Royce, and I need a lot more worries than that to see me through the day. Wait—the reasons get more persuasive. And don't interrupt. A divorced politician doesn't raise too many eyebrows anymore. But hoo boy, step right up, folks, and come vote for the divorced politician who warmed your hearts with all those luxurious home movies of his darling family—and who divorced them all, not so incidentally, to wed the rich lady who invented him. Hoo boy, indeed; that's to be followed with speeches on fealty to law by Agnew and Mitchell.

"You're interrupting. Stop. You're getting reasons. Next: the slipper-fetching factor. I'd expect it, the whole shiny subservience bit, and you'd be lousy at that. No, don't argue; the image of you playing Total Woman to Senator Chauvinist is a side-splitter.

"I love you," he said. He'd never said that before, not after, during, or even before lovemaking, and I tautened like a babe in braids, all thirty-seven-years-old of me. "I don't want to lose you," he went on. "I love you, and I love my children, and I love where I am in the Senate, and I intend to stay with Virginia." A beat. "All clear?"

Another beat. "On the condition," I said, purposely reaching for comedy relief, "that you answer the single burning question: Is Virginia better in bed than I am?"

The corners of his mouth went up. "A truly profound question."

"*Is* she?"

"Different. That's Margaret Mead's favourite copout.

275

When someone asks her, 'Are humans better than other creatures?' she says, 'Different.' "

"Copouts aren't permitted in Maine. What does she do in bed that I don't do?"

"Margaret Mead?"

We both were laughing. I slapped him. "Virginia!"

"Well, she salivates a great deal. She's basically a hillbilly with, they say, pristine gusto; a hillbilly who'd sometimes like to be an empress. You're your everyday empress who'd sometimes like to be a hillbilly. Virginia—"

He stopped. "Enough," he said. "Enough about comparisons. It isn't very dignified."

It wasn't very satisfying, either, this mountain rationalizing why he had to remain with a molehill. I nodded, as if I agreed. Time, time, I thought; he belonged with me, to me. He would come around. That night, I was sustained by his saying *I love you*.

By the fall of that year, the Lou Harris and Gallup polls had Bill placed at the top of the list of freshmen U.S. senators most immediately recognizable to the American public. I was aware of the loud buzzes, that his celebrity was a direct consequence of a massive publicity job by the Scofield press, the president of which was the able senator's able popsie.

Like most vicious stories, there was a tincture of truth in it, though only a tincture. Bill Bradway had come a long distance since his Rhode Island race with old Walter Osborne. If the word *charisma* had died at Dealey Plaza, he brought it back to life, when he was spreading out his philosophic wares on *Face the Nation* or talking pop politics with Barbara Walters or amusing and charming the country on *The Tonight Show*. He was a splendid performer. Character shone from him. Wit sparkled. This wasn't Honest John the snake oil man, or Doubledome the idealist who wished forty acres and a mule for everyone on earth but without a practical notion about implementation. This was William Bradway, Jr, an original, who could reach blue collars and white collars with equal effectiveness.

I helped, yes. I directed *Scofield's* cover stories. I saw that he was mentioned as often as possible in the Letters to the Editor sections of all our papers. I invited our political columnists to file affirmative Bradway essays. If a week went by without a legitimate justification for a Bradway news story, I invented a justification.

By that fall, even Bill believed he was an all-round winner. He relied on me as his sounding board and subtle adviser and nudger. He never said *I love you* again, nor did he thank me in so many words for the use of my magic wand, but that didn't matter; the feeling was there, the closeness, the certainty growing in me that the time was approaching when he would be so firmly accepted by the public as a superstar that his image could survive not only divorce but homicide and arson. After that night in Maine, I carefully veered clear of talking divorce and remarriage. He would come to that himself as his idea, as his own realization that he could go further and be infinitely fuller with me than with the molehill.

A week before Christmas, almost one year after that first night in the John Adams Suite, the molehill came to see me. Alone.

"The big surprise wasn't finding out about Billy and you," said Virginia Bradway. "I've known about you for a good long while now, just like I've known about Billy playing around ever since we got married. After the first couple of years, I never let on I knew. I've always acted dumber than I am; I always figured that's the best way to keep Billy —let him go messing around when he thinks that's what he has to do. I act dumb because he always comes back.

"Last night we were talking," she said. "He told me he wants to try a separation, him and me, that you're in his system, whatever that's supposed to mean, and he's all mixed up and he has to get away from Cheryl and Timmy and I to see where's he's heading.

"Now you listen to me," she said. "If I stayed with him when I was in labour for forty-six hours with Cheryl and I

277

found out he was off humping some tramp, if I stayed with him all this time, with all the lowdown things he's done to me, you can bet all your own I'm not going to hand him over to you like a good little girl.

"You want to find out how dumb I am?" she said. "I'll holler bloody murder. You don't have the only newspapers in the world. I'll holler all the facts and figures; that's how dumb I am. That ruins his career, right? Okay, he can go marry you. You're sure rich enough; you can set him up in some business, or just make him into a playboy for the rest of his life. That doesn't sound to me like the way Billy'd want to live, but maybe you know better.

"So what's it going to be?" she said. "He can go on humping anybody else sevens ways to Sunday, as long as he keeps coming back to me. But *you* better clear out of the picture. If I hear any more of this 'separation' shit, if you're the cause of my marriage folding up, the whole world's gonna hear about it. From me."

I didn't have to tell Bill about that visit. He told me— about the perfect geisha of a wife who had changed, gradually and then fullsteam, into a shrew, an ex-pussycat who might not have been entirely sure I'd fully taken in her reading of the riot act. She was knife-twisting now, Bill said, feeling her power and using it, warning him of what was in store if he didn't dance to her selection of tunes.

"I've never been a good dancer," he said wearily. "To hell with it. In goes the sponge. Out goes the marriage and family made in heaven, all those hypocritical letters to the constituents about moral responsibility, the works. I'm tired. I'm tired of playacting. I'm tired of telling the goddamn Senate and the goddamn country I know all the answers. All I want to do is take off this heavy mask I'm wearing and just sit down."

"That's whining, Senator," I said. "You know it is, and you know it's unworthy of you. Your future is everything. This weak-kitten pose of yours comes to a screeching halt, here and now. We come to a screeching halt as lovers, because I love you much too much to let a two-penny scandal send your future up in smoke. Your *great* future."

"Rah rah."

"Yes, rah rah! You're a winner, my darling. You're strong, and there's greatness in you, and my job's going to be to keep reminding you of that, every hour on the hour."

I helped him. Of course I helped him. He would listen and usually act on my advice and suggestions. That abominable wife of his again became a hands-off subject; neither of us mentioned her. I watched him grow. I helped him grow.

The lovemaking stopped, but the love didn't. In time I could view myself less as Sydney Carton, chanting " 'Tis a far, far better thing I do" on the way to the guillotine, and more and more as a sensible woman who had finally heard what my precious Bill had said in Maine—that he could never have been able to function as Mr Mary Scofield.

Could I have functioned as Mrs William Bradway?

Yes. Certainly. I never stopped believing it . . .

Mary looked up.

Hap Ackerman's plane set down at Gowan, and a Company car drove Mary to Bill's address in Georgetown, a relatively modest house on a tree-lined avenue. The picture window drapes were drawn. There were no signs of activity, of life. A morning newspaper, with a rubber band around it, lay on the front porch. Mary hesitated at the doorbell, and pressed it, once and then again, convinced now that the trip had been for nothing.

She rang a third time. An edge of the drape moved from inside. A moment passed and the door opened. Bill, haggard, wearing a shapeless cotton robe and a day's beard, his hair wild, stared at her, as though trying to place her. He stepped aside, expressionless, neither acknowledging her nor indicating she was unwelcome.

He lumbered into the musty living room. Mary followed him and sat in the chair his hand impersonally motioned towards. A single lamp was lighted. A game show was on television; the sound was off. The airless room smelled of hanging cigarette smoke and dankness, of defeat. Bill,

Mary's beloved Bill, pointed to a nearly empty brandy bottle on a low, paper-strewn table. "There's more where that came from," he said.

"No. Thanks."

"You're entirely welcome." He raised a dark glass, regarded it rather than Mary. "Well, now. You just happened to be in the neighbourhood?"

"Something like that," Mary said softly, hurting for him, hurting with him.

He nodded. "Sorry you missed Virginia. She took the children to visit their grandparents in Akron. So. Here we are, at long, long last. Historic meeting. Which one are you, Stanley or Livingstone? Either one's fine with me. I'm getting generous in my declining years."

"Bill . . ."

"Yep, Bill's my name, and luring tiny tots from the playground with candy bars is my game. Or, as the crusading Scofield press might put it, 'alleged' candy bars. Excuse me." He peered at his glass. "So. Where were we? If you're here to view the remains, you're a bit early. Not by much, but a little early."

"Stop this wallowing!" Mary commanded. "Carole is gone!"

"Wallowing? Wall-lo-wing? Is that like gimble in the wabes? I'm not wall-lo-wing, Scoop. For your gloating edification, I'm applying myself to remembering all the Upanishads and getting stupefied-plastered. I'm not having too much luck in any part of the ball park, but where there's a will there's a whatever." He continued to examine his glass. "Say, I've been meaning to ask you, Scoop, you with the nose for news, you with that commendable stop-the-presses-here's-a-story'll-bust-this-town-wide-open instinct: How is it, with all that savvy genius you have for selling papers, you neglected to print that I used to shack up with Mary The-Truth-Shall-Set-You-Free Scofield? Just asking. Just curious."

Grimly: "We were responsible adults. Those kids weren't."

"Those kids weren't," he repeated. "Mary Freud the omniscient, Mary Freud the pushme-pullyou, sees all, knows all, knows nothing. *Nada. Nada nada*, jing jing jing. Tell you something. You won't hear it, any more than you've ever heard anything in your life except the sound of your royal ass being kissed, but I'll tell you something, anyway. Just pretend to listen, Madam Defarge. After all, you're a guest in my humble home. Just sit there and click your knitting needles, the way you've always done, and pretend to listen."

"Oh, Bill—"

" 'Oh, Bill, oh, Bill!' What I needed, what I've always needed, was warmth, consideration, love without the pay-back hassles. Virginia . . . Virginia gave it to me in spades, and bingo, she turned sour. What I needed I couldn't get from ball-breakers like you—the empresses, always expecting me to live up to *their* expectations, *their* preconceived image of what I was supposed to be, what I was supposed to do for them. For them, always for them."

The contempt, she thought. *This awesome blast furnace of contempt* . . .

"So then I found someone. Just when the eighteen-hour days were turning into twenty-nine-hour days, and I was going to crack if I didn't have something good coming back to me, I found someone. Young, yeah. By the calendar, very young. And soft, affectionate. No strings, just soft and affectionate. I couldn't bring her into my squeaky-clean 'responsible adult' world, those mature Georgetown solid citizens with the Mount Sinai postures and the martini breakfasts and the feverish musical beds, so I put in with her world, her crowd. And all the papers, including guess-whose, made it salacious and dirty."

" 'Responsible adult,' " he said. "That's right, she wasn't a 'responsible adult.' She wasn't mature enough to've learned that love isn't give and take, but buy and sell. Right, Mary? Isn't that the credo you've always lived by, that love can't be for real unless it comes with some kind of price tag?"

"You know that isn't so. You're so full of hate now that you've distorted everything we meant to each other, everything good we shared, the fact that we loved each other."

"Love?" He grinned, a harsh, cold grin. "Oh, no. Oh, no. When do you stop kidding yourself, Scoop? When does everybody stop kidding everybody? We never loved each other, unless using each other is a form of love. Maybe it is."

" 'Using' . . . what a vile—"

"*Loved* each other? Come *on!* I used you to help me get moving in this town. I spent maybe twenty minutes thinking of becoming Mr Mary Scofield, not because there was any love for you, but because I thought it might be good for me. Well, I got over that fast, it would've been too expensive. You used me as a personal Mary monument. You didn't want me, you wanted a winner. Okay, fine, we served up a convenient mutual aggression stew and called it Macaroni. Or we just as well could've. But just spare us the refrain from 'Among My Souvenirs'. And don't roll in here and lay a charge on *me* of distorting the past. Not you, with the solid gold blinders. Who're *you* to sit in judgement on how other people look to be loved? Your whole life's been one big chase after dream material, like some mainliner always looking for just one more vein that hasn't collapsed."

"Why? Why are you doing this to me?"

"Doing what, Mary, rubbing your pretty face in the bottom line—that you give one apple and always expect two back? Why am I doing what to you? What did you come here for? Your two apples? You already took them, don't you remember? When you spelled my name right in the paper, you got your two apples, not to mention two pounds of flesh and both my balls. There's a tasty dish to set before an empress, all right, all right."

Barely aloud: "Carole . . ."

He seemed to soften, though for only a moment. "Ah, yes. Now comes the dawn. Carole's missing, and Mama shows up at big bad Bradway's doorstep, wringing her hands." He did a vicious impersonation of her. " 'Oh, big bad Bill, Carole's missing and I'm annoyed because I was planning to spend the day directing editorials on how beneficent I am to senators and daughters and they pay me back by not being my trained seals. Oh, pamper me, big bad ungrateful Bill, unscramble my eggs, oh—' "

Suddenly, he stopped. "Jesus. Jumpin J. Jesus," he said gravely. "You think—Jesus! Now comes the dawn for real. Big Bad Willie snaps little girls' garters, so it automatically follows: big bad Willie has *your* little girl chained to the bedpost. *Jesus!*"

"No, no, it isn't like that, I—"

"Then what is it like?"

"Carole started to go to you once before when she was upset. I thought she might try to get in touch with you this—time. I'm frantic with worry. I had to look into every possibil—"

"You did, did you? You let it enter your head, even for a split second, that I'd do anything to mix that kid up more than she's been mixed up, that I wouldn't have contacted you right away . . . My Christ, Mary, you and I couldn't have had *any*thing if you could imagine something as grotesque as that."

Fiercely he said, "Get out of that chair. I want you the hell out of here. Now. If I see or hear a glimmer of Carole, if I hear a word about her, you'll know. Now go away from me. Go peddle our Scofield papers somewhere else. You've fucked up my life. You've fucked up Carole's. Go find yourself some fresh meat to manipulate and contaminate and ruin.

"Out!" he shouted, and flung the door open. "Take your goddamn throne and robes and sceptre with you! Don't forget the sceptre! Use it! It'll always stay hard for you! Isn't that all you need?"

Once more, Mary Scofield fled. Once again she slammed Pandora's box shut and flew back to New York, where everything was going to be all right. She would not be sidetracked until Carole was found, and safe.

One of the messages she found when she returned to the town house on that Friday night was from Dr Marco. He was concerned about her having left his office before they

283

could speak. Would she telephone him?

Yes, she thought, and lifted the receiver to call.

And replaced it. I can't, she thought, drained now, limp, cement and mud, both deadened and anxious, battered by the day, sobered and humiliated by it and all the days that had gone before, all the thousands upon thousands of days not without ends but without beginnings (When do you stop kidding yourself, Wonder Woman? When does everybody stop kidding everybody?), too humiliated, too naked to hear yet again the indictable crimes levelled against the sleek zombie with the human name, Mary Scofield.

Instead, she telephoned Joe, precious Joe. All he had to offer was comfort. "You're to take the fastest-working sleeping pill you have in the joint and get under the covers. Starting now," he said. He promised he would ring her as soon as there was reason to ring her.

"You're very dear to me, *Yussele*," Mary said.

"And you have terrific taste. Sleep like a top, kiddo."

She sat near her bedroom phone for moments, trembling now, numb now, waiting for feeling to come, waiting for it to leave. Presently she rose and began to undress, eager for a hot bath after the long day, eager for sleep, too restless for either. ("Get in touch with your feelings." "What feelings?" "You must feel something." "I don't want to be alone. I'm afraid to be alone." "Good. Fear is a feeling.") She pulled off all her clothes. He head throbbed. She pressed the hi-fi button, and *Tannhäuser* boomed. (Owen, who had despised *Tannhäuser*: "It flushes you with this overwhelming urge to rush out and kill a kike. It's surefire Master Race. The only way to listen to most of Wagner is to listen loud." She found a soupy, stringy, likable "The Girl That I Marry." She walked to the bathroom, where the Nembutals were kept. Her headache pounded. She glanced at herself in the full-length mirror, surprised, as if standing outside her own skin, to see her nipples stiffen unaccountably, completely unaccountably. Hastily she turned away from the loathsome sight.

MARY: "A birthday present, at my advanced age? What is it?"

RICK: "A record called *Mantovani Plays Roller Derby Classics*. What the hell do you care what it is till I see you? In the meantime, happy birthday, Miss Newfield."

She distrusted drugs she could not control, but she took two Nembies to the penthouse drawing room and swallowed them, almost as much as a dutiful response to Joe's loving command as for the need to still the knifing tension (*Come see the sideshow freak, between the bearded lady and Tom Thumb: the corpse with twitches*), and washed the tablets down with a scotch, neat, another drug she distrusted. Her hand shook as she held the glass.

"*A doll I can carry/The girl that I marry will be.*"

Walking towards her bed, walking from it, the oversize emptiness of it, walking with a pretence of direction from room to oversize-emptiness room, remembering what Rick had teased, or was it Bill, or was it Weekend Whozis—"When you walk around nude, you walk as though you own the only perfect pair of boobs in the world. So why do they jiggle"—walking, she suddenly thought of Liz Hale, her secretary, thought of phoning Liz:

"I just realized I haven't eaten all day. I don't feel like cooking for myself, or getting involved with the servants. You come on over and we'll poach some eggs."

"Why me?"

"Because you're the only female friend I have."

"Friend?"

"There's no one else. Please."

"What does it pay?"

"Please. You work for me around the clock. Please . . ."

"I'm busy. My boyfriend is here. If you want me to interrupt the closeness we're sharing now, it'll cost you. How much will it pay, and for how long will I have to be your friend?"

She phoned Joe again. "A request. Above and beyond.

285

Would you come here and get under the covers with me?"

Dear, darling Joe, surely bewildered. And finally, understanding: "Yeah."

She buzzed Burt, the town house's night man, on the intercom, and said, "Mr Greenwood will come by. He's to be let up." She showered, still baffled not by the call to Joe but by the hoyden who had placed it, equally baffled by the unrelenting erect nipples. *Sex? Sex isn't what I want. Good God, it's the last thing I want.*

She scrubbed her body hard. *Sex is what I want. A man, a special man, close to me, hugging me, kissing me, next to me, over me, in me. Joe. I need you to be my father, dear Joe, not my lover. Dearest Joe, who knows I was not born but carved out of hollow wood and who will always protect me . . .*

She stepped out of the shower, and dried her body, and viewed it now with appreciation, viewed it as Joe would view it, and drank another scotch. She walked again from room to room, and remembered the evening at Parnassus when she was nineteen, when she sat at the dinner table with Gramp and Venus—Venus, whom Adam had loved and returned to Parnassus where she belonged. Mary was rapturously happy, listening to Gramp praise Joe Greenwood, who had left an hour before to return to the city, as a sensible, sharp young fellow who was going to go places in the Company; when she was dying to blurt out, *Joe Greenwood is sensible and sharp. Joe Greenwood is a magnificent hymen-breaker. Joe Greenwood and I have made love, and Joe Greenwood is still inside me, and I'm in love with Joe Greenwood.*

"—excellent business head on his shoulders," Gramp had said. "Not one of your pushy Jews, either. Still and all, we want to keep him at arm's length. Jews are famous for following you through a revolving door and coming out ahead of you."

"Gramp! What an awful thing to say!"

"Facts speak for themselves. And by the way, young lady, I may be the oldest cuss alive, but my brain's not addled yet and my vision's shipshape. I saw the way you looked at him

286

one or twice, like some moonstruck calf. You want to watch you don't give him any fancy, mistaken notions about his place. I like him, even if he does remind me now and again of Popeye the Sailor with that one eye, but the Jews aren't like us. They'll take advantage of any situation they can, by fair means or foul. It's born in 'em . . ."

Now she heard her doorbell. She dressed in a semi-transparent lavender robe and went to the door, puzzled by the unsteadiness of her gait, and let Joe in.

His smile was as tentative as hers, tentative and quizzical. "A question," she asked, standing near him in the drawing room.

"I'm all ears. And all eye."

"Who owns the only perfect pair of jiggling boobs in the world?"

Joe rolled with it. "Funny you should ask. Some wino stopped me on the street and asked me that very same question on my way over here. Let's see. Ernest and Julio Gallo?"

"No, that's two pairs. But you're close."

"Umm. Whitlow Wyatt."

"Who's Whitlow Wyatt?"

"He pitched for the Dodgers."

"Right! Give the gent a cigar," she said, and opened the folds of the robe.

"Not bad."

"Are they as pretty as you remembered they were?"

"Prettier, younger, and better than all other leading products because of the decay-reducing ingredient, stanous fluoride. Now put them back in."

"M'sieur is bored by Mitzi's silken globes?"

"M'sieur wants to hold the lady of the house, not ze saucy French maid whore. M'sieur can't negotiate friendship and a hard-on simultaneously." Quietly, then: "I know you hurt, honey."

Joe extended his powerful arms, and Mary fitted into them. "Okay," he said as her shoulders hunched. "Okay, Okay. Okay."

287

"What a shit I am!" she cried out. "What a selfish, grubby, horrible, worthless clump of shit I am! What a hateful, motherless, childless—" and her voice broke.

"My baby," she wept. "My baby . . ."

Joe's arms tightened.

"Don't let them hurt her," she whispered.

He rocked her back and forth in those safe arms. He guided her to her bed. "Do you sleep in a nightgown, or raw?" he asked, and then saw the gown on her pillow. "Here we are."

"My darling, darling *Yussele* . . ."

He slipped her robe off, and helped her into the gown, and into the bed, and raised the top blanket up to her neck. His immense hand tousled her hair. His lips kissed her eyes.

"There's so much to say," she murmured.

Joe sat on the bed. "A question. What's the name of Little Orphan Annie's dog?"

"Funny you should ask. I met this wino . . . Wait a moment. Little Orphan Annie's dog. Sandy?"

"Bull's-eye. And what does Sandy say?"

"That I'm a mess. All ye who enter Mary Scofield, abandon hope. That I'll always be the frightened little girl who needs to be tucked into bed."

"Not so bull's-eye. Don't kid around; I'm serious. What does Sandy say?"

" 'Arf.' "

Joe nodded. "Which is more than most of us ever say in a lifetime. Don't *say*. *Schloff*, baby. Sleep. Gorgeous Greenwood's going to stay here with you till you're asleep."

The Nembutals were beginning. She heard the chopping sounds of a helicopter. She tried to capture in her mind a picture of her mother. She imagined herself as very small, her mother cradling her and singing to her. She was able to see Venus Montgomery. Venus, dead now, had played hopscotch with her at Parnassus, had taught her all the words to "I Wish I Could Shimmy Like My Sister Kate," had said to her, "You know your trouble, cutie-pie? You're a scaredy-cat. So's everybody else, one way or another, but they hide it better than you. You gotta learn how to put up a front."

"Some front, huh?" she mumbled sleepily, clutching Joe's hand.

SIXTEEN

GREENWOOD. That Friday night in Mary's bedroom.

I sat with Mary till she was asleep, and realized, once I stood to leave to go home, that I barely had enough energy left to navigate to the door, let alone *shlep* all the way to East River Drive. I went to the guest room nearest her bedroom, punched the button on the night table phone for the Company switchboard extension, and called my office. Cranks were still phoning in, but there was still nothing that added up to a firm ransom demand. The FBI and local cops in different parts of the country were looking into a lead here, a tip there. "Reach me at this number if anything breaks," I said, and lay down, prepared to sleep like the dead, at least.

Fifteen minutes later, I was still awake. Overtired, I thought; that sometimes happens, though I was too overtired to be very philosophical about it. Overtired, I thought, and no more than forty or fifty feet away from Mary . . .

Sure, I'd known exactly what she'd meant when she phoned me and asked me to come over and get under the covers with her. I'd known exactly her game when I'd shown up here, at a little before ten o'clock, and watched the vamp performance that was even more transparent than the purple robe. She'd wanted me under the covers with her, maybe literally, but to hold the dragons at bay, not to play house. Thanks, but no thanks. Lead us not into temptation. I'd delivered myself from the evil—well, the possibility of complications—by keeping my chastity belt bolted. My uncle the rabbi would have been proud of me.

So now I was thrashing around, trying to relax, and getting nowhere. I stared at the ceiling, and then the wall, and then the ceiling again. For a while I wished I hadn't stopped smoking last year.

I loved her.

How about that? After twenty years, I still loved her.

Not that I'd ever tell her, of course, partly because it would have been altogether out of character; I'd locked myself into the role of faithful eunuch, and faithful eunuchs don't suddenly sprout balls. It was partly that and partly—no, mainly—that for all my showy toughness I wasn't up to the risk of letting her know I was crazy about her and having her split her sides laughing. Which she might well do—gently, to be sure ("*And I'm crazy about you, too*, Yussele, *but only as my faithful eunuch*"), but the sort of gentleness I could live without.

The night table clock read 11:30. "Aw, come on, Morpheus," I said, "climb off your ass and come enfold me." Morph answered, "In a minute; just as soon as you figure out what Mary's all about to you. What's to love?"

"A perfectly legitimate question, beautifully put," I said, and pondered it. What was to love?

I remembered one of our midnight Sanka sessions in her office, after a killer of a workday, a week or so before her divorce from Owen Enright was made final. "Two divorces are relatively understandable," she said. "But *three*!" And repeated it: "*Three!* That starts to get a bit tacky. Well, I'm swearing off, *Yussele*. I'm signing the pledge. Some people have no talent for marriage, and I clearly head that list."

"You should've hooked up with me when you had the golden chance," I said. A nervous joke of ours, healed partially by time.

She smiled. "I should've. Think it's too late?"

"You just finished saying you've thrown in the sponge. Anyway, it wouldn't work; the rumour would go out right away that you wanted me just for the prestige."

What if we had married twenty years ago? Would she still be running away? I studied the ceiling some more, and thought back . . .

A week after my discharge from the Air Force in 1945, I took a girl named Melanie Shapyro horseback riding in Central Park. I knew as much about horses as I knew about

291

what I was going to do with my life—next to nothing—but Melanie Shapyro was wild about horses and I wanted to get in good with her. Her father manufactured lamps and was looking to take an energetic son-in-law into the business. Lamps didn't fascinate me much, but marrying money did, for a little while that year, so I decided to be nice to Melanie and see what might happen.

What happened was that my guaranteed-tame horse threw me.

The accident robbed me of an eye. Melanie Shapyro was very solicitous, but then one day she, or her father, concluded that it wouldn't be such a hot idea for her to marry Lon Chaney. (Actually, once I decided that an eye patch made me look like a pirate, the glass eye I was given wasn't all that bad, as glass eyes go. What was the big deal?) Melanie came to see me in the hospital ward and her uh–er explanation for why we should call it quits was that Papa had gradually reached the insight that I was off in the clouds somewhere and not really serious about becoming a responsible businessman and, as night follows day, a responsible husband.

Anyway.

When I flunked out of the lamp and marrying-money business and after two years at City College on the G.I. Bill, seesawing there between business administration and journalism, I went to work for the Company. I didn't storm the corporate castle, but I did go up the rungs. By the time I was in my late twenties and still a bachelor (most of the bums I'd hung out with at the confectionery in Brooklyn were "settled and doing very fantastic, thank you" in *their* late twenties, with their own businesses and families), I was a Scofield trouble-shooter. My job was to travel from city to city wherever a Company newspaper was in trouble, either editorially or financially or both, usually both, try to find out why, and come up with remedies.

I stayed at it because it paid good money and because my immediate boss, Roy Britt, kept dangling the promise in front of me of a lovely future executive post. But it was a frustrating job. I'd analyze a problem, write up solutions, be praised for my perceptions and clarity, and, more often than not, see my recommendations flushed down the john. The flusher, I learned, was the big boss whom I'd never met, Adam Scofield, eighty-three years old and riding his wheelchair at Parnassus, where I'd never been invited. I learned that he wasn't senile so much as incorrigibly stubborn, that his mind was plenty alert enough to recognize that most of his holdings other than publishing—the mills and mines, the real estate, the couple of dozen additional properties—were minting profits without interruption, but rosily deaf to the fact that too many of the newspapers were sinking into the sea. They were sinking because their stark, simplistic, bold-bannered headline approach to complex news had become a hoop skirt in those mid-1950s. Primarily they were sinking because Adam Scofield, who had been their yeast for over a half century, had himself run out of yeast. His brilliant right arm, Caleb Buckminster, was dead. Adam Scofield, once always years ahead of everybody, seemed determined to keep his boats afloat with tattered sails.

I would deliver my reports to Roy Britt: "Fold losers like *The Dayton Light-Union* and *The Butte Star* and *The Charlotte Times-Globe*. Sell or pep up or close up magazine stiffs like *Prayer* and *Queen's Kitchen*." The word would come back to Britt from the big boy: "They're my children. I fathered them and watched them all grow. Would you disown any of *your* children?" Quoth the genius of journalism.

Genius of journalism, my eye. I finally went to see Britt. "Let's talk severance pay, Roy. If I'm not listened to, then I'm not earning my keep. I feel like I'm spending my life with a sexy chick who blows in my ear, and I take her home and she says, 'Let's not spoil it.' "

"Sit tight," he said, and phoned me that night. "Be at Parnassus this Friday, for the weekend. The big boy wants you there." It turned out that with Britt as conduit, the big boy knew all about me, had known about me from my second or third sour report, had been sitting all this time with his binoculars and observing me hop up and down the land.

Parnassus could have housed all the Scandinavian countries. That didn't surprise me; I'd heard about it, read about it. What surprised me was Adam Scofield. I'd expected a Bullfinch relic, mooning into his gruel and recollecting the night he danced with Lillian Russell. Not quite. The only tipoffs that he'd truly passed over the hill were the wheelchair and the claws of fingers under the influence of arthritis; otherwise, I sensed in a hurry, it would be the better part of wisdom to watch him every minute.

His voice surely wasn't eighty-three. He welcomed me and introduced me to Venus Montgomery, a pretty, informal woman, *the* Venus Montgomery every inquisitive Company employee was warned to refer to, if it was necessary for her to be referred to at all, as Mr Scofield's Friend. "This is the young man," Adam Scofield said with a twinkle, "who's been scolding us and telling us all the things we've been doing wrong for fifty-eight years."

The Venus lady winked at me. "I'll get you a drink if you promise not to take this old bastard serious." I grinned, liking her, and asked for a short bourbon. I saw white-coated servants, and supposed there was a retinue, a battalion, of other servants in the wings of the wings, but she fixed me the bourbon herself, a down-home touch there among the breathing dollars.

The old man's reputation for charm was deserved. So was his reputation for caginess; he wasn't going to tell me why I'd been summoned till he was ready. In that motorized wheelchair of his, he took me on a tour of part of the grounds and part of the main house, showing off but as an enthusiastic kid, not as a *grand seigneur*. He negotiated us from one floor to the next by elevator, showing me a five-hundred-year-old printing press and explaining in concise detail how it had worked, naming guests who would be coming for the weekend and asking if I knew them, showing me Florentine fescos and Canary Island grape vines, asking me where I'd gone to school and if I was married, showing

294

me his power plant and private landing field and hand-carved alabaster chandeliers and Persian tiles and four-thousand-year-old Egyptian statuary, asking me without rudeness how I'd lost my eye, showing me a vestibule floor built from Pompeian ruins and ancient ebony jewel cabinets and thousand-year-old Roman archways, asking me if I'd like to go with him to his library for a drink before dinner.

He had sherry. I had another bourbon. "What do you think?" he asked.

"What I think," I said, playing it very carefully, "is that those questions about my education and my eye and whether I'm married and the rest of it didn't fool me for a minute. I think you know the name of my fifth grade home room teacher and where she was born."

He laughed. He nodded. "That's what I get paid for. You're here because the thought began to occur to me fairly recently that I just may not live forever. I may, at that, but there's the chance I won't. *If* I go, I want someone to take over who knows what he's about. I've looked into a lot of candidates, and something about them always seems to be missing. I know you're as fond of Roy Britt as he is of you, and I don't mean to talk him down, but he's a little weak on the trigger. I wish I could give the reins to a son—that's natural—but all I have is my dear wife and my grand-daughter. You'll meet Mary, by the way. She promised me she'll come for the weekend, and she never lets me down. She's the apple of my eye, and smart as a whip, but females don't run companies. Not mine, at any rate. How's your drink? One more?"

"No, sir, this is fine."

"You might be the one. You *might*, assuming you're interested and assuming we have some long talks together and I decide you're the right man."

"Excuse me for blinking hard, sir," I said, "but I was under the impression that the reports I've been sending in have all been adding up to a conviction of mine that some of your papers and magazines are lousy, or they're being managed by my fifth grade home room teacher. And I've reported why, and at length, and I've recommended solutions that took me time and thought, and you've ignored every single one of them. Where does a boat-rocker like me come off being considered, even for a second, for the kind of job you're proposing?"

He nodded again, and there was a polished smile, polished over eighty-three years. "Because you're a tough guy who sticks to his guns. Because maybe I *have* been out of touch with the real world, and the older I get, the more set in my ways I get, and I need to be bashed on the dome now and again—by a tough guy I can respect. Mostly because you may be that rarest thing alive—a newspaperman who knows business and a businessman who knows newspapering. Or so it appears to me, from what they've been telling me about you. I might be mistaken. You might be all wrong for what I need. That's why I want to study you up close. Why don't you finish that liquor or just leave it somewhere? I want to get a nap in before the other guests arrive. We eat promptly at seven here. Promptly."

I knew he had a granddaughter named Mary Scofield. I'd seen her pictures on the society pages: nineteen years old, lean, assured, beautiful, rich-beautiful. Just graduated from Bryn Mawr, having earned a diploma in Debutante, now photographed at the horse show, now photographed water skiing (*and dig those crazy gams*, as the hep-groovy-gone, happily gone, language went in the middle-1950s), now raffling tickets at the charity bazaar, now wafting out of one of the family limousines for the *Kiss Me, Kate* premiere with her current flame, the equally irrepressible, fun-loving Sonny Wasp, himself just graduated from Ivy League College for the Performing Arts where he'd majored in eventually retiring to a home for the destitute in Bel Air.

She did arrive that weekend, alongside her current Sonny Wasp, a.k.a. Bart Clay, which was no sensational improvement. He sported a scrupulously coiffeured ducktail and a bored expression no less scrupulously coiffeured. She swooped down and embraced her obviously worshipful

296

grandfather. She hugged and kissed Venus Montgomery, who hugged and kissed her back. She warmly and some-times wittily greeted each of the Parnassus guests in turn, most of whom she evidently either knew or knew about. She floated past me, not really frosty but simply on some other plane. At one point, talking in Spanish with some diamond-encrusted woman, her head turned, and she saw me and said, "Get me a rum punch like a good fellow, will you?" And turned her back on me, and resumed in Spanish.

Delightful, I thought. She knew who I was, or would make it her Miss Rich Bitch business to find out. Delightful. She goes to Grandpappy and complains, "I told that Green-wood to jump through a hoop for me, and he did; how can you put such a transparent toady in the top Scofield chair?" Or she goes to Grandpappy and complains, "I told that Greenwood to jump through a hoop for me, and he refused; how can you let your precious granddaughter be so insulted?" Oh, yes, utterly delightful.

It couldn't have been more than a minute when she finished the Spanish number and turned to me again, with a lifted-eyebrow type well-where-is-it? gaze. I answered her. I rumbled, "You'll have to find another waiter. This isn't my station."

Her blush was vivid. She smiled a little, and nodded, and made a graceful exit to join a small cluster of people at another part of the lawn. Now and then I saw her glance away when I caught her looking at me. I made an elaborate, probably childish point of ignoring her. I moved around, nibbling at purposely watered bourbons, feeling uncomfort-able partly because I've never been at ease at gatherings con-vened to feature small talk and small hors d'oeuvres, aware that I was there as a guest but feeling more like an on-trial applicant for membership in some cliquish club, aware that Adam Scofield's perhaps-offer that I become a press lord would presently hit me in the ribs with sharper impact than it was doing now. I let myself get fastened into a one-way conversation with Preston Donnelly, an aged syndicated Scofield columnist emeritus who held my arm and explained, through paralyzing denture breath, how They were out to destroy Senator Joseph McCarthy, the greatest American since Washington, how They were in complete control of which anti-patriot buttons Eisenhower was being ordered to push, how They were poisoning my drinking water, how They were intent on murdering us all in our sleep, how They—

Greenwood the *mensch* spoke to me: *Tell this Scofield creation, this rattling Ghost of Christmas Past, to go take a creaking leap for himself. Tell them all to go stuff it. Vamoose, and take your intact soul with you.*

Greenwood the pragmatist spoke to me: *Smile and shake your head up and down and kiss this buzzard on the lips, and he'll report back well, they'll all give you good grades and show the grades to the principal. Tote dat barge, lift dat bale, kiss dat ass, and hokus pokus you're a millionaire, paper-trained but feelthy rich, you're presto a press lord.*

O tempora, O mores, O shit. I released myself from Donnelly's grip and walked away. Just walked away, though that didn't entirely make me a profile in courage. Where I walked was to the sumptuous bungalow assigned to me, the lavish one with the Louis Quatorze bed inside and the stereophonic babbling brook—my own brook, yet—right outside. Where I examined my private kitchen and private bar and other fancy accoutrements never dreamed of in my old neighbourhood, and heard the ring of my private telephone and picked it up and listened to the heiress's thoroughbred voice say unto me, "I apologize for what must have appeared to be finger-snapping. Is it in your fierce heart to forgive me?"

We met at a child's playhouse, a wealthy child's playhouse with a lake shimmering beside it, about a three-minute walk from my bungalow, and she repeated the word "fierce." "You *looked* so fierce," she said. "You frightened me. When I'm frightened, I tend to grapple with it by acting like Lucrezia Borgia. Please don't hate me. I'm really not Lucrezia Borgia."

Nor was she, nor could I understand what I was doing

there, alone and late at night, with not a woman but a girl, a girl of nineteen, a Scofield girl of nineteen. A stunner, to be sure, the kind you never saw anywhere near my old neighbourhood, but nineteen. It wasn't that she could boost or kibosh me with the caliph. It wasn't nearly that simple.

"No one's ever called me fierce before," I said. "I spend twelve hours a day in the library, and I'm always afraid the librarian will go 'Shhh-hh' because I turn a page and it makes a noise."

She laughed. "Oh, sure! How tall are you, six-three, six-four?"

"Four-eleven. And fifty-one pounds. It's the waiter's uniform that makes me seem bigger."

"*Please* lay off. I *said* I was sorry. Would you like to see this playhouse? Or has Gramp given you the full half-dollar tour?"

"This I haven't seen," I said, and then said, " 'Gramp'? You refer to the mountaintop as 'Gramp'?"

"It used to be worse. It used to be 'Grampy.' Now I'm grown up."

"Are you?"

"Oh, getting there. Come on in. At least try," she said, and ducked through the five-foot-high door of what she called a playhouse, actually a plantation mansion, scaled down, but portioned and stately. I managed to follow her by squeezing in sideways. Inside, the feeling was weird, as if I'd stepped through the looking glass into some elfin world. Everything was roughly half normal size, but everything was there—chairs, couches, mirrors, carpets, even kitchen appliances and plumbing. She moved about with head bent. I crouched.

"What is this?" I asked. "Tara for midgets?"

"It is incredible, isn't it? Gramp had it built for me when I was four or five, everything to an exact scale. Here's where I used to have tea parties for my dolls. I could be anyone I pleased here—Joan of Arc, Beethoven, George Sand, Michelangelo, sometimes even myself."

"What's upstairs? Ecuador?"

"A bedroom, and a nursery with toys and cribs and more dolls. And a bathroom."

"Naturally. What's a playhouse without a bathroom?"

My neck ached. "Look," I said, "this is a great place for unbirthday parties and chiropractors, but if I don't get out now they'll be calling me Quasimodo."

Outside, I said, "It isn't much, but it's home."

"And you're a snob. Are you sleepy? Would you like to walk?"

"Fine, if I don't have to do it on all fours."

We must have walked through the garden and woods of Parnassus's sprawling grounds for over an hour that night. I answered her simple, unembarrassed questions about my eye—a subject, incidentally, she never bothered to raise or even allude to, ever again. I answered her other questions about me, though with my guard up; if she was even remotely a Company spy, I wasn't going to cut my throat with her in attendance. Looking back, I guess her guard was up, as well; she clearly enjoyed our being together—I was the one who had to mention it was almost two in the morning—but she bared nothing of substance, not even her soul.

So what did we talk about, that night and at unplanned intervals through that weekend? The verities. The nice trivias. About her itch to read every book, write every play, paint every picture, compose every score, build every bridge, heal every wounded. Her charge that I was laughing at her and my half-sincere denial. Her having heard stupendous things about me from her grandfather. My ho-ho assertion that they were all true. Her shaky belief in herself. Her occasional realizations that she wasn't much. Her observation that privilege had its drawbacks. My observation that I should be so drawn back. Her asking me if I thought she ought to sleep with the current Sonny Wasp. My answering that I was a waiter, not a priest. Her laughing at that. My laughing with her.

We saw each other the next weekend because Adam Scofield invited me back to Parnassus for more relaxed discussions. I'd thought about her more than I'd expected I would, so some of me was hoping she wouldn't be there. You don't get serious with the boss's kid, certainly not at this stage. You especially don't get serious with the boss's kid who's been groomed since inception to walk into the sunset with Sonny Wasp. You don't hit your head with a hammer, no matter how nice the feeling once you've stopped.

When I returned that Friday, Venus Montgomery told me that the old man was napping—"funny; up to five, six months ago he'd never heard of a nap"—and that Mary was at the outdoor pool, alone "I don't know what you have, honey, you're for sure not Gregory Peck," said Venus, a hearty lady I decided I liked a lot, "but you sure got Mary doing headstands. That girl never talks up anybody, but she kept asking what time you'd be here."

"That's because I stole her watch."

"Let you in on another little secret, honey. Adam thinks you're the cat's whiskers, too."

"But do *you* love me?" I said. "That's what I really care about."

"I only date sailors. Go on out there now and play your cards right."

"What do you *mean*, I'm not Gregory Peck?"

Mary was in a chaise at one side of the Atlantic Ocean of a pool, wearing a long beach robe and scribbling notes in the margin of a book. I startled her slightly when I took the book—*Origin of Species*—from her. "This was my favourite movie of all time," I said. "I thought the Three Stooges in the title role was inspirational casting."

She sat up, whipped off her dark glasses, and pitched me a crafty smile calculated to disturb the peace. "Why do you insist on pretending you're an illiterate?"

"Particularly Curly," I said. "Curly's the baldheaded one the other two Stooges keep poking. Curly was stirring and memorable in his role, bringing to it precisely the right shadings and nuances."

"You nut! How about a swim?"

"That's why I came. How are you?"

"Glad you're here. Happy you're here. Go on," she said, and pointed to the bathhouse. "I'll wait for you."

The bathhouse man's name was Jerry; he was a cordial man who knew my name and who guessed, right on the button, my swim trunks size. I picked a brown pair—decisions, decisions—and went back to her. She'd discarded the beach robe. She was (again, in the parlance of those middle-1950s) stacked, had the kind of grand body that would stay fine and fit and firm till the twenty-fifth century, that would never tolerate a sagged breast, a puckered thigh, a—God forbid—varicose vein. "I'm the best swimmer that ever lived," she said.

"So quit boasting and show me."

She showed me, all right. She went off the side of the pool in a long flat dive and came up like a dolphin, her body arched in the classic butterfly stroke, arms reaching forward and legs straight out behind her and kicking down. She hit the other end of the pool, thrust off the wall in a clean backstroke and was back at my end in seconds. She squirted water at me from clasped hands and called, "Catch me, and I'm yours!"

I tried. I leaped at her, but when I hit the water she was gone, slicing away in long racing strokes. I went after her, a first-rate swimmer myself, but midway down the pool, when I was sure I was gaining, I had my foot grabbed and I was pulled under. Humiliating. And nice.

We let the sun dry us. She asked me, "When did you learn to swim that wonderfully?"

"When I was nine. In the Gowanus Canal."

"What a pretty name. Is that in Italy?"

"No, it's a bit west of Nice. Terribly exclusive."

"You're pulling my leg, aren't you?"

"Well, I'm working to resist the temptation," I said. "Listen: whatever happened to Sonny Wasp?"

"Will you stop calling him that! He has a pretty name, too, and it's Bart Clay."

"Bart Clay sounds like the name of the villain in a stag movie."

"Are there villains in stag movies?"

"Oh, *mais oui, mais oui!* You can always spot them. They're the ones who wear the sock garters while everyone else is starky."

"*Sock garters?*"

"In the better stags, the heroine gets to speak lines. She asks the villain, 'Why do you wear sock garters, Sluggo? No one wears sock garters anymore.' And Sluggo is deeply disturbed to hear that, and he sings 'The Last Time I Saw Paris'."

"You nut!"

"You've said that."

"I've never seen a stag movie."

I shrugged. "Seen one, you've seen them all. The same old faces."

"Never saw a stag movie. I've never been on a subway. I've never walked on the boardwalk at Coney Island. Where've I *been* all my life?"

"Take heart," I said. "I'm arranging to have you included in the Hundred Neediest Cases."

"There's something else I've never been: dumb. You like me—I can tell that—but you put me down, you think I'm brainless. I wish you wouldn't."

"Okay. The putting down stops. More or less."

That weekend, and the subsequent weekends, became both a pleasant habit and an exercise in tightrope walking. I would leave Parnassus to go back to New York, where I would work like a truck horse to detail my recommendations of how the Scofield press could be set again on a profitable course, newspaper by newspaper, magazine by magazine, and refine the details in terms as pragmatic as possible to be palatable to the old man. Then I would return to Parnassus for extended conferences, sometimes alone with the old man, sometimes with him and this or that Paleolithic business adviser he'd spring on me to listen in. By my fourth trip there, I was beginning to convince myself I was making dents, important ones. I knew Adam Scofield could be a mercurial old pirate king. I'd heard the stories

303

about his bum son, Harmon, how that son had tried to ride on the family name simply by having the family name, how he'd been kiboshed because the name alone wasn't enough. I had no doubt that the sidelines cavemen, who were sitting in and sucking their pipe stems and scratching their ankles while I was promoting radical changes in the management of a press empire, were doing their best, once I was out of the room, to flatten me.

But I knew something else; I knew the old man wouldn't have kept calling me back if I wasn't getting to him. By my fourth trip there, in early September, I realized that I not only wanted the job, but that I *really* wanted it, that I would be terrific at it.

The old man was at one end of the tightrope. Mary was at the other. I hadn't even kissed her, although all the antennae invited me to help myself. We talked a lot; oh boy, how much we talked! If I was starting to get privately cocky about what a titanic boon I would be to the Company, my mind was still asking what *she* saw in me, why she was obviously so happy when I appeared. In my new pal Venus's words, Gregory Peck I wasn't. Nor was I Moses Maimonides, though I was comparably old.

"Because I can trust you," she said when I finally put the question to her. "Because you can be the most insolent, infuriating man I've ever met, but you'd never let yourself be manipulated or pushed around. Because you're the first man I've ever met under seventy who's ever asked me what I think about anything besides who's going to wear what at Wimbledon. And you listen, and correct me when I'm a ninny and support me when I'm right. Because underneath all that Bogart armour of yours, there's sensitivity and character and intelligence and kindness."

"Here's an exclusive for you," I said. "Outside the protective gates of Parnassus, there has to be a carload of young men who fit somewhere in between the Sonny Wasps and the Joe Greenwoods. Good, bright, unpush-aroundable young men who live a lot closer to Parnassus than I do."

"You do play hard to get, don't you?" she snapped.

"Very well, I'm impressed that your father slaved in a tailor's sweatshop, but that's hardly enough reason for you to be such a pompous snob."

I laughed. "Let's see how I can shut you up." That was when I first kissed her. And let go fast because she was beginning to kiss back.

"What is it?" she asked.

"It's precisely eight minutes before I'm to meet with your granddad."

"He'll wait. I thought you were so independent."

"Oh, no, I'm the original Establishment Indian. Uncle Tom-Tom."

Joe the jokester. Greenwood the gagmaker. I left that Sunday after a long conference with the old man and one of his particuarly unlovable buccaneers, an aged preener named L. P. Lang, who happened to refer during that session, apropos of nothing relevant, to "a bunch of them, sitting on their fat Jew asses in Miami Beach." Adam Scofield didn't react, either because he hadn't heard it or because it didn't matter. I heard it, though, and it mattered. Firmly, but not giving a performance, I said, "Let's get something straight here and now, Mr Lang. I have no patience at all with that kind of talk."

Scofield seemed to come awake. Lang sort of gaped. "What thing? Jews?" He proffered a fatherly chuckle. "Are you Jewish?"

"Yes. Which isn't the point." Like hell; it was almost altogether the point.

Another fatherly chuckle. "Easy does it, there. Considering that whatever it was I said was just a meaningless saying, and considering that my own son-in-law is partly Jewish—"

Adam Scofield appeared bored. "Gentlemen, I can ask my close friend Bernie Baruch or my long-time cronies at the Anti-Defamation League to come by and mediate this dispute," he said, "or we can get back to business."

And I left that Sunday with the deliberate resolve that there wasn't going to be any more of the kissing business with Mary. I didn't need a tablet and pencil to annotate the skillions of sound arguments for me to stay clear of her.

Don't blame me, Your Honour. She called me, that same Sunday night.

"Why don't you ever invite me into the city?" she asked.

"For a stag movie?"

"Yes. And to puff reefers, and mug old ladies in the doorway, and rob a liquor store."

"Who'll spring for the chop suey supper?" I asked.

"You! Whaddaya think, I'm made of money? Actually, I want to drive in to see the Kandinsky at the Modern, and I'll be in the front lobby, at four, picking up men."

"Four," I agreed. "Maybe I'll stroll by. You'll recognize me by my exposed kandinsky."

There was Kandinsky, a tolerable chore on my less than cultured part, and a trip uptown in her insect of a foreign sports car to the Shanghai on 125th Street for roast dumplings and sweet and pungent shrimp, and, prosaic of prosaics, a ride on the Staten Island Ferry. Winding up, or starting up, in my West Seventies apartment.

"Now I know why I had to ring you so many times last night before you answered," she said, one sweep of her hand condemning the flat's mess. "You couldn't find the phone."

"It's the Jewish-son syndrome," I said. "The time we take to make a bed properly steals time we could be using in piety and reflection."

She was no more than an inch away. "And stopping us *shiksas*?"

" 'Stopping'?"

" 'Stopping.' Isn't that the word for sex?"

" 'Stopping'?" A light bulb. "You mean '*shtupping*.' They didn't teach you anything at Bryn Mawr, did they?"

"They taught me that I'd love for you to make love to me."

Which happened. She was a virgin; of all unpredictable magic tricks, she was, for a while that night, a virgin. And tense, and passionate. And, fortunately, not tearful. "How

306

lovely you are," she whispered later.

"You're a fraud," I said.

"You're my lover," she said. And repeated, "How lovely you are."

I was old enough to know better.

Old enough to know (a) that it couldn't go anywhere, (b) that I should have made that plain to her before we touched, and (c) there was thin ice on Adam Scofield's pond, and maybe, just maybe, I was skating on it.

But there I was, closing in on thirty, damn right old enough to know better, and behaving like Harold Teen. Mary began to become important to me. I wouldn't tell her how important—that wasn't the way it was done on my block—but she didn't need long to catch on. There were the meetings at Parnassus, there were the lengthy, meandering, cheery telephone calls, and her drives to the city got more frequent.

Not underhandedly, exactly, though somewhat with the apprehensive eye of a divinity student sneaking out of a burlesque house, I showed her New York. We walked the Coney Island Boardwalk and gobbled franks at Nathan's. We sat in those half-broken seats at the Thalia and saw *The Bank Dick* and *Poppy*. We ate at Frank's Chop House in Harlem. She taught me to be patient with the ballet at City Centre and I taught her what was equally graceful in a heavyweight match at Madison Square Garden. We walked miles of Manhattan. We got so comfortable with each other that sometimes it wasn't necessary to go up to my apartment.

Sometimes it was.

We were a wildly unlikely pair, but it was great. It was great to go to bed with her. It was great to open up at least a piece of a world to her beyond Via Barberini and tennis courts. It was great to hear her tell me, and tell it with a straight face, what a great man I was.

What wasn't great, in time, was that she was starting—it was a gradual thing, not overnight—to develop a bad case of the cloys. She didn't send me a tie on my birthday; she had Sulka hand-deliver a dozen. She got so that experiencing an orgasm wasn't enough; she had to writhe, moan, yelp, bite, and punch, the kind of overdone performance that would have got her justifiably executed if she'd tried it as an audition at the Actors' Studio. She agreed with everything, absolutely everything, I said; I didn't quite say I created the heavens and the earth during a coffee break, but she would have agreed. "Don't hang on so tight," I said. "Talk back."

"I couldn't bear to lose you."

"Well, sitting on my lap while I'm standing up is the quickest way to do it. Relax, girl. Loving me—or anyone— is all to the shiny good. But the whole idea is to feel fond of yourself as well. You have a perfectly good belly button of your own. Now go say hello to it. Take it to lunch."

Her response to those profundities? "We're going to get married. You know that, don't you?"

"*Oi, vay iz mir.*"

"What does that mean?"

"It means you're the one who's the nut," I said. "*If that* ever happens, it'll be only after a gross of obstacle courses've been overcome."

"What's the first one?"

"You have to finish teething."

"O, swear not by the moon, the inconstant moon,
    That monthly changes in her circled orb,
    Lest that thy love prove likewise variable."

"What does *that* mean?" I asked.

She showed me her belly button. "It means, why don't we all go to lunch?"

It ended.

It ended in November, less than a week after I sat in the office of the old man's chief attorney, Noel Lathrop, and signed an executive contract guaranteeing stock options and fat annual raises over five years. It ended when Lathrop phoned me to say Mr Scofield wished to see me at Parnassus. As soon as I could get there. The tone wasn't cordial.

Nor was Adam Scofield. "Back in the forties," he said, in a voice so controlled you could almost see blood vessels bursting, "New York had a Socialist mayor, La Guardia, who was famous for one remark: 'When I make a mistake, it's a beaut.' Now it's my turn to say that, Mr Greenwood."

("Mr Greenwood." I'd been "Joe" for over a month.)

"And don't look around for my granddaughter. She's not here."

"Suppose you get to the point, Mr Scofield."

He did, he sure did. I was a schemer, a conniver, true to the Chosen People's code. All the while he was preparing to hand me the keys to the kingdom, I was busy corrupting all that was left of meaning in his family, his granddaughter, seducing her, surely and systematically selling her a bill of goods. Poisoning her, hedging my every bet, training her to play me up to him. I wasn't only a vicious, heartless son of a bitch, I was a stupid son of a bitch, stupid and Jew-greedy; in my zeal to certify I would own the Scofield press, I'd promised his grandchild I would marry her.

I was out. I had signed a legitimate Company contract, guaranteeing executive escalation. I could honour his honourable request, to agree to destroy it, or I could look forward to a losing court battle. It was quite as simple as that.

"Where's Mary now?" I asked. "I want her here."

"To plead your cause?"

"Fuck the cause, Scofield! The only cause I'm interested in is untangling this bughouse Jabberwocky. Not for your sake; for mine. Where is she?"

"Not here! Not here! Don't you raise your voice to *me!*"

I stormed around the house and grounds of Parnassus, looking for Mary and planning to knock the truth out of her, planning to run away with her, planning Christ knows what non-planning foolishness. I didn't find her, mainly because she was running around New York, looking for me.

She phoned me the minute I was back in my apartment,

and eventually the jigsaw fitted. She'd told the old man we were planning to marry, and we were, weren't we? We both loved each other, so she'd assumed it was merely a matter of time.

"You might've announced all this to me first," I said.

"Yes. I guess. Does it matter so much? You sound mad. You aren't mad at me, are you? I can handle Gramp; I'm sure I can. In no time at all."

In anger, I said things I don't like to remember even now, cruel things. I knew she hadn't meant to be arrogant, but that's what her actions were, and they'd cost me a career *and* the girl I could maybe have got around to marrying, when *I* was ready to propose to *her*. And I never wanted to see Adam Scofield again, or any of his clan, and other choice bits of hurt-little-boy blusters.

I stopped because I heard sobs, and I started to apologize, but before I could get another word out of the phone was dead. I dialled Parnassus. Miss Scofield, I was told, was "unavailable."

It was over.

I didn't see Mary after that until we ran into each other in Bermuda a chunk of years later, but I would occasionally hear about her. She met up and eloped with a minor poet named Tommy Moran, who wrote soaring gems like

> In my generation, where the chapter of history is big
> They say he is mad for he cries for an herb called truth
> They say it can't be obtained, it's priceless, too dear
> He says it is priceless and that means free
> It grows where mountains are in eternity
> By rivers flowing through strange boundaries to the sea
> He says its pollen weights the wind
> So they lock him away for bewitched

while putting down superficial hacks like Dante and Yeats. The short union with the minor poet was followed by a longer one with a professional polo pony named Gil

310

Stafford who moonlighted as the Marquis de Sade. Followed by a number of non-wedlock hits, runs, and extravagant errors, followed by husband number three, the hat rack known as Owen Enright, losers all, as though she was committed to a career of seeking out men guaranteed to prove she was worthless.

Adam Scofield joined the Big Publisher in the Sky about a month after Mary ran off with the minor poet.

His death made the front pages of every newspaper in America, and most of those on the other continents. Not unexpectedly, the Scofield press hailed him as the greatest instrument of communication in the annals of man. The majority of the rest of the press were more restrained in their praise, though they all conceded he had been a monumental force in journalism and public influence. I read the obits and appraisals, read the lionizations and the think-piece blasts, and decided that his most remarkable accomplishment in life was that, despite devastating financial losses as a press lord, as *the* press lord, he left a personal estate of some thirty million dollars and a business empire worth twenty times that.

He left the Company to his wife, Eugenia, who sat as a serene vegetable in Florida, and he left specific instructions that, upon her passing, the Company would go to his granddaughter Mary, his "only other living relative." There was no mention of his son, Harmon, who happened to be very much alive.

He left not a dime of his personal estate to any of the Company's thousands of employees, or to any of his servants.

Half of his personal estate went to Venus Montgomery, "my close and loyal friend."

A quarter of the personal estate was to be dispersed among various private organizations sworn to smite Godless International Communism.

The remainder of the personal estate went to Mary, to be fed her in modest annual allowances until her thirtieth birthday, when she would receive all of it. My understanding is that he had summoned his lawyer to cut her out of the will entirely for having defied him and taken up with the minor poet. And that Venus had cooed him into putting Mary back into the will. I considered that class, of sorts; if she—Venus—had kept her mouth shut, she probably would have inherited all that much more of the pie.

A personal estate of some thirty million dollars and a business empire worth twenty times that . . . Wow, I thought. Wow, thought *Yussele* Greenwood, not the tailor's son but the tailor's assistant's son. Wow, thought the thirty-year-old almost-press-lord, sitting in my West Seventy-fourth Street apartment, contemplating a salami sandwich and seeing myself ending up at the rewrite desk of *The Weekly Bugle* in Armpit, Iowa. (*"Where's Armpit, Iowa?"* *"Shucks, that's just a whoop and a holler from the county seat, Dregs' Landing, Iowa."*)

Okay, it's fairly safe to say that, once old Adam was buried, I could have returned to the Company. There were roundabout feelers and then a criminally overpriced expense account lunch at "21" with an uncharacteristically throat-clearing Roy Britt. "If the papers were sleeping on their feet while the old man was here, they're about to be encased in cement now that he's gone," Roy said. "Lawyers are running the show now, lawyers and editors older than the old man, and their contracts allow them to call the shots, and there's not a damned thing I can do about it. Except offer you a job. And a nice salary, but nothing like a really long leash."

"Will I have to raise my hand to leave the room and take a leak?"

"Pretty much so," he nodded. "But while you're taking that leak, you can be thinking about the nice salary you're getting."

He quoted a very nice salary, to be raised periodically. I nodded, too. "I appreciate it, Roy. I appreciate it, but there's a line in either Numbers or Leviticus that goes, 'What profiteth it a man who canst not take a leak when he damn well wishes?' "

I didn't go to the Company, but neither did I go to Armpit, Iowa. I accepted a job, doing essentially what I'd done at the Company, with the Headley chain of newspapers. Headley didn't pay Scofield money, but they were salivating for fresh ideas, and I gave them a hatful, and before long they made me a dream offer no newspaperman in his right mind could turn down: to take one of their foundering papers and, with no questions asked, make it mine. I landed in Cleveland, but then who wants everything? The point is, I made *The Cleveland Argus-Post* mine, and made it a success.

Cleveland was where Sylvia and I met. Another success.

There were colossal reasons for not marrying Sylvia Saks. She was certainly no looker. She'd been widowed for a year and a half, with two small daughters who took an instantaneous dislike to me. She wanted to talk when I was in the mood for quiet, and she was pensive and reflective when I felt like an all-burners conversation. She was religious, and serious about it; I was all for being Jewish, as long as I wasn't expected to be religious about it. She read Locke and Strachey; I knew who they were, but I didn't much care. She thought—and she wasn't kidding—that Babe Ruth was named after the candy bar.

And yet it worked. Occasional frictions and all, it was a good, workable marriage. The girls discovered they liked me when I discovered I was a mighty good father. Sylvia was the kind of wife the extreme wings of women's lib would call a—well, a *wife*. She saw nothing demeaning in being one. She stayed one, stayed mine, for a shade over eighteen years, stayed through our arguments, stayed with me in Cleveland, and stayed with me when I transferred to the Company in New York, stayed with me. Nine days before that goddamn illness put her in the hospital for the last time, Mary set up a glittery party at her town house, all for Sylvia without letting on that it was for Sylvia, a party jammed to the rafters with movie stars and famous authors, the type of schmaltzy party sure to thrill my basically hick-town Sylvia. That was the night Sylvia sat on a sofa with Sonja Hayes,

313

an in-vogue feminist whose book about the chatteldom of women, *Woman: Condemned,* had that week hit number three on the *Outlook* and *Times* best seller lists. It was presumably a private conversation between them. I was learning not to hover over Sylvia—learning how to appear not to hover, that is—but I hovered and listened in.

HAYES (who had no reason to know that Sylvia was dying, as Sylvia knew; who conceivably wouldn't otherwise have been such a banshee): "I've seen some of your book illustrations. They're excellent. Still sexist—the little girl with the doll, the boy with the fire engine—but sensitive draftsmanship. Tell me: how does your husband help?"

SYLVIA (friendly, misunderstanding): "Help? My husband can't draw a straight line."

HAYES: "No, no. How does he help in the home while you're working?"

SYLVIA: "He doesn't work in our home. He has an office."

HAYES: "I see. Then you have a housekeeper."

SYLVIA: "Well, we have a woman who comes in three times a week to clean. Oh, I see what you're getting at, Miss Hayes—"

HAYES: "Mizz Hayes. Sonja. Call me Sonja. I'm not getting at anything. All I'm questioning is whether you're entirely clear about how much you're giving and how much you're getting in return. I've watched you get up twice to do for your husband, once to get him a drink and once to have a plate of food prepared for him. Not only hasn't he once come by to ask if you'd like something, he didn't even thank you for doing all you did. My question—"

SYLVIA: "All I did? What was all I did? I love him."

HAYES: "You're a *per*son! An *achie*ver!"

SYLVIA (coldly controlled now): "I think you ought to go away."

HAYES: "Sylvia . . ."

314

SYLVIA (all of a viperish sudden): "No, it's Mrs Greenwood. Mrs Greenwood and, for the third and last time, Mrs Greenwood. I like the name. I like my taste in having picked that man. I like his taste in having picked me. I like the way his homely face lights up when he comes home and he smells the potato pancakes I've made for him. I like the way he looks at me. I like the vulgar way he gooses me. I like the way he pretends to pay attention to me chattering at him about my last Great Books class. I like the way he clinks and clunks around in the kitchen to fix me a simple cup of tea when I'm not feeling well. I like the way he screws me. I like the way we hold each other. I like our fights. I like the warmth we both give our children. I like what we have together. What do *you* like, Miss Hayes? What warms you? What comforts you?"

Some woman.

Mary was some woman, too. She was at the funeral with the kids and me, and after, keeping close, letting her own work go by the boards, aware that I couldn't show grief except in private, attuned to me, there for me. She was there when my coronary hit, too, she was on deck all through the spooky ordeal, and after. A friend? You can't buy that kind.

And unless half a loaf is enough, you can't really be loved by them, either. Because all-out love is giving and sharing, trusting the give-and-take of it. And Mary trusted affection only so far as she could control it.

Of course, half a loaf leaves you hungry, whether you're receiving it or giving it.

So what was I doing in a guest room bed in Mary's town house that Friday night, telling myself I loved her? Mary, the un-Sylvia, the Velvet Claw with the half loaf.

Go figure. I couldn't.

Finally, I fell asleep.

For how long? The telephone woke me. It was the Company extension again, I saw by the glowing button. The luminous clock read five past one. Jesus: no sleep at all.

I needed a moment to place Harry. It came—Harry was my chauffeur, and Harry had called the office number when my home phone hadn't answered, and they'd switched him to this line. Harry stammered only when he was upset. At five past one in the morning, Harry stammered.

All I could piece together at first was that he had Rick Tovar in the back seat of my car, that the actor was bleeding like a pig and probably had a concussion.

Eventually I got the story, or some of it. Harry had driven him to Pete Vienna's building on the Upper West Side, was told to wait, and did. Waited, in fact, all these hours, until he looked ahead of him and saw Tovar staggering towards him, not from Vienna's building but from the opposite end of the block. The actor grunted something about having been punched out, coming to in an alley, half crawling, half walking out of that alley and seeing my car. "He needs a hospital, bad," Harry said, "but do I take him, or what? He's passed out. All I know, maybe he's dead, or close to it. Tell you, Mr Greenwood, I'd rather not get mixed up in no hospital stuff, with the police and all . . ."

Move over, I thought. "You're calling from the car, right?" Yes. "Hold on," I said, and pressed the *Hold* button, and puzzled the next step: and *how* you don't go checking mutilated movie stars into hospitals. I thought of my own doctor, Alex Andreas, and marked him off fast; he was a good friend but not that good; if the actor died on him, Alex would insist on making a report, and niceties like that I didn't need.

Then Hagen's name came to me—Hagen, the kind of doctor who advertised his office hours on the walls of subway toilets, but a doctor who, someone or other had once told me, could be counted on to keep his mouth shut if not his fingernails clean. I found his number in the Manhattan directory, and pushed another button and phoned him to verify that he was in. I told him a man who'd had an accident would be brought to him for quiet treatment within

316

a half hour, and luckily remembered the name of Cy Weitman, one of our editors and the guy who'd recommended Hagen, back in the illegal abortion days.

Then I had my office snap it up with the home phone number of Ernie Collinge, who ran Pearlin's in New York, the private cop who'd found Sister Florence at home for me. I called Collinge, waking him but the hell with that, and quickly filled him in: he was to get to Hagen's before my driver and the actor got there—I gave him the mid-town address—pay Hagen's bill, and collect Tovar and deliver him to my apartment. Sure, all of it was dangerous, I realized. But I couldn't afford to have Tovar evaporate until I knew a lot more than I knew at that moment.

"This could mean my ass, Joe," Collinge said.

"It also means a grand, in cash," I said, and pressed the Collinge button out and pressed the Harry button in. "What's going on?"

"Well, he's breathing. I been trying to stop the blood."

I gave him Hagen's address, and told him to deposit the actor and run.

My chest felt heavy.

Vienna, I thought, getting up to dress. So it was the Viennas, after all. And now I'd have to figure out how to deal with Tovar, and the Vienna crowd . . .

Except that while I was standing in the centre of that guest room, buttoning my shirt, Mary called my name from the other side of the door and opened the door. She had been trying to reach me, hadn't known I was here, had phoned my service.

She weaved. I caught her, and squeezed her frozen hands. Harmon had just called her. Drunk and crazy and ranting and desperate, offering Carole's safety in exchange for every overdue Scofield dollar that was rightfully his, rambling curses, warning her that contacting police would guarantee Carole's quick death, ordering her to have one million dollars in unmarked bills ready for the next time he called, that next time to be complete with instructions, goddamning every Scofield but Harmon Scofield, describing the heart-shaped birthmark on Carole's left breast, racing assurances that his long nightmare was over, that every other Scofield's had just begun.

"Call Stefan. I'll be dressed in a minute and a half," Mary said, strong again, and hurried to the door.

"Whoa," I said. "Where are we going?"

"Parnassus. You, I, and the driver. And no police."

"Did he mention Parnassus?"

"No," Mary said, and was gone.

I rang for Stefan, her chauffeur, to come running, and finished getting into my clothes.

Harmon? I thought. *Harmon?* . . .

SEVENTEEN

HARMON SCOFIELD, nineteen years old, and his wife, Eunice, eighteen, took their infant daughter, Mary Elizabeth, home from Ocean City Hospital. Home, that May in the middle 1930s, was a cramped room in a spotless but dark, groaning-old boarding-house, its quarters a far cry from the bright, elegant hotels they had occupied over the past half year in Europe and South America. They walked up the house's five flights of stairs to the cheerless room, cheerless despite the fresh-cut red roses Harmon had bought as a welcome-home present, and Eunice placed the screaming baby on the bed, and tried to comfort her. The baby continued to scream, and Eunice, drawn and near hysteria, glowered at Harmon and cried out, "Thanks a whole lot for everything! We can eat the flowers for supper. Thanks for this real fancy estate I'm bringing my baby to!"

"Shh, honey . . ."

"That's right, tell me to shut up. Mustn't have that old busybody that runs this classy dump think anything's wrong. Where've I been all my life? Your old man, he's got all the money in the world and here we are, sitting in this dark dump I wouldn't invite pigs to live in, and we're poor! I'm more poor now than when I was waitressing. I wanted sunlight for my little baby right from the time she was born. There isn't even no sun or sky for her to look at. A great big billboard right outside the window, a great big ad for Mail Pouch—is that good enough for her, is that good enough for *me*?"

"Shh-hh, something's bound to turn up, honey . . ."

"Oh, go drown in the ocean or something. I want to die. I never been so low before in my life. Wasn't for Mary Elizabeth, I'd want to die." She cradled the still-screaming baby and mourned, "Well, why don't you just take off? That's what you're achin' to do, isn't it, clear out and shut

319

the door after you? Go on, we'll get by. I can wait tables—maybe it's not so classy a line of work, but it's more than you know how to do. You don't even know how to write a letter to pick up a telephone and tell your bitch-bastard father we'll all be starving pretty soon."

Harmon went downstairs, to the drugstore's pay phone. He had sworn to himself that he would never contact his father again. Father could have reached him somehow; he and Eunice had always registered under their right names at the hotels over the months; Father, if he'd wished, could have found them. He hadn't. Dropping a nickel in the phone slot, Harmon placed a person-to-person, collect call to his mother in Arizona, hoping that was where she was, hoping that when he reached her, if he reached her, she wouldn't get too emotional and wouldn't expect him to grovel.

Nothing ventured, he thought now.

Mother was not at Scottsdale, but in Florida. "You're alive," she breathed. "Blessed be Almighty God."

"Are you well, Mother?"

"I had a vision last night. The Lord Jesus touched my shoulder and reassured me you were safe. Where are you? What have you become?"

"You have a granddaughter, Mother. She's one week old, and healthy and gorgeous, and her name's Mary Elizabeth." He explained as little as he could, though she had many questions. "Mother," he said finally, "Eunice and I want to come home and bring you your granddaughter."

". . . That isn't possible."

"Why not?"

"When your father and I went looking for a child to adopt, we could have picked among dozens of others. We picked you. We picked you and we vowed we would love and care for you as if I had borne you." (*Oh, God, that same old crap again*, he thought.) Harmon half listened to the rest of the litany, resting his weight on one foot and then the other, and presently he heard her ask, "Are you paying attention, Harmon?"

"Yes, Mother."

"I've prayed for you, every morning and every night since that day you chose to hurry your father and me into our graves."

Impatiently, with anger building, he snapped, "All of which means what? That you never want to see me again?"

"Your father and I are in agreement. The door will always be open to our son if you're prepared, sincerely prepared to come back."

Brightening, he said, "I am, Mother. I wasn't so hot last year on going to college. I am now—I've been to lots of places and I see the importance now of a good education. And I'll go into the Company. You and Father will never have to have a second's worry about me again. If you can wire us some money right away, we can—"

"Us?"

"Us. Eunice and the baby and me."

"Oh, no, Harmon. Oh, no. That—girl isn't and never will be a member of this family. I'll pray for the baby because I know she's innocent of sin, but no one born in sin will ever be a member of this family, either. Your father and I are quite clear in agreement on that."

"I see," he said huskily. "What does your Christianity advise me to do, then, ankle away from them and let them fend for themselves?"

"That's hardly a concern of—"

Despising her, despising everyone, he stood close to the mouthpiece and declared, "You listen now to your foundling-home son, Mother. Write down this address," he said, reciting it. "I have enough money to see us through another week, if that. Your granddaughter—I don't care what you want to call her, that's what she is, your granddaughter—is going to be hungry for milk. Eunice can't nurse, so we have to buy milk and milk costs money. It's all right if I starve. It's all right if my wife starves. Forget that Mary Elizabeth was born in what you call sin if you can for a minute. Do you want it on your conscience that you're helping to starve an infant? We're living like *de*relicts here! I haven't been loafing all these months. I worked while we were abroad," he lied, "and I made money. It was stolen. That's why we're starving while you and Father are eating. Are you paying attention, Mother? Starving. Starving!"

He slammed the receiver on to its cradle and returned to the room. The baby was sleeping. Eunice, still at the edge of the bed, was slowly rocking her in her arms. "Everything's going to work out just fine, Eunice," he said and kissed the top of her head and touched Mary Elizabeth's tiny, tiny knuckles. "I took care of it. We'll be out of here before you know what hit you."

No wire arrived that day. Or the next. Harmon, who had begun to pawn articles valuable to him a month before—his gold watch, his ring, expensive gifts he had bought Eunice and himself throughout Europe, expensive articles that had brought peanuts in the States—became worried, for there was nothing of value left to hock. He had been calmly positive, before she went to the hospital and during her stay there, that something good would turn up on its own because something good always had.

On the third day after his call to Mother, he counted his money: four one-dollar bills, seven dimes, and nineteen pennies. The landlady, Mrs Hawn, screeched up at him that he was wanted. He tore down the stairs that had become all too familiar and recognized Hatcher, Father's chauffeur. "Good day to you, Master Harmon," the wiry old Cockney greeted him, tapping his forefinger to his cap. "Someone to see you." He walked outside with Hatcher, who discreetly inclined his head towards the long pier across the way. Harmon walked the length of the pier. Father, wearing a broad slouch hat and smoked glasses, sat on a wooden bench that faced the water.

"Hello, Father."

"Sit down."

Harmon sat.

Father glanced at him and then back at the ocean. "You've fleshed out a bit. You're not skin and bones anymore. That's all to the good, but you mustn't put on weight. There's that song, 'Everybody Loves Me 'Cause I'm Fat.'

A funny song but a pack of lies. We ran a slogan contest in the papers for a month, promoting fit bodies. A lady in Dickinson, North Dakota, won first prize, two hundred dollars. You know her slogan? 'Lean is keen.' "

" 'Lean is keen,' " Harmon repeated. "That's nearly a hundred dollars a world. I could've done better than that, a lot cheaper."

Subdued: "You weren't around."

Subdued: "That's true. I wasn't around."

They watched the water, not each other. "I heard from your mother. It took me a while, as you can see, for me to come here. You're not the only stubborn bull in the ring."

"I'm glad you came."

Father's great head nodded. "Your mother claims you were impudent on the telephone, that your language was crude. You mustn't ever do that. She's a fine woman, to be cherished."

"I'm sorry. I'm sorry about a lot of things."

"End of lecture. I've given you a hundred of 'em, up here," he said, poking his temple, "while I was waiting to go to sleep. Where you're concerned, talking with you, to you, I'm the most lucid man on the face of the earth when I'm talking from up here. When I'm anywhere else, I'm not what you'd call an inspired orator."

"I want to come home, Father. With my family. Come home, and start again right."

Father seemed not to breathe for a time, and then he rumbled a sign. "There's no real 'home' anymore, not since you charged off on your own, not since—well, it began before that, didn't it? Funny—I built homes for us all over the lot, and no one really lives in any of them."

A pause. "I'm . . . lonely. All I ever wanted was a family, and sometimes I get so lonely for my family, for us all to be together and happy, that I damn near can't see straight. You—"

A pause. "Goddamn it, but I'm tripping all over my tongue. This is such an important day for me. I can't seem to talk."

A pause. "I'd give nearly everything I own if I could see my grandchild."

"She's not more than a few hundred yards away from you."

Again, Father shook his head. "I might like your wife, and I'm not sure I could handle that. No, it wouldn't do, I'd . . ." He looked at Harmon. "Yes. Show me my granddaughter."

He was puffing and red-faced when they reached the top-floor landing. He nodded awkwardly at the gaping Eunice as Harmon introduced them, and then his eyes fixed on the baby. "May I pick her up?" he asked. "No, I guess I'd best not. She's sleeping. My, isn't she a little dream!"

He remained awkward with Eunice. But soon he said, resolutely, "This is no place for *any*one to live. Come, hurry and get together the things you need. We're all going home, where we belong."

Adam telephoned Eugenia that night from his Manhattan town house study.

"We were fools, Eugenia. We wasted so much precious time being proud and obstinate," he said. "The girl's not nearly what we kept picturing. She's nervous and she doesn't talk much, but that's to be expected. There's nothing trampy about her. The main point is that Harmon's crazy about her. And that baby, Eugenia, that baby! You could just eat her up! We should've done this long ago. I never should've sent him out like some servant we caught stealing spoons."

"How does Harmon look?"

"First rate, first rate. The boy's seriously trying to become a man, Eugenia. He's back home where he should've been all along, where you should be. We talked here for hours, that's why I'm ringing you so late. He's going to bear down now, he gave me his word and I know he's going to keep it. And he *cried*, Eugenia, the boy actually cried! All this past year, you've claimed he was made of icewater. Icewater doesn't cry, Eugenia. Big as he is, old as he is, he said straight out to me that he loves you and he loves me. Can you imagine? I did what savages wouldn't've done —I pushed our own son out of our lives when what he needed was our understanding, and I wouldn't let him back in, and you went along with me—and here he says he loves us!"

There was dead air for a moment and Adam, not expecting her enthusiasm to match his but disappointed that he could almost see the chill, said, "I want you to come back, Eugenia. For good. I want us all to share this."

"Very well, I'll leave my sick sister and rush back to a faithless husband and a son who treats me like a scrubwoman. Let's all of us have an enjoyable time ridiculing decency. Let's take your darling new daughter-in-law to Parnassus so she can meet your actress friend. I'm sure the two of them will find a great deal in com—"

"Please. Hear me. Please."

"What I hear is that you've condoned Harmon's sin by welcoming a prostitute and a love child. I phoned you to see that Harmon has food to eat, not that he be forgiven, certainly not that you open your arms to the kind of life he picked for himself. I tried to instil religion in him. You mocked my efforts, and now *you* can live with the results."

Grady Honeycutt, the *Outlook*'s executive editor, recommended that Harmon be brought into the Company through a side, or preferably back, door. "We've talked, and there's no question he's a sharp young man," Honeycutt conceded, "but he thinks he'd like to be an executive right off the bat. What I suggest is that we start him off running copy. Give me the okay to spread the word he's to be treated like any other copyboy. Let him get his hands dirty. Let him catch hell from the rewrite men. It won't kill him, and he'll learn the business the right way, from the ground up."

Adam fully agreed. Twenty cents an hour was what the other copyboys earned. Harmon would receive twenty cents an hour.

Harmon didn't appear at his second day of work. That

325

night he explained to Adam, "They had me racing like I was a slave. They were bending over backwards to take it out on me because I'm the boss's son. Not that I mind work, Father, you know that, but being a stooge is just a waste of everyone's time."

"Try it again tomorrow," said Adam, warmed by the sounds of youth in the town house, pleased by the bashful sweetness of his son's wife, unable to stay away from the room where his beautiful, perfect granddaughter lay and gurgled happily in her nursery crib. "Give it a little time. Take some lip from the help, if only for appearance' sake. Okay, Commodore? If it doesn't work out, then we'll go on from there."

When it didn't work out; when Harmon wrote a series of sparkling humour columns and Adam proudly printed them and discovered they had been cribbed from a Canadian writer; when the flinty but dedicated Scottish nurse Adam had hired to help care for Mary Elizabeth sniffed to him that the infant's mother was either sleeping or off gallivanting when she should have been showing at least passing interest in the baby's well-being; when Harmon earnestly vowed to change his ways and report to the *Outlook* to really learn the business and then disappeared with his increasingly cheeky wife for a week's "vacation"; when Grady Honeycutt finally had to suggest to Adam that the boy try his wings in some part of the Company other than the *Outlook* ("This may mean my neck for saying so, Mr Scofield, but I can't pamper him and run a staff at the same time. He's throwing snot-nose orders around to men we've had here for twenty-five years. And he's been forging my signature on some pretty hefty expense vouchers") . . . when patience proved exhaustible and profound disappointment became unendurable, Adam gave his son a cheque.

"We'll all be much better off if you and your wife just— go," he said quietly. "The baby will be safe here with me. I'll see that she's cared for."

"Is this kicking me out again?"

"Let's say it's giving you total freedom to be a leaf in the

326

wind. You're faced with only one problem, if you choose to make it a problem. When this runs out," Adam said, indicating the cheque, "you're on your own. This time, any scrapes you get into, you'll get out of without my help."

"I'll have to talk with Eunice. Maybe she'll insist we take the baby with us."

Adam nodded. "By all means, talk with her. And tell her one thing: if the baby goes, the cheque stays here."

The girl, so pleasant and grateful when she had first been brought to this house, was told the condition and screeched at Adam that she loved her baby too much to be black-mailed. And seemed to need time to weigh the condition when Adam held firm, and moved out with Harmon, who declared, "We're coming back for Mary Elizabeth. Don't you forget that. The minute I'm on my own two feet. I'm claiming our daughter. It's going to be sooner than you think. Don't you ever forget that."

Two months after they were gone, Adam learned about Venus. She had married the drunken actor named Bourne, had married him and caught alcoholism from him and kept it until his death. She wasn't drinking now. She was working in a factory in Battle Creek, living alone in a rooming house under her own name, Anita Janusz. She rarely had to deny she was Venus Montgomery any longer, according to the report, for she no longer was Venus Montgomery; her face and figure had bloated beyond recognition as a picture star. When she wasn't at the assembly line, packaging breakfast cereal, she sat in her room, a recluse.

He went to her. She was scarcely older than Harmon, yet her body was a matron's. She wore eyeglasses.

"Let's go home," he said tenderly. "I'll take care of you."

"No. I'll take care of you. Forever, and always. Just don't ever put me inside of a zoo, where I don't belong. Okay?"

"Yes," Adam said and took her home, where they cared for each other and where, lovingly, joyfully, Venus cared for the baby, adored her, knew instinctively how to be a mother, became her mother. Adam, who had always hungered for a family, suddenly saw his family before him. He decided

327

against flying to Eugenia. He wrote to her instead, wrote a reasonable, reasoned letter, devoid of rancour, reminding her of her promise that she would never block a divorce should he wish one. He wished a divorce, he wrote. Judiciously, stressing her goodness, he requested to be let go.

Eugenia's reply was swift. "If my refusal to grant your wish is viewed by you as punishment, then so be it," she wrote. "Until I am summoned to my Saviour's Bosom, I shall remain," and ended it, "Mrs Adam H. Scofield."

On the day Mary Elizabeth was one year old, Adam received a letter, with a Naples postmark, from Harmon.

"Eunice and I miss our baby so terribly," it began on Hotel Vesuvio stationery. "We are having a desperate time here. If you will forward us passage money to get home——& at once!!!!—I swear to you on Mary Eliz's life that my nose will apply itself straight to the grindstone & you will be proud of me yet!!! Father, I am not asking you to help, I am begging you. Don't let Eunice and I down. Blood is thicker than water & we are very, very desperate."

Adam didn't finish the letter. He ripped it into confetti.

After an hour he cabled ten thousand dollars to Harmon, with a message: *Proviso is that you stay away. No need for you here.*

On the day Mary Elizabeth was five years old, as all the Scofield newspaper editorials were stepping up Adam's campaign to persuade public opinion that America must not get involved in Europe's war, Harmon was found in a Roanoke motel bathtub, near death, his wrists cut. Adam flew to the Virginia hospital, paid the officers well for the illegible suicide note and for forgetting to report the incident, and paced a vigil until the point of danger had passed, an agonizing forty hours later. And presently, Harmon, looking white and fragile, was able to speak.

Eunice was divorcing him so that she could marry a mutual friend who was a successful orchestra leader, he explained. She was tired of living hand to mouth, especially knowing that her spiteful father-in-law was made of money.

Harmon had pleaded with her to reconsider. He was served the divorce paper, just as he was about to take a job in Roanoke.

"You did *this* because a tart skipped out on you?" Adam marvelled, awed.

"Let me come back, Father," Harmon pleaded in an almost inaudible voice. "I'm all botched up. However much I try to do something right, I do it all wrong. I can't stop drinking, I can't stop messing up this one life I have . . . Help me . . . somebody help me . . ."

In New York, Adam directed his own physician, George Hunt, to personally examine the boy, to call in as many consultants as desired, and report his findings. "I'm going to strongly recommend a sanitarium," Hunt said. "He's twenty-four now. His body is healthy enough, but emotionally he's walking an awfully taut wire. He's calling for help. If he doesn't get it, he just may not live to be thirty—or even twenty-five."

"Sanitarium. You mean a nut house."

"No, Mr Scofield, I don't mean that at all. I mean a hospital with knowhow supervision, where he's helped not only to quit the liquor once and for all, but to come to terms with himself, to find out what's getting in the way of his moving ahead. He's ripe for help, open to it. There's an excellent private hospital, about midway between here and Parnassus. Let me arrange to have him checked in there. A classmate of mine, a Dr Steiger—"

"I don't want strangers, George. I want you to treat him."

"You still don't follow me, do you? I'm a damned good doctor, but psychiatry isn't my field."

"No. I do follow you, and the answer is no."

"Sir—"

"I said no. I know all about those loony bins. They make you crazier than when you went in. No, Harmon's sure to be all right now that waitress is off his neck. Parnassus will do it. The fresh air there, a romp in the steam room and the pool, his family around him, a little time and plenty of rest and lots of love . . . He'll be fine."

Showing a glint of exasperation, Hunt said, "You asked my advice, and you've rejected it. I think you're making a big mistake. You'll let me know if you change your mind."

Parnassus solved everything.

Within days after he was there, Harmon's colour came back. Mary Elizabeth appeared bewildered to hear him call himself her daddy, but they took to each other almost instantly, played hide and seek together, and Adam watched them, revelling at the extraordinary sight, and exclaimed to Venus, "It's hard to figure which one is the grown-up and which one is the child."

"Okay, if you know what you're doing," Venus said, "but I still think old Sawbones Hunt is right. *I'm* right, and I'm the drink-drank-drunk that's the expert. What started the booze doesn't end by ending the booze."

Adam laughed. "I'm a lucky man. I'm here in the same house with Carry Nation and Sigmund Freud. Easy does it, coal miner's girl. Don't wrinkle your forehead like that. That'll make you old, and you'll become forty, and I'll have to change you for two twenties."

By the end of his first week at Parnassus, Harmon was so buoyant and Mary Elizabeth was so enthralled by him ("He's so nice, Grampy. Can he stay?") that Adam interrupted the busy afternoon—it was the day Germany launched its first major air raid on the city of London—to telephone George Hunt. "How does it feel to eat crow, George?" he exclaimed. "Your diagnosis turned out to be all wet. Everything is glorious here, *glo*rious! Don't feel too bad, George. This boy of mine is going to bury both of us—with his own platinum shovel."

In July of that year, soon after he became seventy, Adam was in Dallas when Venus phoned him from Parnassus. Harmon had taken Mary Elizabeth to the village that morning for an ice cream cone. It was now nearly midnight.

They were found in Havana with Eunice, whose orchestra leader had deserted her, who had contacted Harmon with some fantastic notion that they could ransom the baby and keep her. When his attorney expressed doubt that an abduction charge against natural parents could hold up, Adam sped to Havana himself, where he was met at the airport by a Company detective named Perez, who had tracked them down, who drove him to the hotel and, at Adam's direction, went with him to the room. Harmon opened the door. Adam saw Mary Elizabeth, and she squealed, "Grampy, Grampy!" and they clung in embrace, and Adam told her, "Sweetheart, this man is Mr Perez. I want you to go downstairs with him."

"Are we all going home, Grampy?"

"Yes. Go on now, sweetheart. I'll be along in a minute or so."

Perez took her by the hand. Adam closed the door after them, and faced his frozen-smiling jellyfish son and his son's wife.

"Where do you think you're taking my baby?" the wife hissed.

The flat of his huge hand slapped her with such force that she gasped in disbelief and pain. He lifted Harmon and pitched him across the length of the room, stalked after him, kicked him repeatedly, faintly hearing screams and cries. He moved away at last as the wife grabbed at his arm. He struck her, again and then again, raised her as well and threw her at the cowering, bleeding Harmon. He stood, tensed in readiness to hurt them, to destroy them, straightened, gazed at them through filmed eyes, waited for his breathing to grow less laboured, and said huskily to them both, "If you're ever seen or heard from again, ever, either of you, you'll die. If you try to touch that baby, ever, *ever*, you'll die. I'll see to it. I'll see that both of you die."

He spoke little on the flight back. He held his grand-daughter so tightly that at one point she said he was hurting her. Then she giggled as he apologized, and reached up to kiss his cheek, and soon was asleep, her angelic head on his lap.

At the age of five, and until she was twelve, Mary had a private tutor, Madame deBeauport, who was stricter than

Venus but a nice lady with a smell of peppermint. She had no playmates, except for the caretakers' boy at Parnassus, but she did have Venus, who was often a child with her, and, when he wasn't busy, she had Grampy, whom she adored and who made her laugh. She was never alone. When she travelled anywhere, even with Venus or Madame beside her, Mr Gibbon, a friendly, chocolate-coloured man nearly as big as Grampy, was always nearby, paid by Grampy to watch over her and keep her safe.

She knew early that she was very rich, that she would stay very rich. She became aware that there was a world out there somewhere that contained people who weren't very rich, or even rich at all, but that was where they stayed—out there. At nine, a voracious reader, fluent in Spanish and French, she was Grampy's "hostess" at weekend Parnassus parties.

GOVERNOR MAXWELL: "Tell me, Mr Scofield, is this charming young lady only nine years old? I thought all along I was holding a conversation with a grown-up genius." GRAMPY: "You were".

She would hear Venus complain to Grampy, "You're not doing her any favour, keeping her away from kids her age," and she would retreat to the playhouse Grampy had had built for her, the two-storied miniature mansion that was her fortress, where she could be nine years old or ninety or two, where she could be anyone and anywhere she chose.

When she was twelve, and at Venus's urging, Grampy grudgingly enrolled her at Pearce School for Girls in Westchester, and then only when he was thoroughly satisfied that Pearce had a strict security system, that the whereabouts of every girl there had to be accounted for around the clock, that kidnapping could not be a concern. She vomited and needed to die on the night before she was to go, and admitted to Grampy that she was petrified at the prospect of being with so many people her age. "Never let them know," he roared. "Never let anyone know you're

332

scared, or you'll get pushed around and you'll deserve to be. And anyway, what's there to be scared of? *People?* Don't be snooty or cocky, don't ever be that, but you go in as though you own the place, and pretty soon you will. You'll be looked up to. Your Grampy guarantees it."

She excelled in classes and in athletics. She swam faster, consistently hit more home runs, mounted a horse with more grace, had a stronger tennis backhand than any of her peers. And she was miserable, for they weren't peers; they were giggly sticks who clustered within their own groups and distrusted her because, despite every effort upon strenuous effort to be twelve years old, the impression she gave of snooty-cocky superiority was unmistakable.

At twelve and thirteen, she was pretty. At fourteen, by seemingly sudden magic, she became uncommonly pretty. Her lean athlete's figure rounded and blossomed. She worked to remove the guarded look from her eyes, the defensive dare from her mouth. Some of the girls she had sought to conquer as friends began to include her in their trivial, mindless, meaningless bull sessions, and she joined in, still miserable and unsure, continually ill at ease, yet accepted, for she had taught herself to be sincere; sincerity was agreeing with absurd opinions, laughing at dumb jokes, successfully pretending that she could belong in a group.

At fourteen, there were the hygiene lectures.

MRS WOODY: "Sex is consonant with marriage, gels. Gels who slip before the prized day at the altar never arrive at the altar. Nothing condemns a gel for life so much as being called 'easy'. The highest, noblest passion, gels, is the sense of self-esteem, pride in purity. Let's all say it, shall we: pur-i-ty. Once more . . ."

At fifteen, there was Miss Nesbitt, the math instructor, her idol, pouring tea in her flat on campus.

"You worry far too much about yourself, Mary. You're unquestionably grown-up, and so very beautiful. This

333

shyness of yours simply has to be overcome. Tell me, have you ever been with a young man? I mean *really* been with one? You know what I mean. Or a woman . . .?" "I'll have to go in a minute, Miss Nesbitt, I have an English class in—" "Janet. When the two of us are alone, call me Janet. Let me touch you, like this, let me show you—Ah, you poor, beautiful, frightened thing, don't move away like that, you know I'm not an ogre . . . Very well, then, go. It appears I was wrong. It seems you're not so grown-up, after all."

At fifteen, there were the closely supervised dances arranged by both Pearce and the nearby military academy, Semper Fidelis. There were the boys, with crew cuts and ramrod spines, older than she, yet children, their conversations puerile. At fifteen, the desperate crush on her humanities instructor, Mr Manning, Jason Manning, who was unaware of her except as a student.

At sixteen, her sixteenth birthday, soon to finish at Pearce, soon to enter Bryn Mawr, she lunched in the Plaza's Oak Room with her gorgeous father.

"My, how you've grown! So pretty and mature. Breasts and everything! . . . Very lovely breasts, too, I'm sure. Your young swains must go mad. How many lovers have you captured in your web by now, lovely princess?"

At sixteen and seventeen and eighteen, the chaperoned summer transatlantic crossings, the growing outer confidence, the persistent inner uncertainties, the Monday determination that she had much to give and would, the Tuesday recognition that she dare not step on a crack lest everyone find out her secret: there was nothing at all of substance she had to give. At eighteen, her announcement to Gramp that she planned to shift her major from art history, which she would ever use, to law or economics.

Gramp's large, strong head shaking disapproval: "Not

in my lifetime, missy. You're going to have the Company some day, and the Mr Right you marry's going to run it. You'll have your hands full, giving him handsome babies and all the important dinner parties, the way a wife is supposed to, without having a *career*, too. And a man's career, at that."

At eighteen, warily letting the goony young men kiss and feel her.

"Hey, come on now, Mary, what are you, an Eskimo Pie? You said I could take this lousy brassiere off, and now you're shoving me away." "There's such a thing as finesse." "I'm going crazy here, Mary. What do you want me to do?" "What I don't want is to be asked what I want you to do. I'm not teaching a class. No, stop that adolescent pawing! At once!"

At nineteen, sailing to Le Havre abroad the *France* in first class, reading the passenger list, seeing the names of M/M Jason C. Manning, Scarsdale, New York, phoning their stateroom in second class. Hearing him answer, identifying herself, exhilarated that he remembered her immediately, inviting him and Mrs Manning to dinner. Meeting him alone that midnight on deck by mostly pantomimed prearrangement, trembling as he kissed her, that night and the next night, ready, so very ready, telling him so.

"My wife is watching." "She's asleep, isn't she?" "Yes, but watching. It just won't do." "You don't have to love me. It's enough that I love you. Here . . ." "Ah, but I would have to love you. I'm sorry I let this begin. I have a daughter almost your age. Now we stop. I'm sorry. I'm sorry . . ."

At nineteen, the late summer weekend at Parnassus, signalling Joe Greenwood to get her a rum punch, listening to him say, "You'll have to find another waiter. This isn't my station."

When Gramp failed her, when Joe failed her, she ran.

She ran to Tommy Morgan, who was a scholar and poet and penniless, who made her laugh and who cherished her, who married her and took her to Howth in the south of Ireland. Tommy, who drank hard and who sang and who knew capitalism was finished and who cursed her for tricking him when he discovered she had been cut out of Adam Scofield's will. They were in Parknasilla when the news came over the radio that Gramp had died peacefully in his sleep. They were in Dublin when they learned she would get her inheritance, after all—not all at once, but she would get it. And Tommy drank viciously one night, seven months after they had married, and beat her. And she ran from him, and divorced him.

She ran. She ran to Gil Stafford, who was fond of money but who had it, enough of his own inheritance, handsome and urbane Gil who was a colossal lover, who married her, who taught her that hedonism was everything. The arguments and the hanging tensions and his periodic flights from her began in earnest when they had been married for a little over a year, when his gambling debts grew crushing to them both, when he insisted on more and more kinky sex or none at all, when he airily defended his random affairs with other women, when he repeatedly encouraged her to have affairs of her own and couldn't understand her refusal, when he cursed her for holding on to him too tight. She was twenty-three years old when he called their marriage pointless, called her pointless, wished her luck, and filed for divorce.

She ran. She ran to and from and to lovers who promised to be even more inadequate as human beings than she. She ran. She ran for comfort to Venus, who would live another few years but who, with Gramp gone, herself needed comfort. She ran to Owen Enright and from him. She ran from Carole. She ran to Bill Bradway. She ran to Rick Tovar. She ran from Mary Scofield.

She ran for forty years and three days, and then her town house telephone wakened her from a fitful sleep, from an oppressive dream, the familiar dream wherein she was running over fields upon meadows upon more fields of brambles, and she lifted the receiver and heard her father's voice, heard him describe the heart-shaped birthmark on her daughter's left breast.

EIGHTEEN

GREENWOOD.

The drive from the city to Parnassus normally took forty or fifty minutes, but there was no traffic now, at a bit past one in the morning, and Stefan flew. Mary sat in the corner of the limousine, staring straight ahead. She appeared to be looking inward, and I hated to interrupt her mediation, or whatever it was, but this ninety-mile-an-hour ride was getting to me.

"Okay," I said finally. "Talk to me. Why Parnassus? How do you know he's there?"

She gazed at me as if she'd forgotten *I* was there, then put a hand on my sleeve, a reassuring hand. Instead of answering me, she picked up the car phone, dialled Parnassus, and had herself connected with Mrs Parry, the head housekeeper.

I heard her ask about Harmon. She paused. I heard her, when Mrs Parry seemed to be balking, insist that the call was urgent, and saw her eyes narrow as she listened again, and heard her say, "I'm on my way to Parnassus now, and this is what I want you to do. I want the gateman notified to have the gates open, and every light on the grounds turned on. At once. We should be there in a few minutes."

She put the phone down. Harmon had shown up there yesterday, Mrs Parry had explained, now well and needing a place to rest and needing his presence there kept quiet. The housekeeper, torn between knowing he was never to be a welcome guest and knowing that he *was* a Scofield, nonetheless, had taken it on herself to put him up for a time. He had stayed pretty much to himself, in a back bedroom. She had gone to look in on him late in the afternoon. He wasn't anywhere to be found.

"So he's gone," I said. "What about Carole?"

Mary's face was set, like a stone carving. "Joe, *Yussele,*

338

don't ask now, all right? This is a family thing, and I have to handle it myself. And him. And Carole."

She stared through the window at the flashing lights of the Triborough Bridge. "The bastard," I heard her say softly. "The bastard . . ." Then, after a moment, she turned to me again, and pointed to the limousine's built-in bar. "Is there scotch in there? A stiff one?"

It was before two when we reached Parnassus, but the hundreds of lights switched on from the master control made the place as bright as day. The long, winding driveway led to a circle before the main house, but there was another small road that continued on around the house and disappeared into the woods. Mary knew exactly where to tell Stefan to stop, and she and I walked the ten or twelve yards to a steep stone path. At the foot of that path was the playhouse, partially hidden in a wooded glade by tall trees.

We went down, Mary behind me and tripping once. Just before the playhouse, her steps flagged, almost as if the various possibilities for Harmon mischief had just hit her. "Easy," I said. She nodded.

I moved ahead. I peered in through a window, and relief walloped me like a Muhammad Ali right cross. Carole was inside. Awake. Alone.

Alive.

"She's safe. Thank God. Thank God," Mary breathed, and opened the door and went in and sat across from her rather than stand and hunch. I didn't even bother to try to negotiate the doorway. But I could hear, and I could see.

Carole sat huddled, prettier without the eyeglasses, wearing a white slip, holding a Raggedy Ann doll, smiling at Mary but with a frozen-serene smile that gave me the spooks.

"Carole, dear . . ." Mary said.

The waxen smile stayed. The glazed eyes barely flickered. "Hello, Mommy."

"*Do you know when I realized I was getting old?*" Mary

339

had once said to me. "*When Carole was about twelve and I suddenly became 'Mother.' 'Mommy' was out for good.*"

"What is it, darling? What's wrong?"

Still waxen, still serene: "I love you, Mommy."

"I love you, precious."

" 'Precious' . . . That's so nice. He calls me that, too."

"Who, baby? Who calls you that?"

"He does."

"Who is he?"

"He."

"Where is he?"

"I love you, Mommy. We have so much fun playing here, don't we? I love you, Mommy. Do you love me, Mommy? Do you love Raggedy Ann? He loves me and Raggedy Ann, too."

"Carole, Carole, where is he?"

Her eyes were wide and suddenly bright, and she looked at me for a moment, not seeing me, and then at the open door. She jerked her eyes away, back to Mary.

"I was going to have a tea party, Mommy, and now you're here. Can you stay for the party, Mommy? Please? We can even have real tea."

Mary stood, head bent, and moved towards the girl. And stopped again. "Carole, I don't understand. Your grandfather called me. Is he here?"

The girl twitched, as if she'd been touched by a live wire, but her expression didn't change. "The man was nice, and he was going to come to my party, but he . . . but he . . ." She stopped, and her eyes moved to the door again, and again jerked away.

I motioned for Mary to stay and backed away from the Alice-in-Wonderland door. I went hunting, and with the floodlights that seemed to glare from everywhere, I didn't have to travel far.

I'd checked Harmon Scofield into and out of a number of drunk tanks and euphemistic rest homes without ever having met him; discreet chauffeurs were always the delivery boys. But that was Harmon Scofield, all right, lying face up and

340

naked and very much dead in a shallow fish pond, the blood
still fresh, a kitchen knife deep in his neck.

The details were hard to come by, because Carole with-
drew completely for a shade over a week, neither speaking
nor acknowledging any visitor. "Hysterical withdrawal" and
other terms were slung about, but they all added up to a
catatonic state, broken occasionally by brief flashes of dis-
connected lucidity. From these spurts of frustrating communication, we began to construct that night, piece by
piece, like a jigsaw.

She babbled for a long while to her roommate on that
Wednesday night, the night she was brought back from
Tampa, ashamed of having worried and disappointed
everyone and with the full intention of buckling down to
her responsibilities.

On Thursday morning, with no plan in mind but with
the strong sensation that nothing could work right for her
in the school, with a dream of the recriminations and
punishments to come, she left the school grounds and
spent some time in a diner in town, and then rode a train
to Grand Central, certain that her life at Pearce was over
but not sure what to do about it. She spent that day in
the Public Library on Fifth Avenue, reading through
books about her great-grandfather, Adam Hurd Scofield.
At nine o'clock that night, she ate an egg roll at a Times
Square stand, and saw a double feature on Forty-second
Street, *The Creature from the Black Lagoon* and *It Came
from Outer Space*. At midnight, she paid in advance for
a room at the Dixie Hotel, and slept until noon on Friday.
She ate another egg roll at the same stand, and wandered
past people who dashed past her. At Pennsylvania
Station, she bought a ticket to Viking Hills, bought a box
of Oreos in the terminal, and rode a train to Viking Hills,
eating cookies. She walked from there to Parnassus, an
hour's walk up to the main gate and then another hour's
walk to her playhouse, without being seen by any Parnas-

sus guard because she had memorized all the secret paths.

The playhouse was as she'd remembered it, as if she had never really left it, and she moved from room to room, feeling safe and at home again. She prepared an elaborate tea party for her dolls, but by the time she'd arranged everything it was dark and she was hungry and she realized the Oreos were gone and there was nothing to serve at the party. She stole up to the main house, and entered it by one of the kitchen doors. She waited till she was sure she wouldn't be seen by any of the servants, and then made her way to the giant refrigerator. She gathered up food in her skirt, cheese and fruit and a knife to cut them into neat sections for the party. She turned to hurry again to the door, and gasped. A man stood in front of her, dressed in a bathrobe, holding a glass, looking at her, grinning at her.

She begged him to let her go. He was gentle, friendly; he assured her he had no reason to cause her harm. His name was Harmon, he said, and he asked hers. She slipped past him out of the kitchen and the house, not distrusting him so much as fearful that if she stayed inside another moment, one of the staff would find her and recognize her and have her punished. The man followed her. She didn't run; he smelled of whiskey, but his voice was pleasant and he seemed kind. She needed to be close to someone kind. He took some of the food from her hands and asked if she was going on a picnic, asked if he might come along.

She showed him her playhouse. They laughed when his head bumped the ceiling. She told him her name was Carole. All she could remember for a period of time after was that he was so sweet; he wanted to know the names of each of her dolls, and he promised he would tell no one she was here. He said he knew her mother. He agreed that Mommy was a wonderful lady. He said that the play-house was very familiar to him, that he had played here with Mommy when Mommy was a little girl. He took something from his bathrobe pocket, a small bottle. He poured what was in it into his glass, and he drank, and he made her laugh when he bumped his head again. He picked up the telephone. She could hear the hum as he put it to his ear. He set the phone down. She called him her friend. He called her his precious friend . . .

The rest of the story took time, weeks of time, but it got constructed, too.

Carole's panic didn't begin when that tender, jolly friend suddenly touched her hair and her breasts and took off her glasses and told her she was beautiful. Nor did it begin when Harmon just as suddenly grabbed at her clothes and asked her to be nice to him. It began when she became aware of herself cowering in a corner, undressed, seeing him undressed as well, with no recollection of the seconds or minutes that had lapsed; it built as she saw him weaving away from her, raging into the telephone to someone that all the Scofield money was rightfully his and he intended to have it: grew as his voice grew louder, angry, louder and then louder. She remembered swooping up the knife to pretend to threaten him with it if he touched her again so angrily. She remembered darting out of the playhouse, remembered his catching her, remembered trying to scream, trying to plead, remembered—

Blank. Nothing. Nothing except the need to put her slip back on, and hugging her doll, and thinking how nice it was that her mother had come to her tea party.

The police weren't surprised that a peanut like Carole was able to thrust a knife so deep into the neck. "Strong is strong when you have to survive," a lieutenant named Vaccaro told me after the autopsy. "We had a manslaughter-one, six, seven weeks ago. Woman weighed in at ninety-some pounds. Her husband was two-ten. He must've beaten up on her once too often because she shivved him fifty-four times—while he was awake, yet, and coming at her. Oh, I could tell you cases. When most people figure they have any chance left to keep on breathing, they're gonna find a way to do it. Right?"

At Mary's request, I arranged for Harmon Scofield's

cremation, and I signed the receipt for his belongings.

His weatherbeaten, leather-cracked suitcase, obviously once a fine piece of luggage, contained custom-made silk shirts and Army and Navy shirts; a faultlessly handsome suit with a Savile Row cut and a tweed jacket with a Robert Hall label; socks with holes inside a pair of Lord Shoes; a copy of *How to Be a Better You!* and a porno picture collection of nude broads featuring not so much large bazoomas as contorted faces; the professionally typed manuscript of a play—*Surviving Reality*, a Comedy-Drama by Harmon Scofield—with no fewer than seventeen rejection letters from agents and producers tucked within. An unopened package of condoms. A brassiere. A tube of Preparation-H.

Eighty-seven cents had been found in his pockets, along with two handkerchiefs, one soiled, one spotless. His wallet contained a twenty-dollar bill and four singles, expired credit cards, a dried poinsettia pasted on a card with a pencilled inscription beneath it: *Hi Bonnie!* There were more porn pictures, and a two-by-three photograph of Adam Hurd Scofield, an early and vigorous photograph with a 1923 date on the back and some writing in a young kid's scrawl: *Dear Father: I will Love you allways, your loveing Son, Harmon A. Scofield The First! ! ! !*

Rick Tovar lived.

He had dashed that night to the Vienna crud, in search of Carole because he cared for Mary, to be sure, though probably equally in search of a stagecoach to leap from, the same stagecoaches he'd leapt from as a stunt man. He'd gone there, automatically assuming that Ramon Vienna's kid brother would wrap arms. Vienna didn't, and suggested he get lost, and Tovar barked, "Let's get moving, pal, or I punch you into the Fourth of July." Speak the line on a back lot with cameras rolling, and it parts waves. Speak it in a Central Park West apartment to an animal unused to hearing such language, and it parts skulls. It parted Rick Tover's. Vienna, and several of his animal associates who happened to be there to catch the performance, drove into Tovar with a Mack truckful of fists and groin kicks. He was vaguely aware of riding a service elevator with an animal on either side of him, of being dragged into an alley, of being stomped again, of being warned before he blacked out never to come near anyone connected with the Viennas again.

Yes, Tovar lived. His nearly finished picture in Ireland had its final scenes rewritten and shot without him, but he lived. His cuts and bruises needed many weeks to mend, and his dentist got a lot richer. He made me promise I'd keep the lid on, that under no circumstances was I ever to let it out to anyone, especially Mary—a promise easy enough to keep—and he lived to come back another day to jump from bigger and better movie stagecoaches. I saw him just the other night on a TV talk show. His shirt front was open, and he wore a Dutch boy's cap and a shove-it grin, and Merv Griffin said, "All the reports are that your new picture, *Speak of the Devil*, is going to be the heavy block-buster this winter." Tovar said he'd prefer to talk about a heavier blockbuster, and squeezed the wrist of Joy Gathers, a petite, dense-type blonde with an expression encased in worship. "Ring the bells, Merv," he said. "Tomorrow, Joy and I tie the knot." The whistles and applause from the studio audience were at least twice as loud as on VJ Day. Griffin followed his congratulations by asking Joy Gathers about herself. "Well," she said in Marilyn Monroe's tiny-tot breathlessness, "I did a lot of acting in high school, and Rick and I met on the set of *Speak of the Devil* and, well, we just fell head over heels, and what can I say, he's a devil himself sometimes, only kidding, but he's the finest actor and most considerate doll-baby that ever lived, and I'm going to spend the whole rest of my life making him the happiest fella ever. I mean, ever!" The wedding didn't take place. My guess is that Tovar never entirely came to terms with whether he was more comfortable playing the plastic phony, which he wasn't, or the confident adult, which he wasn't, either. I was never wild about that wild man, but

345

I'd like to think he found some peace for himself.

Carole lived.

Mary, who temporarily went into a miniature comatose state herself, had to have room and time to accept the solemn diagnosis a squadron of psychiatrists were agreed on: that her daughter's kind of schizophrenia, which mightn't have surfaced in quite the way it had if not for Harmon, was too severe and deep-rooted for "cure" to be a practical expectation. "Mightn't have surfaced," meaning what the hell was the difference? The girl had it, and money might eventually help ease it, love might eventually help ease it, but the bedrock truth was that she was not only the third generation of Scofields since Adam; she would, in all likelihood, be the last.

She lived, though. She lived in a mostly rosy cocoon in a private hospital just minutes from the edge of Manhattan. I would take Mary to see her. Sometimes she was fairly focused, fairly alert, giving the appearance of stability. Other times her mouth was slack, her eyes moving slowly in their sockets. But she lived.

Mary lived, too, of course.

On a Saturday night at the end of August of that year, the hottest August in New York since my sisters and brothers and I had fought like savages for the fire escape pillow, Mary and I drove out to Montauk for a lobster. We sat on a wooden veranda to take the air, as my mother used to put it, and faced the sea, and Mary asked, "Who was it who said, 'Those who cannot remember history are doomed to repeat it'?"

"It's 'Those who cannot remember the past are condemned to repeat it.'"

"Same difference. Who said it?"

"Ernest and Julio Gallo."

"That's close," she said.

"Whitlow Wyatt."

"Bingo. What do you see out there, *Yussele*?"

346

"Don't ask me. I have only one eye."

"You've been one up on me, all these years. What do you think, then?"

"What do I think about *what*, dummy?" I growled. "I think for all the lessons I've given you, you still haven't learned how to open a lobster right."

She smiled. "I'll learn," she said. "I promise."

THE END

SEVENTH AVENUE by NORMAN BOGNER

Jay Blackman was a natural-born success in business, making money and, most of all, with women. He had the kind of drive that gets an ambitious man to the top, and he knew all the tricks to help him on the way. He'd married Rhoda to get a foot in the door of the rag-trade, and it was obvious to anybody that the only way he could go was up . . .

Norman Bogner's novel conveys brilliantly the cut-throat business in which Jay is involved: a violent world where sex is used as a bribe, a threat, or a promise.

0 552 10667 4   95p

THE FOUNTAINS by SYLVIA WALLACE

They are some of the most fascinating women in the world. Fabulously wealthy, unbelievably beautiful . . . the cream of the Jet Set elite. Suddenly, they desert their husbands and lovers for The Fountain, California's sun-kissed beauty spa. Here in this sumptuous paradise, they satisfy wild cravings and confess dark desires they would not dare to admit in their ordinary lives . . .

'An emotional explosion that shatters a lot of myths about the sex life of the female . . .'
SIDNEY SHELDON, author of THE OTHER SIDE OF MIDNIGHT.

0 552 10570 8   85p

A SELECTED LIST OF
FINE FICTION
PUBLISHED BY CORGI